Now
I Lay Me
Down

Now I Lay Me Down

Suicide in the Elderly

Edited by

David Lester, PhD and Margot Tallmer, PhD

The Charles Press, Publishers
Philadelphia

Copyright © 1994 by The Charles Press, Publishers, Inc.

The Charles Press, Publishers
Post Office Box 15715
Philadelphia, PA 19103

Library of Congress Cataloging-in-Publication Data

Now I lay me down: suicide in the elderly / edited by David Lester
  and Margot Tallmer.
        p.   cm.
   Includes bibliographical references.
   ISBN 0-914783-65-3
   1. Aged – United States – Suicidal behavior. 2. Aged – Long-term
care – United States. 3. Suicide – United States – Prevention.
I. Lester, David, 1942 - . II. Tallmer, Margot.
HV6545.2.N68   1993
362 ' 8 ' 0846 – dc20   93-25814
                                                                  CIP

Printed in the United States of America

ISBN 0-914783-65-3

Editors

David Lester, PhD
Professor of Psychology
Stockton State College
Pomona, New Jersey

Margot Tallmer, PhD
Professor, Department of Educational
Foundations and Counseling
Hunter College
New York, New York

Contributors

Rochelle Balter, PhD
Institute for Rational-Emotive Therapy
New York, New York

Silvia Sara Canetto, PhD
Assistant Professor of Psychology
Colorado State University
Fort Collins, Colorado

Elizabeth J. Clark, PhD
Director, Department of Social Work
Albany Medical Center Hospital
Associate Professor of Medical Oncology
Albany Medical College
Albany, New York

Nancy R. Covey, MS, RN
Provider Support Coordinator
Virginia Department of Social Services
Richmond, Virginia

Bruce L. Danto, MD
Private Practice
Fullerton, California

Joan M. Danto, MSW
Private Practice
Fullerton, California

Robert Kastenbaum, PhD
Professor of Communication
Arizona State University
Tempe, Arizona

Antoon A. Leenaars, PhD
Private Practice
Windsor, Ontario, Canada

David Lester, PhD
Professor of Psychology
Stockton State College
Pomona, New Jersey

Nancy J. Osgood, PhD
Associate Professor of Gerontology and Social Work
Medical College of Virginia
Richmond, Virginia

Lenore S. Powell, EdD
Assistant Professor of Psychology
College of New Rochelle
New Rochelle, New York

Joseph Richman, PhD
Professor Emeritus
Albert Einstein College of Medicine
New York, New York

Henry Rosenvinge, MD
Consultant in Old-Age Psychiatry
Moorgreen Hospital
Southampton, England

Margot Tallmer, PhD
Professor, Department of Educational
Foundations and Counseling
Hunter College
New York, New York

Beáta Temesváry, MD
Department of Neurology and Psychiatry
Medical University
Szeged, Hungary

Contents

Preface

It has become increasingly clear during the past decade that suicide is not a monolithic condition. Rather, it seems to represent several different entities, sharing only a common endpoint: self-inflicted death.

In nearly all countries, *the elderly have the highest rate of suicide of all age groups* — higher than adolescents and those in mid-life. These latter suicides (especially adolescent) attract much more attention from the media, mental health professionals and society as a whole; indeed, suicide among the elderly has been practically ignored by all.

This paradox can be attributed to many causes, but the key factors are a general lack of understanding of the elderly; the erroneous assumption that old age is a sad period in which depression is normal and to be expected; that older people are ill-suited to psychotherapy; and that attempting to prevent elderly suicide makes little sense because old people won't usually live much longer anyway. In addition, there continues to be an almost total absence of care provided to elderly persons who make nonfatal suicide attempts and research investigation into old people who have committed suicide remains scarce.

All of these (and many other) reasons for not vigorously treating the suicide-bound elderly have recently been shown to be fallacious; now, diagnostic and therapeutic programs designed specifically for the elderly are being developed. Unfortunately, many are unaware of the changes that have taken place and how to implement these new methods and concepts of suicide assessment, treatment and prevention for the elderly.

In a ground-breaking effort, *Now I Lay Me Down: Suicide in the Elderly* discusses in detail how to recognize the suicidal behavior specific to the elderly and how to respond to it - methods that differ significantly from those used with other age groups. The book also describes the full gamut of preventive treatment methods needed to effectively respond to suicide in this age group - from symptom and assessment methods, to individual, family and group therapy, the use of drugs, the role of the social worker, gender differences in counseling, caring for elders in long-term care facilities, and also caring for survivors of suicide. In addition to a chapter on assisted suicide are case histories of elderly people who have commited suicide - one of which covers a woman's entire life, from how she was treated as a child, to her problems (and successes) in mid-life, to her suicide in old age.

In the field of late-life suicide, no other book contains such a wealth of current information or compares in terms of scope, depth or range of topics. It should be read by all those involved in the care of the elderly. Family members, too, will benefit from the insightful and thoughtful understanding of the elderly that this book provides.

The elderly are a valuable part of society, but one that has been horribly neglected. The notion that suicide among the elderly is a health issue not worthy of the time and money it requires is very successfully challenged by this book. With *Now I Lay Me Down: Suicide in the Elderly,* 16 authors from different countries, disciplines and settings offer a broad approach to this area of suicide that has been - until now - so sorely underserved.

1

Suicide in the Elderly:
An Overview

David Lester, PhD

In order to effectively manage suicidal behavior it is important to understand the causes and their correlates of suicide. This book focuses on
suicidal behavior among the elderly, a group that in many countries has
the highest suicide rate of all age groups. This chapter examines not only
what causes suicidal behavior in general but whether there are special
factors that have an influence on the etiology of suicide in the elderly.

EPIDEMIOLOGIC TRENDS

The most striking epidemiologic feature of suicide in America is that the
male suicide rate increases with age while the female suicide rate peaks
at an earlier age, 45 to 54. This pattern is not evident in every nation. Fuse
(1980) described three patterns for the variation of suicide rates with age:
the Hungarian pattern is one in which the suicide rate increases regularly
with age; the Japanese pattern has two peaks, a lesser peak in early
adulthood and a major peak in old age; and the Scandinavian pattern
shows a peak in middle age, not in youth or old age.

Lester (1982) examined the validity of Fuse's hypothesis for suicide
rates in different nations of the world in 1975. The patterns Lester identified
are shown in Table 1. Lester concluded that Fuse's patterns are useful for
describing the age variation of suicide rates, but that his labels for these
groups were confusing; for example, quite a few Japanese males had the
Hungarian pattern rather than the Japanese pattern. Furthermore, not all

Table 1.

Patterns of Suicide in Men and Women

Males	Females
Hungarian (peak in old age)	
Austria	Austria
Bulgaria	Czechoslovakia
Chile	Germany
Cuba	Hungary
Czechoslovakia	Italy
England & Wales	Singapore
France	West Germany
Hong Kong	
Italy	
Japan	
Portugal	
Spain	
West Germany	
Scandinavian (peak at ages 45-54 or 55-64)	
Canada	Australia
Norway	Canada
Poland	Denmark
	Netherlands
	Poland
	Sweden
	United States
Japanese (minor peak for ages 15-24, 25-34 or 35-44)	
Belgium	Bulgaria
Greece	Hong Kong
Puerto Rico	Japan
Singapore	Portugal
Uruguay	Spain
Venezuela	
United States	

Adapted from D. Lester, The distribution of sex and age among completed suicides, *International Journal of Social Psychiatry* 28:256-260,1982.

patterns fit to one of the three proposed by Fuse; for example, Danish and Swedish males did not fit into any of the three patterns.

Lester also separated the nations into four groups on the basis of their gross national product per capita. In general, male suicide rates increased with age for all four groups of nations. For females, the peak age for suicide rose (from the age group 55 to 64 to 75+) as the decreasing gross national product per capita decreased from the first to the third quartile. The rate then dropped dramatically to the 15- to 24-year-old group for the poorest nations (those in the fourth quartile).

Changes in Suicide Rates Since 1970

The suicide rates grouped according to age for some nations of the world who have reported suicide rates to the World Health Organization for 1970, 1980 and 1988 are shown in Table 2. In some of these nations, the peak in old age is striking. For example, in Hungary the suicide rate for men aged 75+ in 1980 was 202.2 per 100,000 per year compared to 31.5 for men aged 15 to 24. The rate for elderly men in Hungary was double that found in Austria, Bulgaria and France, the nations with the next highest suicides for elderly men.

In the 1970s and early 1980s, the striking epidemiologic feature of suicide rates was the increasing rate of teenage suicide. As can be seen in Table 2, the 1980s have been a time of increasing suicide rates among the elderly. In Australia, Bulgaria, Finland, France, Italy and Norway the suicide rates for those aged 75+ peaked for men and women in 1988 (the latest year for which data are available). In addition, the suicide rates for men aged 75+ peaked in 1988 in Austria, England and Wales, Greece, Scotland, the United States and West Germany, while the suicide rates for women aged 75+ peaked in 1988 in Canada, Denmark and Switzerland. These statistics indicate that suicide among the elderly is an area of increasing concern in the 1990s.

It is interesting to note that some countries have witnessed a decreasing elderly suicide rate since 1970 (Japan, the Netherlands and Portugal), and it would be extremely useful to ascertain why this occurred during a period when the majority of nations experienced an increase.

EXPLAINING THE SOCIETAL SUICIDE RATE

Although it is extremely difficult to predict individual acts of suicide (primarily because suicide occurs so infrequently), the suicide rates of most societies have remained remarkably stable over time. For example,

Table 2.

Suicide Rates by Age in Countries of the World in 1970, 1980 and 1988

Ages	*15-24*	*25-34*	*35-44*	*45-54*	*55-64*	*65-74*	*75 +*
Australia							
1970 male	12.4	20.1	26.1	33.6	30.9	31.9	38.5
1980 male	17.6	22.9	23.4	22.3	24.0	22.4	31.9
1988 male	27.8	28.2	26.0	24.4	23.8	27.7	39.8
1970 female	4.7	7.8	11.8	14.6	17.0	14.4	9.5
1980 female	4.5	6.9	9.8	9.2	7.9	7.1	9.1
1988 female	4.5	7.2	7.5	8.2	8.7	7.4	10.0
Austria							
1970 male	27.0	31.7	46.6	58.5	64.6	72.7	77.7
1980 male	28.8	36.3	43.9	59.3	56.3	72.6	85.7
1988 male	27.2	38.6	42.2	48.1	47.6	58.6	107.5
1970 female	5.7	8.2	16.4	22.3	25.7	27.6	29.4
1980 female	6.7	11.1	14.3	20.7	23.0	29.1	33.9
1988 female	4.7	10.3	13.6	16.5	22.5	22.9	29.7
Bulgaria							
1970 male	9.0	11.6	11.3	19.3	27.1	53.2	108.3
1980 male	11.1	12.9	16.3	21.9	26.8	52.2	108.7
1988 male	12.5	15.7	21.8	25.6	33.7	51.2	118.1
1970 female	4.8	4.9	5.3	9.8	15.9	18.4	34.5
1980 female	7.4	5.8	5.7	8.2	14.4	17.0	31.9
1988 female	6.2	6.3	4.1	9.5	14.3	21.6	42.3
Canada							
1970 male	15.6	20.1	26.6	27.9	31.9	28.0	24.6
1980 male	24.8	29.5	25.1	30.7	28.5	26.9	38.1
1988 male	26.9	29.2	26.1	24.2	28.0	26.2	30.6
1970 female	4.8	8.6	10.6	14.5	11.4	9.5	4.6
1980 female	5.4	8.1	8.8	13.7	12.1	9.5	5.9
1988 female	4.9	7.1	9.8	9.9	6.9	6.1	6.2
Chile							
1970 male	14.3	17.7	14.9	16.6	13.9	22.1	19.9

Ages	15-24	25-34	35-44	45-54	55-64	65-74	75+
1980 male	10.8	12.1	13.9	12.5	15.3	10.6	21.2
1970 female	6.1	3.4	1.6	3.2	2.9	3.0	3.5
1980 female	2.9	1.9	0.9	1.7	2.9	1.3	2.4
Denmark							
1970 male	11.1	25.4	39.5	55.9	48.8	45.7	55.0
1980 male	16.3	42.7	61.8	70.7	71.8	60.4	81.3
1988 male	15.9	33.6	44.7	50.5	52.6	47.2	69.2
1970 female	5.7	10.6	22.6	30.2	34.1	26.7	19.1
1980 female	7.7	16.7	35.8	42.8	39.3	32.9	31.6
1988 female	5.5	12.0	20.6	33.2	33.2	36.0	33.1
Finland							
1970 male	22.5	41.5	55.8	60.9	62.6	66.5	50.5
1980 male	37.5	55.7	55.0	60.3	54.9	62.1	60.1
1988 male	39.6	60.4	65.8	64.4	54.7	60.3	65.6
1970 female	6.7	9.4	11.2	20.6	15.9	12.2	7.4
1980 female	9.1	9.5	11.4	16.8	16.2	22.8	9.7
1988 female	7.5	7.7	13.2	25.4	18.3	16.9	14.4
France							
1970 male	9.4	17.1	25.5	36.2	51.1	55.3	74.4
1980 male	15.7	27.4	32.7	39.7	41.2	57.1	99.6
1988 male	13.9	32.5	38.2	40.0	41.2	47.5	109.0
1970 female	4.4	7.4	8.0	11.3	16.3	17.9	18.6
1980 female	5.4	9.6	13.2	14.9	17.2	22.6	24.4
1988 female	4.2	9.0	12.7	19.8	17.6	22.9	25.3
Greece							
1970 male	1.7	3.9	6.1	6.7	10.6	10.7	11.6
1980 male	3.0	5.4	5.6	5.2	5.4	10.1	16.6
1988 male	4.8	7.4	5.7	5.9	9.9	7.5	17.5
1970 female	1.4	1.7	1.0	3.2	4.3	1.7	5.6
1980 female	0.6	1.1	1.9	2.8	2.9	4.5	6.1
1988 female	0.6	1.6	1.5	2.9	3.3	6.9	6.0
Hong Kong							
1970 male	7.2	27.3	23.8	33.8	41.5	50.5	88.7
1980 male	7.9	18.7	17.2	27.6	31.4	53.8	63.0

Ages	15-24	25-34	35-44	45-54	55-64	65-74	75+
1970 female	8.2	11.1	18.9	13.2	26.8	46.4	89.1
1980 female	7.6	12.4	11.8	14.3	21.4	44.4	64.6
Hungary							
1970 male	27.8	48.6	63.6	78.4	85.1	104.9	146.4
1980 male	31.5	58.3	86.8	106.4	96.7	116.3	202.2
1988 male	21.0	57.8	79.4	99.7	84.8	96.0	172.9
1970 female	9.6	11.0	17.5	23.8	33.8	46.2	76.4
1980 female	8.0	16.4	26.7	36.2	42.2	52.9	90.6
1988 female	10.1	19.0	27.2	34.8	35.9	46.8	74.9
Italy							
1970 male	3.5	5.9	7.4	11.4	18.3	24.3	33.3
1980 male	5.3	8.3	9.1	14.0	17.3	26.5	37.4
1988 male	4.9	9.1	9.9	12.1	16.2	28.3	47.4
1970 female	2.3	2.7	3.5	5.2	7.0	7.5	7.8
1980 female	2.4	3.3	4.2	6.8	8.2	10.2	10.2
1988 female	1.4	2.7	3.6	5.7	7.3	9.7	11.1
Japan							
1970 male	14.0	20.1	17.8	20.1	32.3	50.4	82.1
1980 male	16.6	24.9	28.9	33.3	32.2	40.9	73.3
1988 male	10.4	21.9	26.6	41.2	37.8	39.2	72.2
1970 female	11.9	13.8	10.0	13.5	20.6	40.5	66.3
1980 female	8.2	11.4	12.5	15.1	17.8	35.5	60.2
1988 female	6.5	9.3	10.4	16.6	19.3	30.6	54.9
Netherlands							
1970 male	5.8	6.4	11.1	15.7	24.0	25.4	42.5
1980 male	8.3	14.9	15.1	17.1	22.3	26.1	41.1
1988 male	8.2	16.1	14.3	17.2	20.0	21.2	41.3
1970 female	2.1	5.5	7.5	11.0	12.6	14.9	17.5
1980 female	3.7	8.0	8.9	12.4	14.1	14.3	12.0
1988 female	2.4	8.3	9.3	11.2	14.0	13.1	10.7
New Zealand							
1970 male	12.1	10.4	23.1	24.5	16.8	34.6	31.2
1980 male	19.5	17.8	17.4	17.3	22.2	24.4	35.6
1970 female	0.0	3.8	2.9	8.5	12.1	21.1	19.2
1980 female	0.0	8.1	9.3	6.8	15.6	4.4	13.1

Ages	15-24	25-34	35-44	45-54	55-64	65-74	75+
Norway							
1970 male	5.4	15.0	17.4	19.2	24.7	19.6	13.3
1980 male	20.4	18.2	20.6	28.6	31.8	25.5	24.0
1988 male	26.6	31.4	27.5	36.8	34.4	25.4	33.7
1970 female	2.0	4.5	10.1	10.4	8.9	6.9	1.9
1980 female	3.3	9.0	6.7	14.2	12.1	9.6	4.7
1988 female	6.5	11.7	13.8	14.3	13.1	13.0	7.7
Portugal							
1970 male	5.6	6.2	17.5	14.5	27.6	43.4	72.2
1980 male	5.2	7.9	14.7	18.6	24.1	31.0	53.7
1988 male	6.4	8.7	10.7	20.0	23.2	33.4	49.2
1970 female	3.6	2.1	3.0	3.8	6.7	9.2	11.7
1980 female	4.1	5.4	3.8	4.2	5.4	5.6	11.0
1988 female	2.9	2.7	1.8	4.5	5.4	10.2	9.3
Singapore							
1970 male	9.1	8.1	13.3	23.2	39.0	56.5	137.9
1980 male	9.0	17.7	8.1	17.5	32.9	40.9	107.4
1970 female	6.3	15.7	0.0	14.1	14.5	39.9	53.6
1980 female	11.7	10.1	8.3	12.3	17.1	34.5	57.3
Spain							
1970 male	2.0	4.1	7.0	9.6	15.7	21.9	29.0
1980 male	4.3	6.2	6.6	9.7	12.4	18.6	28.5
1970 female	0.9	1.4	1.6	3.8	5.4	5.7	6.9
1980 female	1.1	1.3	2.1	3.3	4.9	4.7	6.4
Sweden							
1970 male	18.5	27.9	44.9	52.5	54.6	46.3	48.8
1980 male	16.9	33.3	37.6	43.9	35.3	39.3	48.9
1970 female	7.9	15.3	19.3	26.0	17.8	15.6	13.0
1980 female	5.8	11.3	16.2	17.8	21.2	14.5	11.4
Switzerland							
1970 male	21.3	27.6	31.2	46.2	49.0	49.5	74.1
1980 male	34.2	36.5	42.2	46.1	63.4	58.9	80.7
1988 male	26.3	38.0	36.6	39.6	41.7	48.5	74.8

Ages	15-24	25-34	35-44	45-54	55-64	65-74	75+
1970 female	4.7	10.2	8.8	19.5	19.1	21.7	16.0
1980 female	12.3	14.8	17.6	21.7	20.8	26.8	23.2
1988 female	7.1	10.0	13.7	17.5	19.7	22.2	26.4

Thailand

	15-24	25-34	35-44	45-54	55-64	65-74	75+
1970 male	7.2	5.7	9.0	8.5	11.7	9.5	10.7
1980 male	12.8	11.1	11.6	13.8	12.9	12.6	(65+)
1970 female	9.9	3.4	3.8	3.0	2.8	2.2	1.1
1980 female	19.6	8.6	7.4	7.1	4.8	3.3	(65+)

UK: England

and Wales

	15-24	25-34	35-44	45-54	55-64	65-74	75+
1970 male	6.0	9.1	11.3	14.1	17.5	20.7	23.9
1980 male	6.4	13.0	15.5	15.4	17.9	18.2	21.6
1988 male	11.0	15.5	18.0	14.7	15.3	16.2	24.3
1970 female	2.6	4.4	7.4	10.3	12.9	15.3	9.7
1980 female	3.0	4.2	8.1	10.9	11.8	13.3	11.0
1988 female	2.5	3.8	4.9	6.4	6.8	8.0	8.4

UK: Scotland

	15-24	25-34	35-44	45-54	55-64	65-74	75+
1970 male	5.8	8.6	15.6	13.1	24.0	12.9	21.7
1980 male	9.6	15.2	19.1	23.4	17.8	18.8	23.2
1988 male	20.5	23.9	22.5	26.6	18.8	12.9	24.1
1970 female	1.8	5.8	8.2	15.1	12.7	5.7	5.6
1980 female	3.1	7.0	9.6	14.3	14.3	10.9	8.1
1988 female	4.9	7.7	9.8	7.9	7.7	12.0	6.0

USA

	15-24	25-34	35-44	45-54	55-64	65-74	75+
1970 male	13.5	19.6	22.2	27.8	32.8	36.5	41.8
1980 male	20.2	24.8	22.3	23.0	24.4	30.2	43.5
1988 male	21.9	25.0	22.9	21.7	25.0	33.0	57.8
1970 female	4.2	8.6	12.1	12.5	11.4	9.3	6.7
1980 female	4.3	7.0	8.4	9.4	8.4	6.5	5.4
1988 female	4.2	5.7	6.9	7.9	7.2	6.8	6.4

Venezuela

	15-24	25-34	35-44	45-54	55-64	65-74	75+
1970 male	14.5	12.6	17.8	19.0	28.8	42.5	47.5
1980 male	10.4	13.9	13.1	18.5	20.6	24.9	46.8
1970 female	11.3	5.6	4.1	4.1	3.0	7.6	5.3
1980 female	3.5	3.2	3.3	2.8	2.4	1.8	2.8

the American suicide rate has stayed at about 12 per 100,000 per year for the last couple of decades.

Durkheim's (1987) theory is still the most popular explanation of societal suicide rates. Durkheim proposed that suicide would be more common when the level of social integration (the number and strength of the social relationships of the people in society) was weaker and when the level of social regulation (the extent to which social norms and rules controlled people's desires and emotions) was weaker. As a result, social and economic variables in the society, such as the divorce rate and the economy, affect the suicide rate of the society by changing the levels of social integration and social regulation. Divorce, for example, breaks social ties and so weakens social integration and at the same time it also implies a reduced level of social regulation.

Lester and Yang (1992) reviewed their own research and that of others on the social correlates of the elderly suicide rate and found that the regional correlates were similar in both the elderly and younger adults. The strongest correlates (in various nations and across the United States) were measures of social integration. The suicide rates of all age groups were higher in places where divorce and migration were more common and church attendance less common.

Over time, at least in the United States, there have been differences in suicide rates by age. The suicide rate of the elderly decreased during times of economic prosperity in America, whereas the suicide rate of younger adults increased during these times. This has important implications for the mental health of the elderly during economic depressions, and it also suggests a way in which the suicide rate of the elderly might be determined differently from the suicide rates of other age groups.

THE CAUSES OF INDIVIDUAL ELDERLY SUICIDES

Childhood Experiences

A good deal of research has documented that particular childhood experiences increase the likelihood of subsequent suicide. Parents who are psychiatrically disturbed, who abuse drugs and alcohol, who are depressed and suicidal themselves, who physically and sexually abuse their children and those who abandon their children (either through divorce or death) are more likely to have children who eventually become suicidal than do parents who do not show these traits and behaviors. For example, when Kosky (1983) compared a group of adolescent suicide attempters with a group of nonsuicidal adolescent psychiatric inpatients, he found that the suicidal adolescents had experienced more violence between their parents, more loss (of any kind, whether through death or separation and of people, pets or possessions), had parents with both medical and psychiatric illnesses, and had suffered more physical abuse from their parents.

This study raises two important questions. The first concerns the direct linkage of suicide to these childhood experiences. It may be that trauma such as physical abuse or the loss of parents through death directly increases the risk of suicide. It is more likely, however, that these experiences increase the likelihood of psychiatric or psychological disturbance which then increases the risk of suicide. Thus, such studies may simply be telling us about the risk factors for psychiatric disturbance and little or nothing about the risk factors for suicide. Be that as it may, such childhood experiences are worth noting in a comprehensive evaluation of a suicidal individual.

The second issue raised by research such as Kosky's is whether these possible etiologic factors are more often found in the backgrounds of young suicidal people than in the backgrounds of elderly suicidal people. For example, Lester (1991) examined the lives of the suicides in the sample of 1528 gifted children first studied by Lewis Terman at Stanford University in the 1920s and followed up carefully ever since. Lester found that suicides that occurred at a younger age were more likely to have experienced the loss of their father by death than were those suicides that occurred later in life.

Physiologic Causes

There has been great interest in recent years in the physiologic causes of human behavior, and this has included suicidal behavior (Lester 1988). The major finding has been that defects in the serotonin-mediated neural pathways in the brain may cause depression and suicidal behavior and depression in general. However, there is a good deal of research that disputes this conclusion and much more research is needed before any kind of definitive statement about the physiologic basis for suicide can be made. At this time no studies exist that explore whether the physiologic basis for suicide is different for the young and the old.

Recent Stressors

Research has documented that suicides often experience a great deal of recent stress, sometimes escalating in the months and weeks prior to the suicide (Litman 1989). However, the kinds of stressors experienced by older suicides differ from those experienced by younger suicides. For example, Eisele and co-workers (1987) found that psychiatric illness and medical illness were more common precipitants of elderly suicides, whereas interpersonal and school and employment problems were more common precipitants of young suicides. Additionally, Rich and co-workers (1988) found that medical illness was a major precipitating cause for the elderly to commit suicide, and that young suicides were precipitated more by legal problems, employment problems and interpersonal separations.

This has led many scholars to comment on the particular losses common to the elderly. Stillion and associates (1989) mentioned the experience of cumulative recent losses, in which a person loses many relatives and friends in rapid succession, often including a spouse, without adequate time to resolve the grief of any of the individual losses. The elderly also often suffer the loss of physical and mental capabilities (frequently in association with medical illness), and they must also often face retirement, inadequate income, social isolation and loneliness. These stressors often have a secondary affect on the elderly person by injuring their body image and their self-esteem (Achté 1988).

These stressors are common to many, if not most, elderly people. What is missing in the discussion of suicide in the elderly is why some elderly people can cope with these stressors whereas others cannot. For even though suicide is more common in the elderly than in other age groups, it is still a very rare event.

Psychiatric Disorders

Suicide is more common in those who are psychiatrically disturbed, in particular in those who are psychotic (especially with an affective disorder), and in those who are substance abusers. Suicide is more common in those with a psychiatric diagnosis of depression, those who show the syndrome of depressive symptoms and those who have a depressed mood. For example, Barraclough and Hughes (1987) found that 93 percent of a sample of suicides in England were judged to be psychiatrically ill, with 70 percent diagnosed as having an affective disorder.

Beck and associates (1974) have argued that one component of depression, namely feeling hopeless about the future, is an especially powerful predictor of suicide. Although a great deal of research has supported this assertion (Lester 1992), the association seems to be weaker, if it exists at all, in the elderly (Hill et al. 1988; Trenteseau et al. 1989).

The most common psychiatric illnesses in suicides change with age. For example, Rich and co-workers (1986) found that elderly suicides were more often diagnosed as having affective disorders and organic brain disorders while young suicides were more often diagnosed as having an antisocial personality disorder or substance abuse problems.

However, in order to show that a particular psychiatric disorder is more relevant to elderly suicides than to young suicides, it would be necessary first to have data on the incidence of the psychiatric disorder at different ages (to show that the incidence was greater in the elderly than in the young) and second to show that a greater proportion of elderly suicides than expected were psychiatrically disturbed and that fewer younger suicides were psychiatrically ill than expected. This has not been done.

Medical Illness

Many elderly suicides are medically ill at the time they kill themselves. Miller (1979) found that about 60 percent of elderly suicides had extreme health problems, while Dorpat's team (1968) found that 85 percent of elderly suicides were ill and that in 69 percent of the cases the illness contributed to the suicide.

Barraclough and Hughes (1987) found that 59 percent of suicides in England were medically ill before death; however, this percentage did not differ from that found in nonsuicidal people matched for age. Although some studies report more medical illnesses in elderly suicides as compared to those dying of accidental deaths (Barraclough 1971), more recent research has failed to replicate this finding (Cattell 1988).

On the other hand, suicide in general is reported to be more common in those suffering from certain diseases such as AIDS, epilepsy, peptic and gastric ulcer (though possibly because many of these patients are alcohol abusers), lupus, kidney disease, multiple sclerosis, Huntington's chorea and spinal cord injury (Lester 1992). The findings for cancer are inconsistent, though some studies do report a high suicide rate in cancer victims, especially among the elderly (Olafsen 1983).

However, the existence of a medical illness does not necessarily mean that it is a precipitating factor for suicide. Vogel and Wolfersdorf (1989) studied elderly psychiatric inpatients who committed suicide and found that only 7.5 percent were apparently motivated by an acute illness and 20 percent by a chronic incurable illness.

The disturbing question remains why, if medical problems are more common in the elderly, both in suicides and in nonsuicides, does medical illness provoke suicide in only a very small minority of the elderly?

Double Suicides Because of Illness

One noteworthy trend is the growing number of double suicides and euthanasia deaths among the elderly. Especially with the rise in the incidence of long-term degenerative diseases (of both the body and the mind), more elderly are turning to suicide as a way of avoiding prolonged suffering. This trend is evident in the books being written about children helping aged parents commit suicide (Rollin 1985) and the recent publicity given to physician-assisted suicide.

Wickett (1989) examined almost a hundred cases of double suicides and found that two-thirds were mercy killings followed by suicide and one-third double suicides. In the typical case, the wife or both partners were suffering, and the husband was the instigator. The couple was usually living alone, and they killed their pets too. The couple felt exhausted and helpless and had a fear of being institutionalized and separated. Usually the husband could not bear his wife's suffering or the prospect of life without her.

MOTIVES FOR SUICIDE

We have seen that, although the elderly in some nations do have higher suicide rates than younger adults, the etiologic factors seem similar to those for younger suicides. However, analyses of the suicide notes left by the elderly suggest different motives for their suicides.

Farberow and Shneidman (1957) found that the suicide notes of the elderly reflected more of a wish to escape from suffering and less of a wish to punish themselves or to punish others. Capstick (1960) similarly noted that the suicide notes of the elderly more often referred to illness, the hereafter, management of affairs and directions intended to protect survivors from distress or danger. Finally, the notes were also less wounding and malicious toward others. In line with these findings, Leenaars (1989) found a lesser emphasis on interpersonal relationships and ties to others, less ambivalence or anger toward others and less discussion of their inability to overcome personal difficulties in the suicide notes of the elderly. Also, like the young, but unlike middle-aged adults, the elderly show an imitation response to media news of famous suicides; there is an increase in the suicide rate of the elderly in the weeks following a famous suicide (Stack 1991).

LESS LETHAL SUICIDAL BEHAVIOR

It has long been held that the elderly use more lethal methods for suicide, although they are less likely to attempt suicide than younger adults (for example, Templer and Cappelletty 1986). In the United States, elderly male suicides more often use guns and hanging (more lethal methods) than do young male suicides, while elderly females use medication overdoses for suicide more often than do young female suicides (McIntosh and Santos 1985-86). (Since all of these suicides died, all of their methods were lethal!)

How do we explain the lower incidence of suicide attempts in the elderly? Although this belief is widely held, Osgood and his co-workers (1991) documented a high incidence of self-destructive behavior by the elderly in nursing homes. The suicide rate was 16 per 100,000 per year, the attempted suicide rate was 63, the rate of death from indirect self-destructive behavior was 79, and the rate of nonlethal, indirectly self-destructive behavior 228 per 100,000! Indirectly self-destructive behavior was defined as "repetitive acts by individuals directed toward themselves, which result in physical harm or tissue damage and which could bring about a premature end of life," and included active methods such as self-mutilation and ingesting foreign substances and passive behaviors such as refusing to eat or drink or refusing to follow the medical regimen. Those over the age of 75 were more likely to use the passive forms of indirect self-destructive behavior, but they were also more likely to die as a result.

It seems very likely that Osgood's research will cause others to revise their opinion about nonlethal suicidal behavior in the elderly. Perhaps the elderly who act in a suicidal manner, but who survive, are less likely to be brought to medical emergency rooms or to the attention of authorities who could count the incidence. The acts are often responded to by the family caretakers or nursing home staff who do not typically report such behaviors (unless especially asked to do so, as Osgood did).

CONCLUSIONS

The elderly often suffer from overwhelming and often repetitive losses— the loss of physical and mental capacities as a result of aging and illness, the loss of employment and meaningful activity, as well as the loss of social interaction. It makes sense, therefore, that in many nations the elderly have a very high suicide rate.

It is remarkable that the suicide rate in the elderly, though high, is not even higher. The vast majority of the elderly suffer many, if not most of the above-mentioned losses, but do not turn to suicide. This is puzzling and it is important for scholars to ascertain what prevents so many elderly people with the risk factors for suicide from killing themselves.

On the basis of this review, our conclusion concurs with that of others (for example, Carney et al. 1991); the general determinants of suicide among the elderly are similar to those for younger adults, even though the specific psychiatric disorders and stressors differ. Much more research is needed to identify the ways in which suicide differs for those of different ages.

REFERENCES

Achté, K. 1988. Suicidal tendencies in the elderly. *Socijalna Psyhijatrija* 13:57-66.

Barraclough, B.M. and J. Hughes. 1987. *Suicide*. London: Croom Helm.

Beck, A.T., A. Weissman, D. Lester and L. Trexler. 1974. The measurement of pessimism. *Journal of Consulting and Clinical Psychology* 42:861-865.

Capstick, A. 1960. The recognition of emotional disturbance and the prevention of suicide. *British Medical Journal* 1:1179-82.

Carney, S.S., C.L. Rich and P.A. Burke. 1991. Suicide over Sixty. In D. Lester, ed., *Suicide '91*. Denver: American Association of Suicidology.

Cattell, H.R. 1988. Elderly suicide in London. *International Journal of Geriatric Psychiatry* 3:252-261.

Dorpat, T.L., W.F. Anderson and N.S. Ripley. 1968. The Relationship of Physical Illness to Suicide. In H.L.P. Resnik, ed., *Suicidal Behaviors*. Boston: Little, Brown.

Durkheim, E. 1897. *Le Suicide*. Paris: Felix Alcan.

Eisele, J.W., J. Frisino, W. Haglund and D.T. Reay. 1987. Teenage suicide in King County, Washington. *American Journal of Forensic Medicine and Pathology* 8:208-216.

Farberow, N.L. and E.S. Shneidman. 1957. Suicide and Age. In E.S. Shneidman and N.L. Farberow, eds., *Clues to Suicide*. New York: McGraw-Hill.

Fuse, T. 1980. To be or not to be. *Stress* 1(3):18-25.

Hill, R.D., D. Gallagher, L.W. Thompson and T. Ishida. 1988. Hopelessness as a measure of suicidal intent in the depressed elderly. *Psychology and Aging* 3:230-232.

Johnson, B.D. 1965. Durkheim's one cause of suicide. *American Sociological Review* 30:875-886.

Kosky, R. 1983. Childhood suicidal behavior. *Journal of Child Psychology and Psychiatry* 24:457-468.

Leenaars, A.A. 1989. Suicide across the adult life-span. *Crisis* 10:132-146.

Lester, D. 1982. The distribution of sex and age among completed suicides. *International Journal of Social Psychiatry* 28:256-260.

Lester, D. 1988. *The Biochemical Basis of Suicide*. Springfield, IL: Charles C Thomas.

Lester, D. 1991. Childhood predictors of later suicide. *Stress Medicine* 7:129-131.

Lester, D. 1992. *Why People Kill Themselves*. Springfield, IL: Charles C Thomas.

Lester, D. and B. Yang. 1992. Social and economic correlates of the elderly suicide rate. *Suicide and Life-Threatening Behavior* 22:36-47.

Litman, R.E. 1989. 500 psychological autopsies. *Journal of Forensic Sciences* 34:638-46.

McIntosh, J.L. and J.F. Santos. 1985-1986. Methods of suicide by age. *International Journal of Aging and Human Development* 22:123-139.

Miller, M. 1979. *Suicide after Sixty*. New York: Springer.

Olafsen, O. 1983. Suicide among Cancer Patients in Norway. In J.P. Soubrier and J. Vedrinne, eds., *Depression and Suicide*. Paris: Pergamon.

Osgood, N.J., B.A. Brant and A. Lipman. 1991. *Suicide among the Elderly in Long-term Care Facilities*. Westport, CT: Greenwood.

Rich, C.L., D. Young and R.C. Fowler. 1986. San Diego suicide study. *Archives of General Psychiatry* 43:577-582.

Rollin, B. 1985. *Last Wish*. New York: Simon & Schuster.

Stack, S. 1991. Social Correlates of Suicide by Age. In A.A. Leenaars, ed., *Life-Span Perspectives of Suicide*. New York: Plenum.

Stillion, J.M., E.E. McDowell and J.H. May. 1989. *Suicide across the Life Span*. Washington, DC: Hemisphere.

Templer, D.I. and G.G. Cappelletty. 1986. Suicide in the elderly. *Clinical Gerontologist* 5:475-487.

Trenteseau, J.A., L. Hyer, D. Verenes and J. Warsaw. 1989. Hopelessness among later-life patients. *Journal of Applied Gerontology* 8:355-364.

Vogel, R. and M. Wolfersdorf. 1989. Suicide and mental illness in the elderly. *Psychopathology* 22:202-207.

Wickett, A. 1989. *Double Exit*. Eugene, OR: The Hemlock Society.

2

Symptoms and Assessment of Suicide in the Elderly Patient

Margot Tallmer, PhD

It is difficult to decide if an individual older patient is at risk for suicide for several reasons. One of the main problems is that there is no combination of indicators that is accurate enough to correctly predict whether a particular person might kill himself—neither clinical judgment, rating scales, physical health assessment, nor knowledge of demographic data. Suicide is such an individual act that general principles cannot be identified and risk factors cannot be applied to all people across the board because they are not useful when assessing an individual person. Psychological autopsies—information from friends, family and acquaintances of the suicide—often useful for understanding some of the reasons that a person committed suicide, are often not used with elderly suicides because many investigators feel that there will be a lack of informants with whom they can speak because of the fact that many elderly people typically live in social isolation. Actually, this is not at all true; many elderly people who kill themselves were (or are still) married (Younger et al. 1990) and at least one knowledgeable informant (i.e., someone who knew the suicidee well) has been found in 90 percent of the cases studied and other informants have been located at least 50 percent of the time. Additionally many people assume that the many negative aspects of old age are an acceptable (in other words, an understandable) reason to commit suicide and, as such, feel that there is no reason to study the many other factors that cause the elderly to kill themselves.

It is a well-publicized fact that most suicides (both young and old) have communicated their suicidal intentions to a health professional shortly before they made their suicide attempt; studies show that over 50 percent of adults have voiced their intentions within 1 week of the act and 90 percent within the last 3 months (Barraclough 1971). This fact alone should make the helping person especially keen to the need to carefully search for and to be especially alert to any hidden clues. That adults so often voice their suicidal intentions to their physicians may often cause retrospective data to be distorted to assuage or deny the guilt that is experienced by the person or persons responsible for missing clues (if they did in fact exist); had they recognized or taken these clues seriously, the suicide could possibly have been prevented.

Suicide attempts by elderly people are more deliberately planned and they also use more lethal means; therefore, their attempts are more often successful than the suicide attempts of younger adults. The usual predictive signs for suicide (see Brown and Sheran 1972) are more equivocal with older persons, therefore suicide prediction of the elderly is often difficult (MacKinnon and Farberow 1976), as well as impractical (Murphy 1972). There are many questions about suicide that cannot be readily answered. Who will commit suicide soon and who, despite severe distress, will delay the act and possibly never choose to kill themselves? Are the clues that a suicide attempt is imminent the same for those who are short-term and long-term risks? Are there age-specific factors that must be considered? Does age correlate with suicidal ideation and suicidal action?

In this chapter we will discuss certain clues that may assist in the diagnosis and assessment of whether an elderly person is suicidal. Demographic data, clinical judgment, rating scales and psychological histories will be part of this discussion.

DEMOGRAPHIC FACTORS

Although we cannot rely on statistics, they are certainly useful information. The following are some broad data that may assist the mental health professional. The number of elderly suicides is actually not that large, but considered as a whole, their rate of suicide certainly exceeds expectation. Therefore, elderly, especially white Protestant males who are widowed or divorced, with blue-collar or low-paying jobs form a disproportionately large percentage of suicides in the United States today. Married persons are at lower risk, perhaps because they are more integrated into a supportive social network, or perhaps those who marry and remain so may be psychologically and physically more fit than their single counterparts.

The suicide rates of black people decline as they age more than white suicide rates, perhaps through a "survival of the fittest" selection process; have blacks learned how to function in the system in a better way than whites? For women, suicide rates peak in the age range 45 to 55, while suicide rates increase consistently with age for white men. Suicide rates are higher in those widowed or divorced, in those who sleep more than 9 hours a night and in those who have three or more drinks a day (Ross et al. 1990). Interestingly, a history of cigarette smoking is also strongly associated with suicide.

PHYSICAL ILLNESS

The presence of a serious physical illness has proven to contribute to suicide (Dorpat and Ripley 1960) and this is especially true in older men. Common illnesses among those who commit suicide are peptic ulcers, cardiovascular disease and malignancies (Sainsbury 1955). Epilepsy is also a high-risk factor (Barraclough 1981), as is rheumatoid arthritis and stress. General Health Questionnaire scores are also significantly correlated with suicidal intent (Power et al. 1985). There is no question that certain types of stress are more prevalent in old age—for example, stress caused by the loss of social roles and physical abilities—especially among older men. Of course suicide cannot be explained by this fact alone. We must assist the elderly patient to uncover the psychological meanings behind all physical symptoms. For example, loss of hearing, relatively common in old age, can lead to an overwhelming sense of isolation. Physical decrements have been demonstrated to have a great impact upon social disengagement— greater than retirement or changed marital status (loss of spouse, for example). An individual's high-risk health issues cannot, however, be generalized to the larger population and the high-risk factors in the larger population do not necessarily apply to the individual person.

When discussing suicide, distinctions also must be made between the effects of aging and the effects of psychiatric disorders. If they occur together, it must be ascertained if age played an independent part in causing the suicidal action, separate from the influence of the illness itself. Age is an independent risk factor and should not to be confused with psychiatric morbidity (Osgood 1982).

The elderly have increased psychiatric symptomatology—psychopathology that might be less easily recognizable than it is in younger persons and therefore less accessible to treatment. Important interpersonal losses or breakdowns play a larger part in suicide among the elderly, such as the death of relatives, loneliness, family conflicts and isolation. Even if mental illness plays a part in the suicide, motives often reflect chronic stress rather than psychopathology.

Suicidal ideation appears more often in young people than it does in the elderly—in other words, older people tend to carry their suicidal thoughts through to completion. Perhaps we think less about suicide as we grow older.

ASSESSMENT SCALES

Clearly, the most desirable tool for assessing suicidal risk—particularly sought after by psychologists, but wished for by all—would be some kind of valid predictive test, a scale, a measuring device that would separate those who will attempt suicide and carry it out from those persons who pose very little or no suicidal risk. Unfortunately, such a scale as a part of the mental status exam has never been developed well enough to be widely accepted (Murphy 1983). Many scales are based on prediction rather than assessment—in other words, the present risk is inferred from the likelihood of a future event.

Suicide is such a personal and idiosyncratic act that it is nearly impossible to include in one assessment scale all the possible variables that may contribute to the potentiality of the event. Therefore, a rating scale has to be situational and the setting specific (Brown and Sheran 1972; Litman et al. 1974; Motto et al. 1985). Data show that sometimes persons who seem most clearly to be a high risk survive a serious suicide attempt, whereas those at the opposite end of the intentionality spectrum, that is, low-risk persons, are ultimately unsuccessful in their suicide attempt, either because of a lack of knowledge, poor judgment or a miscalculation in their suicidal planning. For example, Sylvia Plath, who clearly cannot be considered to have been a low-risk type, nonetheless killed herself because of careful planning to survive that serendipitously went awry. Another possible situation is where one commits suicide long after the situation that originally caused his suicidal thinking has passed; he acts suicidally despite the fact that conditions have changed. We have no way of forecasting new precipitating events, new opportunities or the sudden availability of methods that people devise to kill themselves.

As attractive as scales would be, they can only be used to supplement clinical judgments. Maltsberger (1988) suggests concomitantly using clinical material, the presenting illness and the mental status exam. As we have said, no scale has really been widely adopted (Motto et al. 1985). Certainly scales are understandably attractive to the less experienced practitioner, but they have an enormous appeal to all, despite the widespread dissatisfaction with such measurements (Brown and Sheran 1972;

Litman et al. 1974; MacKinnon and Farberow 1976; Motto et al. 1985). Short-term prediction of individual suicidal behaviors is nearly impossible (Pokorny 1983) and even long-term predictive value falls substantially after a year or so. Some of the scales that are currently in use follow:

1. Lettieri (1973) developed scales to predict suicidal risk in aging men and women with good reliability.
2. Miller (1978) composed a profile of the typical suicide completer, but the sample size was small and limited to white males.
3. The MMPI (Minnesota Multiphasic Personality Inventory) probably is the most widely researched test, but because it has provided inconclusive results, it has limited use.
4. Beck's Suicidal Intent Scale and the Beck Depression Inventory have been carefully and fully studied (Beck et al. 1974), though Salter and Platt (1990) have challenged the construct validity of these scales. Hopelessness, discussed later in this chapter, must be taken into account as an important link to suicidal wishes and behavior. Beck and his colleagues (1985) demonstrated the role of current hopelessness in prediction of future suicides among ideators over a reasonably long time span. Their instrument did not carefully distinguish between those ideators who ultimately suicide and those who did not, but it did demonstrate that depression alone is not significantly related to suicidal intent unless hopelessness is also a factor.

We repeat, then, that one must be wary of depending on measuring instruments. No one scale has ever been widely adopted. Too many variables contribute to outcome, variables we cannot reasonably forecast such as intervention efforts, critical life events, health factors, family resources and the like. Lifestyle changes may occur that affect the outcome of original suicidal intent, such as a grandchild being assigned to a school near the elderly grandparents home, diminishing isolation and establishing a needed relationship for a lonely, isolated person. We need a very large sample to profitably use a prospective design and it must have a long follow-up period. Any reliance on a single scale can be quite dangerous in planning an effective treatment and assessing suicidal disposition.

MENTAL ILLNESS

There are many that believe that all people who commit suicide are emotionally disturbed or—to use a term Shneidman likes—perturbed. Some estimates say that 50 percent of older persons are mentally ill or that

30 percent of those over 65 are depressed. These statistics could then account for the large percentage of suicides that occur in old age. Moscicki (1989) states unequivocally that the strongest risk factor for eventual suicide is a life-time diagnosis of psychiatric disorder. However, psychiatric diagnosis is often problematic (there is almost always more than one diagnosis) and, even if the diagnosis is made correctly and agreed upon by several people, it cannot explain why some patients with a particular diagnosis commit suicide while others with the same diagnosis do not. We also know that a large majority of psychiatric patients do not kill themselves. Unfortunately, even if the patient is diagnosed and other factors considered and even if serious suicide attempts have been made, we still cannot accurately predict suicide. Finally, to make a diagnosis after death is difficult; any findings will obviously be inconclusive. As a result, in an attempt to help explain a seemingly inexplicable event, a hindsight view often tends to overestimate the severity of the suicider's mental illness.

Nonetheless, most studies do conclude that there is a widespread prevalence of psychiatric symptoms in suiciders and while figures vary, it is generally thought that about 1 in 2 suffer from affective disorders, 1 in 4 from alcoholism and 1 in 20 from schizophrenia (Clark et al. 1987). The formal elements of mental illness may be secondary to suicide, necessitating that attention be paid to psychological explorations of psychodynamic material.

Depression is by far the most common symptom for psychiatric referral. Guze and Robins (1970) estimate that 15 percent of those with affective disorders commit suicide, a rate 30 times greater than the general population (i.e., those without affective disorders). In a retrospective study of suicide, Barraclough and Pallis (1975) found a good deal of diagnosable depression. The distinguishing symptoms for suicide were insomnia, impaired memory and self-neglect. Since half of the population studied showed psychomotor retardation, we must redefine the old dictum that retardation tends to prevent suicide. Suicide usually occurs during episodes of depression, not remission. As well, the rate of self-murder appears to be highest in the early course of an illness (Guze and Robins 1970). Depression is also the most frequently diagnosed condition after a suicide attempt (Schmidt et al. 1954) and over half of the people who have attempted suicide have had a depressive disorder (Harrington and Cross 1959). Others have replicated this finding (Robins et al. 1959; Yessler et al. 1961; Flood and Seager 1968; Robin et al. 1968; Silver et al. 1971). Of course, depression may be present in many disorders even if it is not assigned primary significance (Vanderivort and Locke 1979). Because suicidal wishes are more prevalent in depressed patients (Beck 1967) and suicidal feelings often lead to suicide (Paykel et al. 1974), suicidal ideation should be studied in the general population (Schwab et al. 1972).

Depression may be a necessary ingredient to suicide, but alone it is usually not a sufficient reason. If suicide is mood-dependent, that is, if suicide rarely occurs unless a person is going through a depressive episode (Murphy 1983), that state may very well not remain constant. We look then to factors closely linked to and associated with depression, such as hopelessness, which appears to exacerbate the intention to commit suicide (Murphy 1963). Minkoff and associates (1973), Weissman (1974), Wetzel (1976), Drake and Cotton (1986) and Fawcett and co-workers (1987) all have found hopelessness to be a direct causing factor in suicide and one that is fortunately subject to direct clinical intervention. Not potentially fatal by itself, hopelessness is a risk factor, but it is a state of mind that rises and falls, mirroring the depression. Some people feel constant hopelessness, but it should always be considered an important clue to suicide, even if it is not a main symptom (Beck et al. 1975). As well, hopelessness may have good predictive value for future acts of self-destruction. One should suspect depression a priori whether or not the patient so states.

If depression is such an important element in elderly suicide and is so common, albeit not universal (affective psychosis and neurotic/personality disorders are supposedly twice as common after the age of 65 than before), why is it so frequently misdiagnosed and even overlooked? One possible answer is that the elderly patient often couches his difficulties in terms of somatic complaints—they have no energy, cannot sleep well, have backaches, constipation, joint pains or may lack interest in sex. In response to these complaints, physicians often prescribe drugs and this may be far from the appropriate choice of treatment. Many of the early signs of depression are treated as normal, expectable parts of the aging process and are not perceived as evidence of depression. For example, many elderly people experience sleep difficulties and a lack of libido, but contrary to popular belief, these symptoms are not necessarily an expected part of growing old, but rather may be clear symptoms of depression. Also, sometimes elderly people see several doctors at once and this may mean that the patient is being given and therefore is taking different or duplicate prescriptions. If the combination of drugs is dangerous, it may induce or even worsen a depression. Another frequent problem with elderly patients is that their medication becomes expired and therefore their effectiveness is reduced. Finally, older persons frequently share drugs with friends or purchase over-the-counter medications and this means they often take drugs they should not be taking or they may run into problems with drug interactions.

Another complicating issue in assessing and preventing suicide among the elderly is that many medical and psychiatric illnesses in the elderly do not have strict boundary lines; they mimic each other and both can be present at the same time. An undiagnosed or untreated illness can lead to a depressive state and, as well, many ailments include depressive symptoms. The depression can serve as a prodromal warning to illnesses such as diabetes, thyroid disease, cardiovascular accidents, brain tumors, rheumatoid arthritis and chronic fatigue syndrome.

The elderly may also tend to conceal their intention to end their life by non-violent and often indirect means, such as refusal to eat or non-compliance with required drug treatment. In fact, this is the preferred method of suicide for the depressed, bedridden elderly.

Finally, depression can also be understood as dementia, actually pseudo-dementia, so that the symptoms are inaccurately diagnosed as organic rather than functional. A differential diagnosis and evaluation must be made between affective disorders and cognitive difficulties. Cognitive intactness may survive throughout a depression. To make matters worse, depressed people may not question or complain of their lack of competence and therefore reject treatment as unnecessary. True organic brain syndrome would necessarily diminish the intentional ability to deliberately and sequentially plan a suicide. The possibilities of committing the act are thus proportionately diminished. Also closely related to depression is the process of bereavement, which makes one more vulnerable to depression and suicide (Dorpat et al. 1965). Of particular significance is recent bereavement over the death of a spouse or a parent (MacMahon and Pugh 1965). The risk of a suicide attempt is high during the first 4 to 5 years after a death of a loved one and highest in the first 2 years, particularly for those with previous important losses, histories of psychiatric disorders or lack of a family support system (Bunch 1972). Early loss of a parent, and especially the loss of a mother, has been associated with nearly every kind of psycho-pathology imaginable—schizophrenia, juvenile delinquency, somatic ailments, persistent depression and many other ailments. However, it is hazardous to attempt to pinpoint the effects of early deprivation on late-life suicide. We often witness the death of the remaining spouse soon after being widowed. Some of these deaths are probably silent suicides resulting particularly from noncompliance with drug regimes that one spouse may previously have monitored for the other.

Another group at high risk for suicide are alcoholics. It is estimated that 15 percent of all alcoholics may kill themselves (Bassuk 1982); their risk of committing suicide is 10 times as great for non-alcoholics. The majority of persons with this disease are depressed (Barraclough et al. 1974). One must differentiate between two types of alcoholics: (1) those who started to drink heavily as young adults and who also have a history of social and psychological problems and a long history of alcohol abuse and (2) the older adult who began to drink in reaction to specific problems—such as aging and life stresses—who begins to drink in late life. Clearly, the latter is the focus of our attention here, for the loss of a spouse or close relative occurs more frequently as one ages. The most dangerous time for suicide appears to be 6 weeks after a death of a loved one (Murphy et al. 1979) and when there are available methods to kill oneself. Clearly, the presence of a primary depressive disorder is not necessary for this to occur.

In terms of psychiatric history, one simply cannot assess whether or not an inpatient is likely to kill himself (Hawton 1987). On the acute units, suicides are 50 times greater than in the general population (Fernando and Storm 1984), where the week before and the month after admission are the times of greatest risk. Additionally, the patient has an interactive relationship with hospital staff who may become more ambivalent and hostile the longer the person remains hospitalized (at times mirroring the patient's own attitude). As a result, attempted suicides may often be viewed by staff as attention-getting acts (Goldfrey and Bottrill 1980; Ghodse 1978; Patel 1975). The "genuinely" suicidal person may be viewed more sympathetically by hospital staff, and because they may be the only "friends" an elderly patient has, the suicide *attempter* may be converted into a person who seriously intends to kill herself in order to ward off perceived negativity from the staff (Salter and Platt 1990). Neurotics tend to have the highest risk the first year after discharge, with the greatest risk being those with a panic disorder (Conwell et al. 1990). There are few data on those with personality disorders. In 1977, schizophrenics made up a minority (5 percent) of all adult suicides, but the diagnostic criteria that have been used are vague (Miles 1977). Drake and his co-workers (1984) found a number of suicides during the non-psychotic phase, particularly among those with higher educational level who had voiced prior suicidal intentions and who lived alone. It is tempting if the diagnosis is uncertain to label the person psychotic, but this is, of course, not a fair practice. Investigation of the person's complete pattern of causation is truncated. Certainly, if delusions are present and persistent, the suicide risk is elevated considerably.

CLINICAL JUDGMENT

Suicide may be a behavior outcome reached through so many different pathways that no constant set of clinical features can serve as an accurate prediction equation (Clark et al. 1987). As we have discussed, many variables necessarily effect our clinical judgment—demographic factors, diagnostic issues and medical and psychiatric histories. As well, there is the issue of the diagnostician's own feelings toward suicide and death that can often complicate judgment. There is also a clear need to explore the circumstances and meaning of any suicidal attempts and ideas and the fantasies of death elaborated by the patient. The patient's present crisis must be taken into account. What are the meanings and context of the precipatory stress? How has the patient dealt with crisis in the past? Did he have problems in the past? What life-stage issues might be involved in evaluating the present crisis? And, a favorite question of all clinicians, Why now? We have agreed that even given all this information, we may still be unable to predict accurately on an individual basis who will or will not commit suicide. We need also to know whether the patient has a support system and whether he has interpersonal relationships and if so what they are like. Are they rewarding? After discharge from the institution, will others be there to help? Will the patient accept help if it is forthcoming? It must also be determined whether there are genetic factors and biological correlates, whether there is a family history of depression or alcoholism and an attempt should be made to determine what the nature and precipatants of the suicide attempts were.

An assessment must also be conducted of patients' philosophical approach to life, in other words, do they believe that people have the right to take their own lives? What exactly does suicide mean to the patient? Does he see suicide as an act of weakness, of fear or perhaps strength? As well, the caretaker's personal belief system often interacts with the patients credo. If the helper has an obvious negative judgment about the right to die, the suicidal person will most likely not feel comfortable about discussing the matter with the caretaker and will therefore not have the opportunity to discuss the problem. The result of this situation is often that the patient intentionally conceals his dysphoria and ends up committing suicide. Obviously, the major difficulty is that the suicidal intention is not always clearly revealed to the clinician. For example, the patient's presenting complaint may not be related to suicidal thoughts. The question becomes whether the patient is displaying masked depression or its depressive equivalent, or is the clinician, because of countertransference problems related to aging and death (personal belief systems about suicide, death and dying) interfering with the ability to make a correct assessment. While it is vital to determine whether the patient shows any hostility, it is equally important for caregivers to be aware of their own feelings about suicide.

Miller (1979) has defined it well: suicide occurs if a patient reaches a line of unbearability, a completely and previously unconscious individual point, a line that says the quality of life is so poor and intolerable that he no longer desires to live. When hope is present, a person may ask for help; without it, he may choose to kill himself.

REFERENCES

Barraclough, B. 1971. Suicide in the elderly. *British Journal of Psychiatry* (Special Supplement 6: Recent Developments in Psychogeriatrics).

Barraclough, B. 1981. Suicide and Epilepsy. In E.H. Reynolds and M.R. Trimble, eds., *Epilepsy and Psychiatry*. Edinburgh: Churchill Livingstone.

Barraclough, B., J. Bunch, B. Nelson and P. Sainsbury. 1974. A hundred cases of suicide clinical aspects. *British Journal of Psychiatry* 135:355-373.

Barraclough, B. and D.J. Pallis. 1975. Depression followed by suicide: a comparison of depressed suicides with living depressives. *Psychological Medicine* 5:55-61.

Bassuk, E.L. 1982. General Principles of Assessment. In E.L. Bassuk, ed., *Lifelines*. New York: Plenum.

Beck, A.T. 1966. *Depression: Clinical Experimental and Theoretical Aspects*. New York: Harper & Row.

Beck, A.T., G. Brown, R.J. Berchick, et al. 1990. Relationship between hopelessness and ultimate suicide: a replication with psychiatric outpatients. *American Journal of Psychiatry* 147:190-195.

Beck, A.T., M. Kovacs and A. Weissman. 1975. Hopelessness and suicidal behavior: an overview. *Journal of the American Medical Association* 234:1146-1149.

Beck, A.T., R.A. Steer, M. Kovacs and B. Garrison. 1985. Hopelessness and eventual suicide: a 10-year prospective study of patients hospitalized with suicidal ideation. *American Journal of Psychiatry* 145:559-563.

Beck, A.T., C.H. Ward, M. Mendelson, et al. 1961. An inventory for measuring depression. *Archives of General Psychiatry* 4:561-571.

Beck, A.T., A. Weissman, D. Lester and L. Trexler. 1974. The measure of pessimism: the hopelessness scale. *Journal of Clinical Psychology* 42:861-865.

Brant, B.A. and N.J. Osgood. 1989. The suicidal patient in long-term care institutions. *Journal of Gerontological Nursing* 16(2):15-18.

Brie, D. and J.T. Maltsberger. 1983. *The Practical Formulation of Suicide Risk*. Cambridge, MA: Firefly Press.

Brown, T R. and T. Sheran. 1972. Suicide prediction: a review. *Suicide and Life Threatening Behavior* 2:67-98.

Bunch, J. 1972. Recent bereavement in relation to suicide. *Journal of Psychosomatic Research* 16:361-366.

Clark, D.C., M.A. Young, et al. 1987. A field test of Motto's risk estimation for suicide. *American Journal of Psychiatry* 144:923-926.

Conwell, Y., M. Rotenberg and E.D. Caine. 1990. Completed suicide at age 50 and over. *Journal of the American Geriatric Society* 38:640-644.

Dorpat, T.L., J.K. Jackson and H.S. Ripley. 1965. Broken homes and attempted and completed suicide. *Archives of General Psychiatry* 12:213-216.

Dorpat, T.L. and H.S. Ripley. 1960. A study of suicide in the Seattle area. *Comprehensive Psychiatry* 1:349-359.

Drake, R.E. and P.G. Cotton. 1986. Depression, hopelessness and suicide in chronic schizophrenia. *British Journal of Psychiatry* 148:554-559.

Drake, R.E., C. Gates, P. Cotton and A. Whitaker. 1984. Suicide among schizophrenics. *Journal of Nervous and Mental Disease* 172:613-617.

Dyer, J. and N. Kreitman. 1984. Hopelessness, depression and suicidal intent in parasuicide. *British Journal of Psychiatry* 144:127-133.

Fawcett, J., W. Scheftner, D. Clark, et al. 1987. Clinical predictors of suicide in patients with major affective disorders: a controlled prospective study. *American Journal of Psychiatry* 144:35-40.

Fernando, S. and V. Storm. 1984. Suicide among psychiatric patients of a district general hospital. *Psychological Medicine* 14:661-672.

Flod, R.A. and C.P. Seager. 1968. A retrospective examination of psychiatric case records of patients who subsequently committed suicide. *British Journal of Psychiatry* 114:443-450.

Ghodse, A.H. 1978. The attitudes of casualty staff and ambulance personnel towards patients who take drug overdoses. *Social Science and Medicine* 12:341-346.

Goldfrey, R.D. and A. Bottrill. 1980. Attitudes to patients who attempt suicide. *Medical Journal of Australia* 2:717-720.

Guze, S.B. and E. Robins. 1970. Suicide and primary affective disorders. *British Journal of Psychiatry* 117:437-448.

Harrington, J.A. and K.W. Cross. 1959. Cases of attempted suicide admitted to a general hospital. *British Medical Journal* 2:463-467.

Hawton, K. 1987. Assessment of suicide risk. *British Journal of Psychiatry* 150:145-153.

Jeffrey, R. 1979. Normal rubbish: deviant patients in casualty departments. *Sociology of Health and Illness* 14:90-107.

Lettieri, D.J. 1973. Empirical prediction of suicide risk among the aging. *Journal of Geriatric Psychiatry* 6:17-42.

Litman, R.E. 1987. Mental disorders and suicidal intention. *Suicide and Life-Threatening Behavior* 17:85-92.

Litman, R.E., N.L. Farberow and C.I. Wold. 1974. Prediction Models of Suicidal Behaviors. In A.T. Beck, H. Resnik and D.J. Lettieri, eds., *The Prediction of Suicide*. Philadelphia: The Charles Press.

MacKinnon, D.R. and N.L. Farberow. 1976. An assessment of the utility of suicide prevention. *Suicide and Life-Threatening Behavior* 6:86-91.

MacMahon, B. and T. Pugh. 1965. Suicide in the widowed. *American Journal of Epidemiology* 81:23-31.

Maltsberger, J.T. 1988. Suicide danger: clinical estimation and decision. *Suicide and Life-Threatening Behavior* 18:47-54.

McCann, J.T. and R.E. Gergelis. 1990. Utility of the MCMI-II in assessing suicide risk. *Journal of Consulting and Clinical Psychiatry* 42:861-65.

McHugh, P.R. and H. Goodell. 1971. Suicidal behavior: a distinction in patients with sedative poisoning seen in a general hospital. *Archives of General Psychiatry* 25:454-464.

Miles, C.P. 1977. Conditions predisposing to suicide. *Journal of Nervous and Mental Disease* 164:231-246.

Miller, M. 1978. Towards a profile of the older white male suicide. *Gerontologist* 18:80-82.

Miller, M. 1979. *Suicide after Sixty: The Final Alternative.* New York: Springer.

Minkoff, K., A.T. Beck and R.E. Bergman. 1973. Hopelessness, depression and attempted suicide. *American Journal of Psychiatry* 130:455-459.

Moscicki, E.K. 1989. Epidemiologic surveys as tools for studying suicidal behavior: a review. *Suicide and Life-Threatening Behavior* 19:131-146.

Motto, J.A. 1980. Suicide risk factors in alcohol abuse. *Suicide and Life-Threatening Behavior* 10:230-238.

Motto, J.A., D.C. Heilbron and R.P. Juster. 1985. Development of a clinical instrument to estimate suicide risk. *American Journal of Psychiatry* 142:680-685.

Murphy, G.E. 1972. Clinical identification of suicidal risk. *Archives of General Psychiatry* 27:356-359.

Murphy, G.E. 1983. On suicide prediction and prevention. *Archives of General Psychiatry* 40:343-344.

Osgood, N.J. 1982. Suicide in the elderly. *Postgraduate Medicine* 72(2):123-130.

Pallis, D., J.S. Gibbons and D.W. Pierce. 1984. Estimating suicide risk among attempted suicides. *American Journal of Psychiatry* 144:139-148.

Patel, A.R. 1975. Attitudes towards self-poisoning. *British Medical Journal* 2:426-430.

Paykel, E.S., J. Myers, J. Lindenthal and J. Tanner. 1974. Suicidal feelings in the general population. *British Journal of Psychiatry* 124:460-469.

Pierce, D.W. 1985. The predictive validation of a suicidal intent scale: a five-year follow-up. *British Journal of Psychiatry* 147:655-659.

Pokorny, A. 1960. Characteristics of 44 patients who subsequently committed suicide. *Archives of General Psychiatry* 2:314-323.

Pokorny, A. 1964. Suicide rates in various psychiatric disorders. *Journal of Nervous and Mental Disease* 139:499-506.

Pokorny, A. 1966. A follow-up of 618 suicidal patients. *American Journal of Psychiatry* 122:1109-1116.

Pokorny, A. 1983. Prediction of suicide in psychiatric patients. *Archives of General Psychiatry* 40:249-257.

Power, K.G., D.J. Cooke and D.N. Brooks. 1985. Life stress, medical lethality and suicidal intent. *British Journal of Psychiatry* 147:655-659.

Robin, A.A., E.M. Brooke and D.L. Freeman-Browne. 1968. Some aspects of suicide in psychiatric patients in Southend. *British Journal of Psychiatry* 114:739-747.

Robins, E., S. Gassner. J. Kayes, et al. 1959. The communication of suicide intent. *American Journal of Psychiatry* 115:724-733.

Ross, R.K., L. Bernstein, L. Trent, et al. 1990. A prospective study of risk factors for traumatic death in a retirement community. *Preventative Medicine* 19:323-334.

Sainsbury, P. 1955. *Suicide in London.* London: Chapman & Hall.

Salter, D. and S. Platt. 1990. Suicidal intent, hopelessness and depression in a parasuicide population: the influence of social desirability and elapsed time. *British Journal of Clinical Psychology* 29:361-371.

Scale, A.B. and C.M. Hamilton. 1963. Attempted suicide in Glasgow. *British Journal of Psychiatry* 109:609-615.

Schmidt, E.H., P. ONeal and E. Robins. 1954. Evaluation of suicide attempts as guide to therapy; clinical and follow-up study of 109 patients. *Journal of the American Medical Association* 155:549-557.

Schwab, J.J., G.J. Warheit and C.E. Holzer. 1972. Suicidal ideation and behavior in a general population. *Diseases of the Nervous System* 23:745-748.

Simon, R. 1989. Silent suicide in the elderly. *Bulletin of the American Academy of Psychiatry and the Law* 17(1):83-95.

Silver, M.A., M. Bohnert, A.T. Beck and D. Marcus. 1971. Relation of depression of attempted suicide and seriousness of intent. *Archives of General Psychiatry.* 25:573-576.

Smith, J.C., J.A. Mercy and J.M. Conn. 1988. Marital status and the risk of suicide. *American Journal of Public Health* 78(1):78-80.

Stelmacher, Z.T. and R.E. Sherman. 1990. Use of case vignettes in suicide risk assessment. *Suicide and Life-Threatening Behavior* 20:65-84.

Stengel, E. 1972. A Survey of Follow-up Examinations of Attempted Suicide. In J. Walden, T. Strone and T. Larson, eds., *Suicide and Attempted Suicide.* Stockholm: Nordiska Bokhandelns Forlag.

Vogel, R. and M. Wolfersdorf. 1989. Suicide and mental illness in the elderly. *Psychopathology* 22:202-207.

Walden, J., T. Strone, T. Larson, et al., eds., *Suicide and Attempted Suicide.* Stockholm: Nordiska Bokhandelns Forlag.

Weissman, M.M. 1974. The epidemiology of suicide attempts, 1960-1971. *Archives of General Psychiatry* 30:737-746.

Wetzel, R.D. 1976. Hopelessness, depression and suicide intent. *Archives of General Psychiatry* 33:1069-1073.

Yessler, P.G., J.J. Gibbs and H.A. Becker. 1961. On the communication of suicidal ideas. *Archives of General Psychiatry* 5:34-51.

Younger, S.C., D.C. Clark, et al. 1990. Availability of knowledgeable informants for a psychological autopsy study of suicides committed by elderly people. *Journal of the American Geriatric Society* 38:1169-1175.

3

Suicide Across the Life Span with Particular Reference to the Elderly

Antoon A. Leenaars, PhD

In recent years, a great deal of interest has been focused on suicide among specific age groups, for example, adolescents and the elderly. However, the modern trend in psychology, sociology, psychiatry, anthropology and other human health fields has now shifted to the examination of suicide across the life span, from childhood through adulthood to old age, in other words, how suicide methods and motives change with age (Leenaars 1991a). This chapter addresses suicide within this developmental framework, although particular emphasis will be given to the suicide of the older adult.

One difficult problem in assessing suicide is the matter of obtaining suitable data. Shneidman and Farberow (1957) and others have suggested the following alternatives: statistics, third-party interviews and the study of nonfatal suicide attempters and documents (such as personal documents). Each of these sources has its limitations (Leenaars 1988a; Maris 1981), yet each has also brought social scientists closer to understanding the event of suicide. Although there is considerable controversy surrounding the admissibility of introspective accounts as opposed to objective reports (Runyan 1982; Windelband 1904), Allport (1942) notes that personal documents have a significant place in social science research and makes a clear case for their use: they provide intimate information about the person, advance both nomothetic and idiographic research and they aid in the aims of science in general—understanding, prediction and control.

THE SUICIDE NOTE

Perhaps the most personal documents of all are suicide notes. They are unsolicited material provided by the suicidal person, usually written minutes before the suicidal act. They are an invaluable starting point for comprehending the suicidal act and for understanding the special features about people who actually commit suicide. They can often shed light on suicide—an act that seems incomprehensible to those of us who have never had such emotions (Leenaars 1988a; Shneidman 1980, 1985; Shneidman and Farberow 1957).

Early research on suicide notes (e.g., Wolff 1931) largely utilized an anecdotal approach that incorporated descriptive information. Subsequent methods of study have primarily included classification analysis and content analysis. Currently, there are over 80 published articles on suicide notes and Leenaars (1988a) presented an extensive review of the literature including an annotated bibliography. Only a few of these studies have utilized a theoretical-conceptual analysis despite the belief, since the first formal study of suicide notes, that such contributions offer rich potential (Shneidman and Farberow 1957). In a series of studies spanning the last 15 years (Leenaars 1979, 1985, 1986, 1987, 1988a and b, 1989a and b, 1990, 1991a and b; Leenaars and Balance 1981, 1984a and b; Leenaars, Balance, Wenckstern and Rudzinski 1985), Leenaars and his colleagues have introduced a logical empirical approach, which not only presents a method for the theoretical analysis of suicide notes but was also calculated to augment the effectiveness of previous controls.

Essentially, this method (outlined in detail in Leenaars 1988a; Leenaars and Balance 1984a) states that suicide notes should be treated as an archival source and should be subject to the scrutiny of a control hypothesis, following an ex post facto research design (Kerlinger 1964). Suicide notes are recast in different theoretical contexts (such as hypotheses, theories and models) for which lines of evidence for each of these positions can then be pursued, utilizing Carnaps (1931) logical and empirical procedures. These positivistic procedures call for the translation of theoretical formulations into observable and specific statements in order to test the formulations. These statements embody the meaning of the theory as they are matched empirically, by independent judges, with the actual data. Next, conclusions are developed from the verified statements. This method allows predictive validity or its equivalent to be introduced into the investigation of suicide notes and also allows testing between theoretical positions, discriminations within theoretical positions and facilitation of model building.

To date, the theories of ten suicidologists have been investigated

(Leenaars 1988a). Specifically, these are the studies of Adler, Binswanger, Freud, Jung, Menninger, Kelly, Murray, Shneidman, Sullivan and Zilboorg. From these investigations, 23 key statements were found that were able to frequently describe the content of suicide notes (i.e., one standard deviation above the mean of all observations) and 18 statements that significantly differentiated between genuine suicide notes and simulated suicide notes (written by non-suicidal people and used as control data). Both sources of information have utility in understanding suicide. These investigations have not only provided a basis for understanding suicide but have been shown to have clinical and legal implications for assessment and intervention (Leenaars 1988c, 1989c, 1991c, 1991d).

Suicide Notes and Age

The first controlled study of suicide notes indicated that the dynamics vary with critical demographic variables, notably age (Shneidman and Farberow 1957). However, very few subsequent studies on suicide notes have examined such variables. Previous research on age (Cohen and Fiedler 1974; Darbonne 1969; Leenaars 1987, 1988a, 1989a and b, 1991a and b; Leenaars and Balance 1984c; Lester and Hummel 1980; Lester and Reeve 1982; Tuckman, Kleiner and Lavell 1959) has been summarized by Leenaars (1988a). Briefly, this research indicated the following: suicidal ideation varies with age; inwardly directed aggression is more prevalent in younger adults; younger adults are more harsh, self-critical and self-depreciative; and older adults exhibit a greater wish to die. Though similar in some respects to suicide notes of young people, the most noteworthy observation from analysis of the suicide notes written by older adults is that they have a strong wish to die.

A problem with present-day age-related studies is that various researchers have divided their age samples differently, resulting in some difficulties in directly comparing studies and various definitions of "young" and "old" that are used in the literature. This problem is largely caused by the difficulty of obtaining adequate samples of suicide notes. Using my current archive of over 1200 suicide notes, an a priori classification of age has been proposed (Leenaars 1987a, 1988a). The following schema was suggested for our sample groups which was based not only on extensive research on adult development (Colarusso and Nemiroff 1981; Kalish 1975; Kimmel 1974; Troll 1975), but also on Erikson's theoretical model of the stages (i.e., time lines) of such development (Erikson 1963, 1968), with the understanding that overlap between these groups as well as even more refined classifications within these groups are possible. The three groups Erikson defined are :

- Young Adulthood; chronological age: 18-25
- Middle Adulthood; chronological age: 25-55
- Late Adulthood; chronological age: 55 and over

SUICIDE ACROSS THE ADULT LIFE SPAN

Suicide is best understood as a multidimensional human malaise (Shneidman 1985). It would seem most accurate to define suicide as an event with biological (including biochemical), neuropsychological, sociocultural, interpersonal, philosophical/existential and psychological aspects. From a psychological point of view, suicide has been structured differently by various suicidologists. As mentioned above, Leenaars attempted to define suicide in terms of suicide notes by studying ten suicidologists. From this work a number of predictive (23) and differentiating (18) variables were isolated that could be used to understand suicide from a psychological perspective. These variables were reduced to a meaningful study, consisting of eight clusters (Leenaars 1989a). Specifically, suicide was defined psychologically with the following variables: unbearable pain; interpersonal relations; rejection-aggression; inability to adjust; indirect expressions; identification-egression; ego; and cognitive constriction. These eight clusters provide a basis to understand the common patterns of suicide across the adult life span including the elderly:

Unbearable Psychological Pain. The most common stimulus in suicide is unendurable psychological pain. Although, as Menninger (1938) noted, other motives (elements, wishes) are evident, the person primarily reports in the suicide note that he wants to flee from a trauma, a catastrophe. The suicidal person feels boxed in, rejected, deprived, forlorn, distressed and especially hopeless and helpless. The person communicates in the note that his situation is unbearable and that he desperately wants a way out (Jacobs 1971; Shneidman 1980; Wagner 1960). As Murray (1967) noted, suicide is functional because it abolishes painful tension for the individual and provides relief from intolerable suffering.

Interpersonal Relations. Previous research on suicide notes (Bjerg 1967; Darbonne 1969) and my own research (Leenaars 1988a, 1989a) indicate that the suicidal person has problems establishing and maintaining relationships. Suicidal persons frequently describe in their letters a disturbed, unbearable interpersonal situation. Achieving a positive development in these disturbed relations was said to be the only possible way to go on living, but such a development was not usually seen as forthcoming. Suicide appears to be often related to unsatisfied or frustrated affiliation (attachment) needs, although other unfulfilled needs may also be evident (e.g., achievement, autonomy, dominance).

Rejection-Aggression. The rejection-aggression hypothesis was documented by Stekel in a famous 1910 meeting of the Psychoanalytic Society in Freud's home in Vienna (Friedman 1910/1967). Adler, Jung, Freud, Sullivan and Zilboorg have all expounded variations of this hypothesis. In the first controlled study of suicide notes, Shneidman and Farberow (1957) reported that self-blame and hate directed toward others are evident in many notes. My research (Leenaars 1988a, 1989a) suggests that although the person may be ambivalent, a characteristic of some suicidal people is that they turn back upon themselves murderous impulses (wishes, needs) that they had previously directed against a traumatic event or person, most frequently someone who had rejected them. Suicide may be masked aggression—it may be murder in the 180th degree.

Inability to Adjust. Depressed people are not the only ones who kill themselves, although depression is very frequently observed in suicidal people (Leenaars 1988a, 1991a). Although the majority of suicides may not fit into any specific disease classification, the "down phase" of manic-depressive disorders, obsessive-compulsive disorders, schizophrenic disorders, psychopathic disorders and other disorders has been related to some suicides (Leenaars 1988a, 1991a; Sullivan 1962, 1964). In their notes, suicidal persons themselves often state that they are unable to adjust. These adults, considering themselves too weak to overcome difficulties, reject everything except death. They do not survive life's difficulties.

Indirect Expressions. Complications, ambivalence, redirected aggression, unconscious implications and other indirect expressions or behavior are often evident in suicide. Tripodes (1976) also indicated in his studies of suicide notes that the suicidal person often confuses real and not real, objective and subjective feelings and so on. The suicidal person may see the note as a clear, obvious message, but it is often confusing and contradictory to others. Furthermore, there are usually many more reasons that caused the suicidal person to commit the act than he is consciously aware of when making his decision to kill himself; the driving force may well be an unconscious process.

Identification-Egression. Freud (1917/1974, 1920/1974) hypothesized that an intense identification to a lost or rejecting person or, as Zilboorg (1936, 1937) showed, to any ideal (e.g., health, youth, employment, freedom) is crucial in understanding the suicidal person. Here, identification is defined as an attachment or bond based on an important emotional tie with another person (Freud 1921/1974) or any ideal. If this emotional need is not met, the suicidal person experiences deep pain and wants to egress, in other words, to be gone, to be elsewhere. Suicide becomes the only solution.

Ego. My research (Leenaars 1988a, 1989a) suggests that adults frequently exhibit in their suicide notes a relative weakness in their capacity to develop constructive tendencies and to overcome their personal difficulties. Their egos have likely been weakened by a steady toll of traumatic events (for example, loss, rejection, abuse, failure).

Cognitive Constriction. The common cognitive state in suicide is constriction (Shneidman 1985). Previous research on suicide notes (Henken 1976; Leenaars 1988a, 1989a; Neuringer 1976; Osgood and Walker 1959; Shneidman and Farberow 1957; Tripodes 1976) shows that constriction—rigidity in thinking, narrowing of focus, tunnel vision and concreteness, among other things—is the major component of the cognitive state in suicide. The suicidal person exhibits in the suicide note only permutations and combinations of reflections on a trauma (for example, poor health, rejection by spouse).

THE ELDERLY

A life span developmental perspective is essential in understanding suicide and suicidal phenomena. Despite considerable similarities between the above described eight patterns, the comparison between the age groups above-described suggested that individuals describe their behavior as different in some critical respects, depending on age (Leenars 1985). The notes of the age group 18 to 25 years are the most different from those of other adults (Leenaars 1989b). The notes of older adults differ in some respects, but in terms of degree, not in presence or absence, since these patterns occur across the life span. With particular reference to the older adult, Leenaars (1989a) has observed certain patterns discussed below:

Indirect Expressions. The older adult exhibits this pattern less than other adults. Suicide in late adulthood appears to be less a function of ambivalence, redirected aggression or unconscious implications. The suicide notes of the elderly are less contradictory and more direct and they are more aware of their reasons for killing themselves than are other age groups. This observation has direct implications not only for understanding suicide in the older adult, but also for intervention (Leenaars 1991d). It also raises a large number of questions about suicide in the older adult. Are there fewer contradictions for suicide in late adulthood and if so, what sort of feelings, attitutes and interests do the elderly have? Why is there less submission, humiliation and self-flagellation? Is this related to a higher level of desire to die? Are the elderly conscious of their motivations or are unconscious processes less evident in their notes?

Interpersonal Relations. Although no age differences were noted per se on interpersonal relations across the life span, an age-by-sex interaction was found relative to this variable (Leenaars 1989a). Older males exhibited a problem in establishing and maintaining a relationship more frequently than their female counterparts. Males with this problem very frequently described a disturbed, unbearable interpersonal situation in their suicide notes. This is particularly noteworthy because the reverse pattern is evident in younger adults. For this author, this raises more questions.Why are relationships more of a problem for older suicidal men? Do they have more problems with attachment and separation? What other needs are operating in males? Since the relation may be toward other ideals (e.g., health, work), is this relevant? Why are older females less likely to describe problems they have with relationships in the suicide notes they leave? For males, is the relation primarily with the spouse? Do females have more alternative supports?

SUICIDE NOTES OF OLDER ADULTS

Several genuine suicide notes written by individuals in their later years follow. The writing style itself provides information on what it was like for these individuals as they engaged in the penultimate act of writing the note.

Elderly male:

I'm tired of the pressure for so long.
I'm too old to fight any longer.
I'm sick.

70-year-old male:

Dear Mary,
You could of averted this had you been sincere
in your love. It is sure to bad I had to meet you on the
river last Spring. I was in very good shape both

healthy and financially. Now I have neither. My
heart is pounding like a sledge hammer. You could of
made up with me as easy as you said Yes. I can't take
it any longer. May the good Lord forgive me. I hope
you will be happy and satisfied. I am only praying to
God for forgiveness. It is hard decision to make but I
must go through with it. You know at 70 all alone
it is no fun. Yours for happiness if you can find it.

                                                        Bill

I always did love ya.

Elderly male:

IN CASE OF EMERGENCY

CALL M at _____ (phone number)

I MAILED MY PAYMENT BOOK TO (insurance co., address)

AGENT'S NAME (name)

MY RENT IS PAID UNTIL APRIL _____

ED I'M SORRY THAT I COULD NOT DO BETTER IN
EVERYTHING. SORRY I HAVE TO LEAVE SUCH A MESS.

YOU WERE THE ONLY DECENT PERSON TO HELP ME. THANK
YOU.

GOD BLESS YOU

                                                        BILL

LANNY
I AM IN SUCH BAD PAIN, I CAN'T TAKE IT ANYMORE. I ALSO
CANNOT TAKE MY MONEY PRESSURES ANYMORE. I OWE BOTH
BANKS FOR LOANS BESIDES MY CAR, MY BUSINESS HAS FAILED
AND I HAVE NO OTHER WAY OUT.

                                                        Bill Smith

CALL SUSAN YOU HAVE HER PHONE NUMBER IN MY WILL.
SHE HAS MY INSURANCE POLICY (name of woman, address, phone
number)

NOBODY TO ATTEND MY FUNERAL

DO NOT PUT STATISTIC IN NEWSPAPERS

Elderly female:

11:30 A.M.
Bill & my family

I've decided that I can't live my life this way anymore. I have no more ambition and I can't even do my housework anymore. I'm sure I'm headed for a mental break down. If I'd had a kind + understanding husband things might have been different. You've let money take over your whole life. I have to beg you for everything. I thought when I got my social security I'd be able to have a little independence and travel some but you took that. Tell my family not to grieve for me. At last I'll be happy. I put the bills on the corner of the table.I know you will get by with DAVID'S help. I know I should see a doctor but I've been afraid to ask you. More expense you know. I've thought about this for a long time and I know it's the right thing to do. My life is a living hell every day. Tell every one I'm sorry but it has to be. Good Bye and good luck.

Love Mary

Please take care of Susan please. love my family with all my
heart. I want you to show this letter to the family.

Elderly female:

My son,

cannot tolerate this illness of mine any more. Pardon me if you can.
You are too good. Love

Mummie Mary

Elderly female:

Couldn't stand being a burden *any longer,* after what I did there was no road back. Today you hated me so I had to go away. You said I shock *everyone.*

REFERENCES

Allport, G. 1942. *The Use of Personal Documents in Psychological Science.* New York: Social Science Research Council.

Bjerg, K. 1967.The Suicidal Life Span: Attempts at a Reconstruction from suicide notes. In E. Shneidman, ed., *Essays in Self-Destruction.* New York: Science House.

Carnap, R. 1959. Psychology in Physical Language. In A. Ayer, ed., *Logical Positivism.* New York: Free Press, (originally published in 1931).

Cohen, S. and J. Fiedler. 1974. Content analyses of multiple messages in suicide notes. *Suicide and Life-Threatening Behavior* 4:75-95.

Colarusso, C. and R. Nemiroff. 1981. *Adult Development.* New York: Plenum.

Darbonne, A. 1969. Suicide and age: A suicide note analysis. *Journal of Consulting and Clinical Psychology* 33:46-50.

Erikson, E. 1963. *Childhood and Society,* 2nd Ed. New York: W.W. Norton.

Erikson, E. 1968. *Identity: Youth and Crisis.* New York: W.W Norton.

Freud, S. 1974. Mourning and Melancholia. In J. Strachey, ed., *The Standard Edition of the Complete Psychological Works of Sigmund Freud* Vol. XIV. London: Hogarth Press (originally published in 1917).

Freud, S. 1974. A Case of Homosexuality in a Woman. In J.Strachey, ed., *The Standard Edition of the Complete Psychological Works of Sigmund Freud,* Vol. XVIII. London: Hogarth Press (originally published in 1920).

Freud, S. 1974. Group Psychology and the Analysis of the Ego. In J. Strachey, ed, *The Standard Edition of the Complete Psychological Works of Sigmund Freud,* Vol. XVIII. London: Hogarth Press (originally published in 1920).

Friedman, P., ed. 1967. *On Suicide.* New York: International Universities Press, 1967 (originally published in 1910).

Henken, V. 1976. Banality reinvestigated: A computer-based content analysis of suicidal and forced death documents. *Suicide and Life-Threatening Behavior* 6:36-43.

Jacobs, J. 1971. A Phenomenological Study of Suicide Notes. In E. Geddens, ed., *The Sociology of Suicide.* London: Frank Cass.

Kalish, R. 1975. *Late Adulthood: Perspectives in Human Development.* Monterey, CA: Brooks/Cole.

Kerlinger, F. 1964. *Foundations of Behavioral Research.* New York: Holt, Rinehart & Winston.

Kimmel, D. 1974. *Adulthood and Aging.* New York: John Wiley & Sons.

Leenaars, A. 1979. A Study of the Manifest Content of Suicide Notes from Three Different Theoretical Perspectives: L. Binswanger, S. Freud and G. Kelly. Unpublished Ph.D. dissertation, Windsor, Canada.

Leenaars, A. 1985. Freud's and Shneidman's formulations of suicide investigated through suicide notes. Paper presented to the American Psychological Association Meeting, Los Angeles.

Leenaars, A. 1986. A brief note on the latent content in suicide notes. *Psychological Reports* 59:640-642.

Leenaars, A. 1987. An empirical investigation of Shneidman's formulations regarding suicide: Age and sex. *Suicide and Life-Threatening Behavior* 17:233-250.

Leenaars, A. 1988a. *Suicide Notes.* New York: Human Sciences Press.

Leenaars, A. 1988b. Are women's suicides really different from men's? *Women and Health* 18:17-33.

Leenaars, A. 1988c. A thematic guide for suicide prediction: A proposal. American Association of Suicidology Conference, Washington, DC.

Leenaars, A. 1989a. Suicide across the adult life-span: An archival study. *Crisis* 10:132-151.

Leenaars, A. 1989b. Are young adults' suicide psychologically different from those of other adults? *Suicide and Life-Threatening Behavior* 19:249-263.

Leenaars, A. 1989c. Suicide notes in the courtroom. American Academy of Psychiatry and the Law Meeting, Washington, DC.

Leenaars, A. 1990. Do the psychological characteristics of the suicidal individual make a difference in the method chosen for suicide? *Canadian Journal of Behavioral Science* 22:384-392.

Leenaars, A., ed. 1991a. *Life Span Perspectives of Suicide.* New York: Plenum.

Leenaars, A. 1991b. The suicide of young adults. In A. Leenaars, ed., *Life Span Perspectives of Suicide.* New York: Plenum.

Leenaars, A. 1991c. Suicide Notes, Communication and Ideation. In R. Maris, A. Berman, J. Maltsberger, et al., eds., *Assessment and Prediction of Suicide.* New York: Guilford.

Leenaars, A. 1991d. Suicide notes and their implications for intervention. *Crisis* 12:1-20.

Leenaars, A. and W. Balance. 1981. A predictive approach to the study of manifest content in suicide notes. *Journal of Clinical Psychology* 37:50-52.

Leenaars, A. and W. Balance. 1984a. A logical empirical approach to the study of the manifest content in suicide notes. *Canadian Journal of Behavioral Science* 16:248-256.

Leenaars, A. and W. Balance. 1984b. A predictive approach to Freud's formulations regarding suicide. *Suicide and Life-Threatening Behavior* 14:275-283.

Leenaars, A. and W. Balance. 1984c. A predictive approach to suicide notes of young and old people from Freud's formulations regarding suicide. *Journal of Clinical Psychology* 40:1362-1364.

Leenaars, A., W. Balance, S. Wenckstern and D. Rudzinski. 1985. An empirical investigation of Shneidman's formulations regarding suicide. *Suicide and Life-Threatening Behavior* 15:184-195.

Lester, D. and H. Hummel. 1980. Motives for suicide in elderly people. *Psychological Reports* 47:870.

Lester, D. and C. Reeve. 1982. The suicide notes of young and old people. *Psychological Reports* 50:334.

Maris, R. 1981. *Pathways to Suicide.* Baltimore: John Hopkins University Press.

Menninger, K. 1938. *Man Against Himself.* New York: Harcourt, Brace.

Murray, H. 1967. Death to the World: The Passions of Herman Melville. In E. Shneidman, ed., *Essays in Self-Destruction.* New York: Science House.

Neuringer, C. 1976. Current Developments in the Study of Suicidal Thinking. In E. Shneidman, ed., *Suicidology: Contemporary Developments*. New York: Grune & Stratton.

Osgood, C. and E. Walker. 1959. Motivation and language behavior: A content analysis of suicide notes. *Journal of Abnormal and Social Psychology* 59:58-67.

Runyan, W. 1982. In defense of the case study method. *American Journal of Orthopsychiatry* 52:440-446.

Shneidman, E. 1980. *Voices of Death*. New York: Harper & Row.

Shneidman, E. 1985. *Definition of Suicide*. New York: John Wiley & Sons.

Shneidman, E. and N. Farberow, N. 1957. *Clues to Suicide*. New York: McGraw-Hill.

Sullivan, H. 1962. Schizophrenia as a Human Process. In H. Perry, N. Gorvell, and M. Gibbens, eds., *The Collected Works of Harry Stack Sullivan*, Vol. II. New York: W.W.Norton.

Sullivan, H. 1964. The Fusion of Psychiatry and Social Sciences. In H. Perry, N. Gorvell and M. Gibbens, eds., *The Collected Works of Harry Stack Sullivan*, Vol. II. New York: W.W. Norton.

Tripodes, P. 1976. Reasoning Patterns in Suicide Notes. In E. Shneidman, ed., *Suicidology: Contemporary Developments*. New York: Grune & Stratton.

Troll, L. 1975. *Early and Middle Adulthood*. Monterey, CA: Brooks/Cole.

Tuckman, J., R. Kleiner and M. Lavell 1959. Emotional content of suicide notes. *American Journal of Psychiatry* 116:59-63.

Wagner, F. 1960. Suicide notes. *Danish Medical Journal* 7:62-64.

Windelband, W. 1904. *Geschichte und Naturwissenschaft*. Strassburg: Heitz.

Wolff, H. 1931. Suicide notes. *American Mercury* 24:264-272.

Zilboorg, G. 1936. Suicide among civilized and primitive races. *American Journal of Psychiatry* 92:1347-1369.

Zilboorg, G. 1937. Considerations on suicide, with particular reference to that of the young. *American Journal of Orthopsychiatry* 7:15-31.

4

Psychiatric Treatment of the Elderly Suicidal Patient

Bruce L. Danto, MD and Joan M. Danto, MSW

As the population of the United States ages, there is a growing number of people with medical and mental health problems who require care. Advances in medicine have increased the longevity of our citizens and certainly this is a positive aspect of medical technology. The negative side is that as we prolong life we also prolong the length of time that people must live with a serious illness. Many people are unable to provide for the needs of their aging loved ones and as a result, alienation often occurs. It is not surprising that depression among the aged, who are now faced with living for a longer time with a debilitating disorder and old age with or without suicidal ideation, is a growing menace. Depression tends to diminish communication in all ages and this is especially true for the elderly. Kastenbaum (1992) states that an elderly person's perspective about death rarely reaches the eyes and ears of an observer because many seniors live alone and lack the opportunity to share feelings of depression or suicidal thoughts with another person, let alone a caring person. The aged, many of whom reside in low-income urban areas, tend to be socially invisible.

Kastenbaum (1992) points out that awareness of an elderly suicidal person's view of his future and how he wishes to cope with it may also be limited because of a tendency to mirror the caregiver's lack of interest. All too often physicians are quick to prescribe medication to elderly persons, but they rarely talk or listen to them. According to Kastenbaum, elderly men and women often accept the inevitability of death with a sense of quiet composure. He also feels that advanced age, chronic illness and the probability of death do not necessarily lead to a high suicide risk. He concludes that death is not necessarily the most potent enemy for the elderly. It is essential to listen to the messages that our aging population provides about their attitudes toward life and death.

McIntosh (1992) observes that rates of suicide peak in older age groups. He offers data that show that at the present time in the United States there are approximately 30,000 deaths annually that are recorded as suicide. Some 6000 involve older adults. Specifically, in 1988 there were 30,407 suicides and 6363 were committed by Americans 65 years of age and above. Of 83 total suicides per day, 17 were by those aged 65 and older. In 1993, the highest suicide rates were for persons over the age of 65 at 20.6 per 100,000.

The suicide rate of the general population in the United States in 1988 was 12.4 per 100,000 compared to 21.0 per 100,000 elderly Americans and 13.2 for the young. Older adults, therefore, have a risk of suicide that exceeds the rates for the nation by more than 50 percent. Among the elderly, the demographic subgroups at greatest risk are males, the widowed, the divorced, the very old and whites.

Miller (1979) studied a group of men and women over the age of 60 and found a number of factors that he felt related to suicide. He felt that the most important determining factor for suicide in old age is an underlying mental illness from which the older suicidal person may suffer, and it is true that many elderly suicides suffer from a psychosis or organic dementia. However, the most common mental problem in the elderly is depression. Only a small number of seniors attempt suicide during a state of confusion. Some elderly people experience delusions of poverty, of having a fatal illness and of becoming insane. He comments that physical illness is also frequently a contributing factor to suicide, particularly chronic obstructive pulmonary disease and other degenerative diseases. Physical illnesses may cause brooding and introspection or may eventually cause the older person to come face to face with the frightening reality of his frailty or the threat of permanent invalidism and dependency. The diagnosis of an incurable disease frequently leads to the same result.

Social factors, according to Miller, also must be taken into account. These factors involve lack of employment or meaningful purpose to life, alcohol abuse and solitary living arrangements that are frequently associated with estrangement and isolation from family members. The highest suicide rates occur among men who are divorced, followed by those who are widowed and those who have always been single.

Miller quite properly points to retirement as another related causative factor for suicide. Those from an upper socioeconomic class who retire have greater security and stability and more freedom to live more easily as a retiree by being able to travel, attend the theater and other social activities. Lower-class retired persons are often confronted with a dreary and restricted lifestyle with very little to look forward to. Thus, remaining gainfully employed seems to be a vital factor that will inhibit suicidal behavior among the elderly. For the older male especially, being employed not only means having an income, but also having a purpose to life; he has a valued social function and is a productive and useful member of society.

A crisis may also be the precipitating agent for a person who has been contemplating the thought of suicide. However, one factor that separates the elderly person from other age groups is that once suicidal intent has been formed it becomes very serious and intense.

SUICIDE PREVENTION: STRATEGIES FOR INTERVENTION

Psychiatric and mental health treatment of the aged is so difficult because the elderly are often stereotyped as senile, sexless and nonproductive (Osgood 1985). Some therapists are reluctant to treat the old, rationalizing that the elderly are poor candidates for treatment because of their age. Osgood (1985) comments that when some therapists deal with elderly patients it brings out conflicted feelings about their own aging. Some feel that aging inevitably represents decline and that they cannot influence change in an older client. Others even feel that it is not practical to treat an elderly person because they have a limited life expectancy. Sometimes, when an older patient dies, either from natural causes or suicide, it encourages the therapist to develop a geriophobic attitude; they are seen as the enemy that deprives the therapist of his own sense of importance.

Today, in the field of psychogeriatrics, according to Osgood, there are several kinds of professionals working with the elderly in a variety of settings, employing various intervention techniques. Making up the ranks of this group are psychotherapists, psychoanalysts, psychiatrists, geriatricians, nurses, social workers, recreational therapists, pastoral counselors and peer counselors. This chapter concerns itself with the private practice treatment, but obviously there are other settings for treatment in the community: nursing homes, day care centers, nutrition program sites, senior centers, retirement communities, hospitals, churches, local neighborhood programs and the community at large.

In the private practice treatment of the elderly, the therapist must always be sensitive to the impact of multiple loss. The elderly may have lost their health, attractiveness, youth, spouses, friends, careers and possibly their savings. Therapists must have knowledge about the physical, psychological, economic, social and other changes that accompany the aging process. There should be an appreciation of the demographic factors that place the aged in a high-risk category, discussed earlier in this chapter. Obviously, therapists must be able to recognize, distinguish and assess depression, loneliness, stress and unhappiness. They also have to recognize somatopsychic types of depression arising from organic brain dysfunction.

As has been suggested earlier, therapists who work with the depressed, angry and suicide-prone elderly must come to terms with their own attitudes toward aging and death, their relationships with parents and grandparents as well as their own feelings regarding pain, illness and bodily physical changes.

Some factors that complicate the treatment of the elderly patient, particularly in a private practitioner's office, are the problem of transporting the patient; the attitude of family members toward helping an elderly loved one who is depressed; the coexistence of organic brain disease; and the unrelenting problems of physical illness, particularly with respect to cardiopulmonary disease.

Treatment may require home visits (which we do regularly) or visits to a senior center, hospital or retirement facility for the aged. The use of existing support systems (friends, relatives or church members) is important, not only to offer friendship and basic assistance to the patient, but as a means of providing transportation.

A close relationship between those providing custodial, medical and nursing support for the elderly is vital in organizing an overall program. Efforts to coordinate treatment or to participate in an existing plan are much easier to arrange in the private practice office because there are no bureaucratic limitations that mental health and psychiatric staff and other types of facilities have to contend with in order to try to help the patient. One of the most important factors in providing treatment for the elderly is to avoid being part of the largely unintentional process of dehumanizing the older person. Older patients, especially, should be listened to carefully. Dehumanization, boredom or lack of purpose in life represent secondary causes of depression, similar to the pain experienced by loss of loved ones, health, economic security and employment. They should be encouraged to exercise by walking, swimming or by doing other forms of physical exercise that they can tolerate.

The psychiatrist and mental health worker must realize the fact that the elderly have more discretionary time available and more of a chance to engage in various forms of leisure. For the aged, leisure is mainly motivated by a need for affiliation and social integration. As long as boredom can be overcome and meaningful relationships can be made available, depression tends to diminish or can be prevented from developing.

Techniques of Psychiatric Intervention with the Elderly in the Private Office

Psychotherapy provides an opportunity for early detection and treatment of psychiatric disorders. Psychiatric treatment must be adapted to the resources of the individual, not only in terms of insurance coverage, but also support systems and medical and social resources. The therapeutic approach has to be active and direct; it cannot involve short-term therapy because, as people get older, they seem to accumulate additional problems. Loving-kindness, warmth and support are of the utmost importance in working with the aged and a sense of humor and a friendly smile by the therapist are important.

According to Osgood, empathy and a brief, problem-centered focus are useful. Listening is critical, along with a hug for reassurance and, above all, respectful treatment. The elderly should be assisted in maintaining coping mechanisms. Some degree of dependency in this situation may be appropriate for the elderly and may even be life-saving. Setting goals is also very important. In offering psychotherapy, it is necessary to build trust and rapport, handle any resentments that the patient may have and, of course, try to manage any suicidal feelings or impulses. Above all, avoid stereotyping the senior patient.

The need for medication must be evaluated in each patient. Special care must be taken in determining the types of antidepressant medications that should be prescribed for depressive illnesses. Although all tricyclic antidepressants are inexpensive and easy to use, Pamelor is less likely to cause cardiac arrhythmias and can be used very successfully. Small amounts of tricyclic medication may be used effectively, particularly if psychic energizers such as Ritalin are used. Prozac must be given in very small doses as it can induce confusion in the aged. Monoamine oxidase inhibitors (MAOIs) are rather risky for the elderly because it takes so long for them to work. Moreover, the aged may be confused about avoiding the foods that are high in tyramine (beer, wine, cheese, chocolate, etc.) and which can lead to serious side effects.

For psychotic patients, it is necessary to use neuroleptics, but these drugs must be used in very small doses, for example, 1 mg of Stelazine two or three times a day to suppress the psychotic features that are associated with depression. It should be remembered that hypnotics, sedatives, neuroleptics and even tricyclics can produce confusion. However, because antidepressants themselves can precipitate a psychosis, a neuroleptic must be added.

Anxiety and restlessness are very common symptoms and a small amount of Xanax is usually enough to handle these problems. For obsessive-compulsive disorders, Anafranil can be used effectively, but usually in doses not exceeding 75 mg daily. If that dose produces too many stressful side effects, then Klonopin can be used at 0.25 mg three times a day very effectively.

Placement on a chemical dependency unit may be necessary if there is a history of alcoholism or drug abuse. This is important not only because of the intensity of the program which can be offered, but because it also provides medical management as well as psychiatric and chemical dependency management of the patient.

Zoloft, a relatively new drug, is now available for the treatment of depression. Cohn and associates (1990) conducted an 8-week double-blind study of Zoloft on 241 elderly depressed patients. This drug produced a response similar to amitriptyline. On the basis of depression scale scores, 69 percent of the Zoloft patients and 62 percent of the amitriptyline patients responded positively to treatment. Approximately 28 percent of the Zoloft patients and 35 percent of the amitriptyline patients withdrew from the study because of treatment-related side effects. Zoloft was associated with a statistically lower frequency of somnolence, dry mouth, constipation, ataxia and pain, but a higher frequency of nausea, anorexia, diarrhea, loose stools and insomnia.

In addition to psychotherapeutic and psychopharmacologic management of the patient, it is frequently helpful to work with the spouse, children or other relatives of the patient. Periodic contacts may be necessary to help cultivate a support system for the patient and to make sure that all treatment efforts are coordinated so that everyone can share the same treatment goals.

CASE STUDIES

Case 1

A 74-year-old widow called our office, pleading for emergency admission to a hospital because she felt she was imminently suicidal. She remained in the hospital for 2 weeks and was given the antidepressant Pamelor, 10 mg at night. She was treated with intensive psychotherapy, occupational and recreational therapy as well as group therapy, and was in a supportive nursing milieu.

The woman had experienced multiple losses of significant others over the years. Her mother had died at age 28 during the flu epidemic in 1919 and this ultimately led to a breakup of her family. She was raised by a paternal aunt and uncle to whom she was very close and she lived with them until she went to college. Her father died in 1972 from pneumonia.

Her husband had been a manic depressive for 7 years and had talked of suicide in 1972. He wanted her to travel with him but she refused because she wanted to continue working to qualify for Social Security. Her husband's psychiatrist suggested that they separate. His brother found him dead the next day, hanging in the closet. She felt guilty about having turned down his request to travel with him. Her brother-in-law, who was the best man at their wedding, committed suicide in 1981.

In 1990, her son attempted suicide by cutting his throat and although he survived, he sustained severe brain damage. This injury contributed to his death in August 1991. (This is the event that triggered her severe depression, which led to her hospitalization.) Another son, a disabled Vietnam veteran, returned from the war as a drug addict and became schizophrenic at the age of 45. Her oldest brother, the last of her siblings, died in October 1991, 2 months after her son died. All of her brothers and sisters were now dead.

Her only remaining child, a daughter in her 40s who had been divorced twice and had 3 children, showed very little interest in her mother. The daughter would make humiliating remarks to her mother, urging her to get control of herself. The patient would drive to her daughter's home on the weekend to visit, only to find that her daughter, son-in-law and grandchildren would actually move into another room in the house, excluding her. The only time she heard nice words was when her daughter wanted money from her.

Her health history was also complicated. She had been hospitalized for repair of an abdominal aneurysm and had also had a heart attack in 1989.

Her mental status examination revealed depression and lowered self-esteem and feelings of hopelessness. It was apparent that she was suffering, not only from the loss of people close to her, but also from a feeling of social estrangement and isolation. There were no signs of organic brain syndrome or dysfunction of intellectual performance.

We rated her intention for suicide as low because she had not developed a suicide plan; however, I felt that her mood would deteriorate if she were not admitted to the hospital. Her admission diagnosis was major depression, recurrent type.

She had been a grammar school teacher for 10 years and a Hollywood movie studio tutor for 30 years. She was an alcoholic when she was in her 40s, but stopped drinking in 1982. She was a college graduate who had done some postgraduate work at two local universities. She stopped school just short of receiving her master's degree. She retired from teaching in 1982. Economically she was comfortable, receiving Social Security, a motion picture industry pension, as well her late husband's pension.

Following her discharge from the hospital, she was continued on Pamelor, Trilafon for severe anxiety and Benadryl to help control some of the excitement caused by the medication.

As her anxiety became fairly well controlled, the Trilafon and Benadryl were discontinued. Because she started to show obsessive preoccupation with her losses, she was put on Clonopin which was effective in relieving anxiety and obsessive thinking.

With her retirement came the end of adventure in her life, that had involved traveling to different states and countries to teach child movie stars. Her life became placid. She realized she had retired too early and that her life was devoid of any meaning or important relationships.

Efforts to encourage her to work as a volunteer tutor at a local school were useless because she felt she could not handle the strain and was concerned about her aortic aneurysm. She did attend AA meetings but resisted attending a local senior citizen center.

Ultimately, she was able to call her schizophrenic son and talk with him about his brother's death. Although he took the news well in the beginning, he responded by going on a drinking binge and has not been heard from since.

She began to verbalize feelings of anger toward the people in her family who had committed suicide: "I wanted to pull their hair out as I felt abandoned by all of them." She particularly missed her husband and adoptive parents. She complained of having nightmares involving some spinning object coming after her. This may very well have represented death.

Significant improvement was noted when she responded to suggestions to follow through on a move to a beautiful new residential retirement home. The home caters to older people and has excellent programs with frequent field trips to various museums and entertainment activities. She has her own apartment and is checked on daily; she can cook some of her own meals even though excellent dining is available. She is making friends, seems optimistic about the future and appears to be on the mend.

Case 2

This patient is a 68-year-old white female who has been widowed since 1953. Her 10-year marriage to her husband, who served as an officer with the airborne unit of special forces, ended when he died from injuries sustained in a training accident at a military base. She then fell in love with another man who died later of a heart attack in 1985. After that she felt incapable of having another relationship with a man.

She was referred to us by a psychiatrist who had gone into retirement. She had been in treatment with him for 5 years prior to seeing us. He had treated her for bipolar disorder with lithium. She had been hospitalized for 1 month at a local hospital where that psychiatrist resided.

Her medical history was unremarkable in that she only suffered from diverticulitis, which was now controlled. She had a partial hysterectomy in 1970 and a uterine suspension in 1945. In 1982 she underwent removal of a congenital cyst and a cataract in her right eye. There was no history of severe accidents or allergies and her vision was corrected with her global implants and eyeglasses.

She was not clearly depressed when I saw her, although she had some crying spells and had depressed periods associated with loneliness. She had paranoid delusions of persecution and there was also evidence of thought disorder. Her intellectual function was entirely intact. She had been hearing voices since 1987, but these hallucinations were not persevering. Her anxiety level was high and her self-esteem was reasonably good. She had a stable weight and appetite. The diagnosis was bipolar affective disorder, mixed type. She was seen on a supportive basis and was given lithium plus Haldol.

She has a daughter who is 47 years of age and is widowed and two sons, 38 and 36 years of age, both of whom are married. All of her children are normal and she currently lives with her older son, his wife and their children, all of whom enjoy her company.

When she first entered treatment here, she lived in a residential treatment center. She was beginning to show effects of isolation when a severe depression brought her to the point of pseudo-dementia. In 1990, she was picked up by the police for walking down the street with her dog, barefoot and in her underwear. Because of this confusion, I wondered whether she was overmedicating herself. As a result of her behavior, she moved in with her son and his family.

After she moved in with her son, she showed a remarkable improvement and she experienced far less depression. She became mentally clear after her medications were properly controlled. She now had company and began to feel very good.

Shortly before this writing, she was brought to our office by her son for her usual 3-week medication check. She was crying, her facial expression suggested deep depression and she appeared to be totally helpless. I had never seen her this way before. She talked about "kicking the bucket" because this seemed to her to be the only possible way to get relief. She said that she felt she was a burden to her son and was of no use to anyone.

The psychiatrist seeing her at this time decided that humor, although somewhat risky, might provide some relief. She procured a wash bucket from the kitchen, brought it into the room and announced, "Martha, here is your opportunity—you can kick the bucket right now in this office." Her response and reaction, as well as that of her son who was sitting with her, was encouraging and very reassuring. She broke into intense laughter and then kicked the bucket with her foot two or three times, laughing and giggling the whole time. She then complained that she was suffering from tunnel vision in one eye and the psychiatrist told her that it was no problem, "Just stay out of tunnels." This brought on more raucous laughter. It was obvious to me that she was not suffering from organic brain dysfunction because she fully understood the humor, respected it and profited by it. After this incident, her depression seemed to lift and she appeared to be in much better spirits.

She is now in a stable and loving environment, she has people to interact with, including grandchildren, and aside from some guilt feelings that any woman who had always been self-sufficient might feel under these circumstances (having to rely on her children for support), she is doing much better. Her family obviously does not feel she is in the way and they reassure her of this and offer their love.

The psychotherapeutic approach to this patient has involved and will be a combination of medication (lithium and Haldol), supportive psychotherapy, humor and family support to help her achieve whatever her situation will permit her to achieve.

COMMUNITY RESOURCES IN THE MANAGEMENT OF THE DEPRESSED AND SUICIDAL ELDERLY

Obviously, the primary resources available to the senior citizen who requires support, either financial or emotional, should be the spouse and children. Caregiver "burnout" is a problem that is seen increasingly in involved relatives. In California recently, a woman was charged with injuring her terminally ill husband for whom she has been the sole caregiver. She is now in jail, accused of elder abuse and attempted murder. Apparently, she felt frustrated and angry because her sick husband ate her chocolate Easter bunny. Although this may be an extreme case, it illustrates caregiver burnout well. It occurs when a spouse or child feels anger and stress from having to cope with the illness of their loved one. These reactions are common in those who are tending to the seriously ill elderly person, particularly if the "patient" suffers from psychiatric impairment. Caregivers may experience a variety of feelings ranging from depression to complete physical exhaustion. Unfortunately, this can sometimes lead to the murder of the spouse and the suicide of the caregiver. At the least, it may lead to serious depression which then brings another patient to a psychiatrist or mental health worker's office.

Frequently, as an elderly spouse provides care for a mentally and physically ill wife or husband, the health of the caregiver may begin to fail. In one case, a husband put so much effort into providing care to his sick wife that he neglected his own health, had to be hospitalized for pneumonia and actually ended up dying. His spouse was admitted to a nursing home and lived for 2 more years.

Many caregivers are unaware of the pressure they are under and do not know where to turn. At a recent workshop, some spouses agreed that caring for an ill person at home can make them angry and physically ill (Jones 1992). It may be helpful for caregivers to attend a support group that will allow them to share feelings and get support from one another.

Additionally, caregivers should be made aware that Medicare will pay for the services that are provided by family doctors, psychiatrists and other mental health specialists who are in private practice. Many private practitioners have a wide range of experience in dealing with various private community resources, are usually available, even after office hours, and often have more patience in dealing with problems related to the elderly than persons connected with community agencies. The waiting lists are long in community agencies, the time between appointments is great and they generally have fewer community resources. It should be apparent that the level of care rendered by professionals in private practice is often superior because they have more time to spend with patients and often have experience working not only with senior citizens but with their families as well.

FINANCING THE PRIVATE CARE OF SENIOR CITIZENS

Many senior citizens with Medicare are seen in private practice. Most of these people also have secondary insurance which they assume will cover the cost of treatment that Medicare does not cover; unfortunately, most people are not aware of how their insurance works.

A doctor submits a bill for his medical services to Medicare and they in turn determine the amount they will pay for that service. If the physician is a provider of service, he will receive a statement called an Explanation of Benefits (EOB). It consists of the doctor's charges, what is allowed by Medicare and the amount being paid. A copy of the EOB is then sent to the Medicare recipient. A formula is used to determine payment. For psychiatric treatment, this is usually 62.5 percent of the amount allowed.

The entire process is confusing for both patient and doctor. Adding to the problem is the fact that many people are not aware of what their secondary insurance will pay on the unpaid allowed portion of Medicare. If patients enter a doctor's office and assume that since they have Medicare they will be covered for medical services, they are making a big mistake. For those who do not have to worry about money, this is not a problem, but for those on limited budgets, it may mean that they need to schedule fewer visits to the doctor, which is, of course, not always safe for patients who need to see their doctor frequently. Most doctors attempt to schedule their patients according to the patient's needs and some are willing to write off a portion of the payment.

Among the financial problems that people discuss is their concern over living arrangements. Some seniors must sell their houses because their spouse has died and in some cases living with their grown children is an unacceptable option. There are several possibilities open to people in this predicament. There has recently been a proliferation of retirement homes. They all offer similar services, although some are fancier than others. These homes are usually large, apartment-like buildings that serve meals, provide activities and offer services such as banking or shopping trips, busing to a doctor's appointment or visiting museums and parks.

There are also board and care facilities that provide more specialized services such as assistance with bathing, dressing and monitoring medication. Most will also take a limited number of residents who are non-ambulatory. These facilities are licensed in most states by the State Department of Social Services.

For those patients who have less limited incomes, there are retirement communities across the country in which people can actually buy their living quarters in the same way they would buy a condominium. These retirement communities also offer meals, activities and even nursing care similar to that available at managed retirement homes.

In marked contrast, there is a growing number of homeless elderly. Many of these persons suffer from psychiatric illnesses or from organic conditions such as alcohol-related dementia. Others suffer from chronic health problems. Since some of these elderly people have Medicare benefits, they occasionally show up in the office of a private practitioner.

It is important for private practitioners to be aware of the community services that are available for their patients. This applies to the psychiatrist as well as any other type of physician. There are senior centers in most cities and towns that provide a variety of activities such as lectures, travelogues, crafts, card games and other interesting programs that will appeal to many elderly persons. There are also volunteer centers for seniors who wish to volunteer their time to help other needy seniors. Often, seniors who speak a foreign language can be paired with one another to promote communication. The former teacher of child movie stars, described in the first case history, has developed a program in her own retirement complex that involves teaching English to members of a predominantly Spanish housekeeping staff.

Private physicians should also be aware of the hospice programs that exist in their communities. They may be asked to suggest such a setting for one of their patients who has a terminal illness. Also, membership in the American Association for Retired Persons (AARP) should not be overlooked. It offers many services, including discounts, for senior members. AARP also has an insurance program that provides secondary coverage to Medicare that includes psychiatric benefits as well.

With the expanding growth of the elderly population, many insurance companies are expanding the types of coverage that they offer. There is an increased need for insurance benefits that cover nursing homes, home health care and adult day care as well as psychiatric treatment. The cost and length of service varies according to the plan that is chosen. Medicare only pays for a small portion of skilled care for those in nursing homes. For this reason, it is important for people who are still young and in good health to acquire insurance protection for their later years.

REFERENCES

Cohn, C.K., R. Shrivastava, J. Mendels, et al. 1990. Double-blind multi-center comparison of sertraline and amitriptyline in elderly depressed patients. *Journal of Clinical Psychiatry* 51(12, supplement B).

Crawford, D.E. 1991. Insurance options expanding to meet long-term needs. *New Lifestyles,* Summer-Fall, p. 49.

Jones, L. 1992. Caregiver "burnout" hits many, experts say. *Los Angeles Times,* April 27, Section B:1,7.

Kastenbaum, R. 1992. Death, suicide in the older adult. *Suicide and Life-Threatening Behavior* 22:1-14

Kutza, E.A. and S.W. Keigher. 1991. The elderly "new homeless." *Social Work* 36:288-301.

McIntosh, J.L. 1992. Epidemiology of suicide and the elderly. *Suicide and Life-Threatening Behavior* 22:15-35.

Miller, M. 1979. *Suicide after Sixty.* New York: Springer.

Osgood, N.J. 1985. *Suicide and the Elderly.* Rockville, MD: Aspen.

Osgood, N.J. 1992. Environmental factors in suicide and long-term care facilities. *Suicide and Life-Threatening Behavior* 22:98-106.

5

Individual and Group Therapy for the Suicidal Older Person

Margot Tallmer, PhD

Whether psychotherapy or psychoanalysis is effective with older persons has been a controversial issue for some time. Certainly, our analytic progenitors were not kind to the notion. In fact, Freud found his own mental thoughts (but not his theoretical writings) boring after the age of 50 and proclaimed that psychoanalysis was unsuitable for older people. Many believed that older people were cognitively too rigid and inflexible to profit from psychoanalytic treatment. How is it that some mental health practitioners subscribed to this thinking, especially despite clear evidence of brilliant creativity in Freud, Sophocles, Dostoyevsky and Verdi when they were older? Today, too, many analysts decline to work "analytically" with older patients. (And, as a corollary, some institutes even prohibit analysts over the age of 65 to commence extended analyses.) Robert Butler would probably attribute this attitude to a form of prejudice—gerontophobia. Many of us fear and dread what age will do to us (Woodward 1986). Aging can be seen as a moral crime; it invades our bodies, creates ugliness, weakness and frailness, and eventually causes physical and mental decline. A serious mistake often made is that society does not differentiate, even today, between normal aging and the existence of physical and mental disorders among the aged. However, today's emphasis and research on life-cycle psychology, the current increase in the number of older persons in the population—and particularly the increase in the number of successfully treated older persons—along with Medicare financing for mental health practitioners, have made part of this debate irrelevant. There is no question that today older patients are indeed undergoing psychotherapy and psychoanalysis, whether some disagree with its effectiveness or not.

This issue has been confronted by researchers, even if only minimally, but the substantiating literature and research has increased significantly. I started this chapter in this way, partially to give a historical view (albeit a birds'-eye vision), but also to suggest that some practitioners who treat the elderly may be less experienced and therefore obliged to deal with the more difficult, elderly patient because they see it as a stepping-stone leading ultimately to a less time-consuming, less stress-inducing and a more financially profitable practice. In addition, the problems addressed in this chapter will help improve the skills needed to treat the elderly. This is particularly important because the elderly differ from each other more than any other age category and therefore do not fall into neat, easily understandable treatment categories.

Is it true that elderly, suicidal patients are more formidable to work with, to be avoided, if at all possible, by practitioners? Shneidman (1981), an eminent voice in suicidology, feels that "working with a highly suicidal person demands a different kind of involvement. There may be as important a conceptual difference between ordinary psychotherapy (with individuals where dying or living is not the issue) and psychotherapy with acutely suicidal persons as there is between ordinary psychotherapy and ordinary talk." (I would amend that statement by noting that while dying or living is not the immediate issue, death is always a consideration in an in-depth scrutiny of the intrapsychic processes for any age group.)

Our original inquiry regarding how worthwhile it is to treat older adults is further compounded by this question: Why even attempt to treat older people who wish to kill themselves? And this question only leads to other questions: Is old age itself a reasonable justification for committing suicide? Is rational suicide a reasonable act in light of the fact that an older person's life may very soon be over anyway? Living wills and organizations like the Hemlock Society suggest that rational, voluntary, nonpsychotic suicide is indeed possible, and this includes the elderly who may be terminally ill. If one believes this, as many do, our initial questions are answered, at least in part. This issue will be discussed in further detail later in this chapter.

The role of the therapist in suicide prevention or assistance has not been well studied. It is a difficult role, particularly for nonmedical psychotherapists who are often unaccustomed to dealing professionally with suicide and death. They are also often unfamiliar with the team work with other professionals that is usually mandated in this situation. The psychologist or social worker who works with elderly suicidal people must be alert to mood swings, psychotic thinking and signs of depression, and ought to be prepared to cooperate, if necessary, with a medical professional, especially if the patient is mentally too impaired to make use of psychotherapy. This is important because many therapists are only used to working alone with their patients, accustomed only to the private patient/therapist dyad. The question of whether antidepressant medications can effectively alter the chance of suicide has not been determined (although there is no contrary evidence that they increase the risk of suicide). Research shows that pharmacological treatment is helpful in acute cases of affective and other mood disorders. This is discussed later in this chapter. When intervening with elderly suicidal patients, therapists must consider the possibility of hospitalization and possibly electroconvulsive therapy. Non-medical professionals must also realize that they alone may not be able to treat the elderly patient during a suicidal crisis. In fact, physicians are the primary source of referral of older suicidal persons. The recent research finding that a very high percentage of those who have committed suicide sought medical and psychiatric care within the year and often within the week prior to their suicide only reinforces this fact. Some believe that the suicidal elderly will turn to therapy only as a last resort and this causes relatives, family and friends to feel beleaguered, and physicians to feel frustration and failure. When it becomes apparent that an elderly person has reached a crisis situation, the problem should be treated as such and necessary help should be sought immediately. Sometimes the crisis is short-term, and sometimes it is long-term. As in any other crisis situation, a solution will be found—the crisis will end one way or another. However, the way in which it will end is unpredictable, that is, the crisis can provide an opportunity for a positive solution and growth or it may cause further problems.

Psychotherapists are often in a very good position to help the suicidal elderly. If a person has the basic desire and will to recover, clearly this will be of help to the analyst (Nunberg 1948). There is no longer any doubt that psychotherapy can prevent or at least lessen disorders formerly assumed to be untreatable in the elderly. Here I will mainly consider the outpatient treatment of older suicidal patients, assuming, however, that most of our discussion will apply to any psychiatric milieu—any hospital or institution that provides psychotherapy. I will address possible techniques for treatment, note the impact of suicide on the therapist, describe potential errors that might inhibit positive contributions, and finally, look at transference and countertransference issues.

POSSIBLE TECHNIQUES FOR PSYCHOTHERAPY

Suicidal intent is a crisis situation that, depending on various issues, will either last for a short or long period of time. A short-term crisis may necessitate temporarily providing a protective environment so that the person cannot inflict self-harm. Significant others in the person's life may need to be recruited to help with this action. As well, many of the problems that cause suicidal feelings are often caused by issues concerning family members and close friends, and even if this is not so, by bringing family and friends into the treatment plan, it can sometimes help elderly persons feel that they are not being conspired against by strangers, helping them to comply with the advice they are being given. It is usually a good idea for every therapist to contact those people who are closest to their client so that they can obtain information needed for a well-rounded understanding of the patient. While this is often a necessary step in a suicidal crisis, as a word of warning, bringing a fragmented or dysfunctional family together can often create an uncomfortable situation for both the therapist and the family member. Some patients have spent a lifetime achieving necessary distance from their parents (or whole family) and a therapist's attempt to reestablish that relationship with their parents would only be a setback for their client. This is often a real problem because the family may provide financial help. Also, significant others may be entirely unaware of the person's problems because they have fallen out of touch or, if they do know what is going on, they may be in denial about the cause of the patient's destructive behavior. In any event, family relations should always be discussed and therapists should be aware of the nature of their clients' family makeup. Usually, major changes must be made in the client's lifestyle and the therapist should therefore be aware and up-to-date on what treatments are effective and what community resources are available. Perhaps the client needs to move to a halfway house or attend a day treatment center. It is essential for nonmedical professionals to work as a team with the family, avoiding conflicts regarding decisions and minimizing distorted views of reality.

Another group of patients, long-term suicidal patients, may not be in a crisis situation but are nevertheless chronically suicidal and have lengthy histories of repetitive, nonsuccessful suicidal attempts often associated with a history of chronic drug and alcohol abuse, anorexia and other serious destructive behavior. Chronic suicidal conditions develop when the issue that originally precipitated the suicidal distress was never sufficiently worked through or resolved. Interestingly, there is a positive side to chronic suicidal intent; the knowledge that suicide is always an option makes people feel that they always have a "way out," giving them a sense of false control (false because it is not known whether death is a peaceful solution). It can be a soothing feeling to know that one can end one's life at any time and perhaps in some ways this can be considered preventative medicine in that it might make one wait until a later date to commit suicide instead of doing it right then and there. It is somewhat comparable to the use of morphine and other pain killers in hospitals; when narcotics are available to patients at all times, studies indicate that their use is greatly diminished.

Efforts should be made to alter negative lifestyle habits of the chronically self-destructive individual. For some, the fear of survival may be as great as the fear of death—in other words, having to endure the endurable. This same feeling was observed in survivors of the Holocaust; surviving was a fate worse than death and prisoners would rather have been killed than endure their horrible existence.

THE INITIAL INTERVIEW

The initial interview with an elderly patient, as with all patients, is of strategic importance. Harry Stack Sullivan said that information not obtained at the very onset of treatment can sometimes take years to uncover and then to understand. Unfortunately, with elderly patients, time is often not available. Therapists will have personal questions regarding the treatment of an elderly patient: how will it affect them as therapists? How much time and energy do they want to invest in this patient? How much can they tolerate? How useful do they think they can be? These reactions will affect others who are involved in assessing the patient, and it is important for the therapist to be aware of these psychodynamic feelings. But practical issues are also vital. Having more than one suicidal patient at a time may be a strain on the rest of a therapist's practice and personal life. The therapist should consider all the practical and emotional issues involved in treating a suicidal patient. The more positive and optimistic the therapist is, the better the treatment outcome will be.

If a patient has been referred because of a suicidal possibility, self-destructive tendencies will probably be evident to the therapist at the onset of treatment—for example, how they choose to seek relief from unbearable pain, the nature of their dependency on others, whether they lack feelings of self-worth, if they have fear of the future and, often most important, have they reached a point where they have lost hope. According to Rangell (1988), the range of motivations for those who resort to suicide is not all that wide. "The moment of decision always rests on deeper states: on the relative degrees of satisfaction or frustration; on hopes and expectations of the satisfaction or frustration; on hopes and expectations of the satisfaction of instincts (loving and aggressive), or their opposite; on the possibility of ego mastery or its unlikelihood; on superego tranquility or savagery toward the ego and the self. Again, the range is not wide. A small number of crucial ratios are the determining factors."

Two main forces are at work in the initial interview. One is (hopefully) the existence of interest, attention and therapeutic vigilance on the part of the therapist and the other is the counterforce that a therapeutic alliance establishes (which at early stages will not have had sufficient time to develop) which will eventually help control destructive impulses. If a client commits suicide in the middle of treatment, it will usually be a true surprise to the clinician, whereas if it occurs near the end of treatment, when there are plans for reentry into life, changes in personality and attempts at new activities, all of which reactivate anxiety, it cannot be entirely unanticipated.

DEALING WITH SYMPTOMATOLOGY

It is imperative to meet the patient, as the saying goes, "where she lives." For our purposes here this means that therapists must try to get into their clients' heads. They should try to uncover any defenses their clients may have and whether they have feelings of loneliness or lack of self-worth. It is important to come right out and openly discuss their suicidal fantasies. The superego's harshness must be watched carefully; many patients cannot distinguish between feelings and actions; for example, to them, crimes of the mind may merit punishment. If possible, a therapist should try to determine why the client wants to kill himself. While elderly people generally have many different reasons for committing suicide, they some-times do it as a means of atoning for their sins (Havens 1967). While wanting to obtain as much information as soon as possible, the therapist should not overwhelm the patient with questions regarding the cause of his troubles; these subjects may often exacerbate feelings of self-con-tempt. When a person feels alone, isolated and unconnected, there is little chance that he will be able to be comforted. Nevertheless, therapists should always encourage their clients to purge their feelings. Suicide among the elderly is often caused by intolerable feelings of hopelessness, self-contempt and isolation, feelings so terrible that death seems better than life. These topics should be discussed and the therapist can try to help the client work through them.

Elsewhere in this book depression is discussed at some length, but here I wish to distinguish it from despair. Depression often results after a loss of one sort or another and is sometimes accompanied by feelings of anger and protest. Despair is qualitatively different from depression, because with it comes the feeling that the future will never be better and that life will never change. In this position of despair, people often feel extremely alone and that no one else can understand their distress, and even if they did, they wouldn't be able to help. Roth (1955) says that the therapist "must reach through the gray web of depression and strike a personal relationship with the patient that contains support and the possibility of hope, even while hitting the stance of despair and accepting the possibility of failure."

This is a difficult goal for the therapist to reach. Because many suicidal patients have ambivalent viewpoints, if the therapist overemphasizes the positive and hopeful aspects of their lives, patients cannot maintain the fulcrum position and instead tend to absorb and retain only negative aspects. If the patient descends into serious despair, the therapist must be able to tolerate it (no easy task) and focus on helping the client to assume some sense of self-worth. By delving into the causes of despair, a therapist often causes the client to confront misery he may not wish to uncover, and reveal surface issues the therapist may not be able to help solve. This is a crucial issue with the older patient for, as Erik Erikson notes, it is the final development task—that is, we achieve either ego integrity or accept despair in old age. Patients should be permitted to experience this unwanted affect (fear and pain about delicate issues) with a therapist who is willing to share the client's pain and be, at least, a temporary sounding board for her misery. If the therapist can tolerate these dark feelings, the patient may gain the strength to follow the therapist's direction.

In therapy, it is axiomatic for therapists to attempt to move patients away from their current, usually painful psychological state of mind to a more realistic and positive, less punitive position—in other words, to take her away from where she used to be to where she may not want to go, but needs to go if treatment is to be successful. For example, when a new patient complains about certain things that her former therapist did that irritated her, the current therapist should try to do things in a different manner. Similarly, if the patient concentrates solely on outside issues, the therapist should direct attention to the dyadic relationship in the room. Should transference be the exclusive object of the client's concentration, reality situations outside the office should be discussed. In other words, the therapist should address and try to relieve the patient's feelings of self-concept by correcting distortions that refute her evidence for self-scorn. Suicidal persons often introject—in other words, they unconsciously incorporate untrue (or perhaps partially untrue) ideas into their personality, turning hostility they feel toward others onto themselves. As a result, the therapist is right in the middle of this—not an easy situation.

HOW THERAPY WORKS

The therapist must be able to feel empathy for the patient's despair, his potential desire for death, murderous hate, intensity of hopelessness and helplessness. Can one person (for our purposes, the therapist) ever feel the depth of another's despair? And if so, how will it assist the patient? Havens (1967) suggests that therapists should try to delve into the lower dark corners of their patients' lives by finding something in their own lives that can approximate (even if only slightly) the intolerable suffering that their client feels. Therapists can then demonstrate to their clients that not only can they bear intense pain, but more importantly, that they understand it, have even gone through it, and that they will try to go where the client may not want to go, or perhaps does not know how to get there. Moreover, the therapist must do this without pressing the client in terms of time. Most affects diminish with time. With the suicidal older person therapists do not usually have the luxury of waiting for a resolution; but they must stay patiently with the client and wait until her feelings unravel. Understanding is needed, not direction, reassurance or judgment.

As with any therapy, the helping professional is interested in how the patient applies her beliefs to other aspects of her life, especially during earlier times and with a different cast of people. Grief work certainly mandates attention to earlier losses and repetitive patterns in coping. A therapist must trace the anger and note how rage is self-directed.

Certain mechanical changes in the therapeutic situation are necessary with suicidal patients. The therapist must be as available as possible, must tolerate the client's dependency on the therapist by being willing to make additional appointments, must be willing to make unscheduled emergency appointments and must accept (sometimes constant) phone calls, which may often come in the middle of the night. Not infrequently, as mentioned, the therapist may have to work with an unfamiliar hospital team, although the adjustments in practice efforts just described hopefully will make hospitalization unnecessary. Years ago, when I started my training, contracts with the patient were made only as a putative security measure: "I, the therapist and you, the patient both agree you will not hurt yourself—that you will call me whenever you think you need to do so." We would then shake hands. This provided a false sense of security—lulling therapists into complacency, for the contract could be easily forgotten.

Above all, the therapist must bring hope into what is a seemingly hopeless situation. If suicide is an attempt to restore the sense of self (at the ultimate cost), hope must be introduced as an alternative—that is, there has to be a reasonable expectation that the present conditions can be overcome or ameliorated. "The ultimate but crucial dynamic spurring the suicidal impulse to destruction of the self is the status of hope—the ego's deep, pervasive unconscious assessment of the potential for overcoming conditions that have brought about the present internal condition of a traumatic state with no expected path of escape. The differences among anxiety, depression and a suicidal state have to do with the status of the complex ego affect of hope. With a suicidal urge, there is no future. Hope neither is present now nor will ever appear" (Rangell 1988). Correcting distortions regarding time will help create hope for the suicidal person. The truth is, as I have stated, that time does alter the situation and that most suicidal crises are usually transient. Hope often appears to arise from having good early experiences with the patient. Gambling with suicide may keep a scintilla of hope alive for the patient as she plays with fate and relies on an alliance with someone (perhaps the therapist) that she perceives as more powerful than herself. The therapist must believe that the crisis can be weathered and that she can withstand fatalism; therapists should not think they can get away with false reassurances—without doubt they will quickly be spotted by the patient.

TRANSFERENCE

The appearances of transference phenomena always seem to be an evidence of the persistence of the unconscious throughout the life span. Grotjahn (1955; 1978) suggests that the older patient's constricted social ambiance gives the transference situation a greater emotional investment. Van der Kolk (1983) agrees that the intensely idealized transference reactions that arise during childhood and old age are often a defense against isolation. The relationship with the therapist, who is often seen as the patient's child (Krassner 1977), may be the sole meaningful interpersonal interaction in the patient's current life. At the same time, the transference objects are more varied (they may be children, parents, grandchildren, even in-laws) due to the broader, longer life experience (Meerloo 1955). Consequently, there are more frequent shifts between positive and negative feelings. Sometimes, establishing a strong enduring object in the suicidal person's life, even when they may say they want to be left alone, at the same time they actually crave their presence, and this appears to be a necessary aspect of effective treatment. The therapist's inexorable patience and empathy provide the patient with relief and a self-object that is more self-sustaining than directive or authoritarian. Where the omnipotent authority role is part of the transference, it can be used temporarily to allow the release of hopelessness and helplessness and then "transferred" to the patient. The patient's own sense of mastery is enhanced and he can use the therapist as an ally.

For women in therapy, the deepest resistance can often be a reawakening or recognition of the earliest primitive love and yearning for their mothers—a considerable amount of submerged libido that has been translated into rage and aggression. The elderly patient needs the same amount of help to work through the mourning process that comes from early lack of mothering as do younger age groups. Recognizing anxiety and being patient with the client often reveals the persistent desire for final reunion or rebirth with her mother figure. For many women, this desire is often denied and hidden deep inside because this strange, fearful mother often is a figure that has overwhelmed the patient for a long time—and this is especially true for the elderly woman who has had more time. The therapist may be targeted for such a reunion. The rage against the self may then also protect the other person. Or he may become the dependent, hopeless, constructed object the patient perceives herself to be. Hope is rekindled by "hunting for the lost libido" (Lazarus et al. 1987).

For many researchers, countertransference, not age per se, is the limiting factor in successful treatment of the elderly (Grotjahn 1955; Meerloo 1955: Linden 1957; Blum and Tallmer 1977; Krassner 1977; King 1980), but others argue in the same way for the use of transference (Blau and Berezin 1982). They believe that early object ties and level of maturity determine the type of transference more than chronological age does. I suggest that with the elderly suicidal patient, both of these forces are maximized due to the severe nature of the crisis. Both the transference and countertransference come into play very quickly, shift rapidly and their importance waxes and wanes. These alterations necessitate careful and ceaseless scrutiny and tolerance on the part of the therapist.

COUNTERTRANSFERENCE

All therapists have some particular blind spot that prevents them from listening objectively to their patients. This countertransference need not necessarily hinder work if the therapist recognizes it, works on it and allows these feelings to be monitored. The opportunities for such blind spots are increased when the patient is not only old, but suicidal, or not only suicidal but also old. I have briefly referred to the phenomenon of gerontophobia—the widespread, irrational dread of becoming old. Woodward (1983) states that the fear of difference forms the basis for this prejudice and that being old is indictable as a moral crime. She quotes Simone de Beauvoir (1973) who speaks of the ugliness, decrepitude and frailty that invades our bodies as we age. De Beauvoir, however, fails to distinguish old age from a disease process. The senescent, the victim of the prejudice, is urged to fight societal bias—equating age with death. When you are old, you are close to the end of life in the mortal world, but, of course, there is often a long span of old age before death. Older persons are a direct, omnipresent reminder of the fact that humans are immortal, assaulting, of course, the illusion that we are invulnerable. In a research study, I found a large number of older psychoanalysts who avowed repeatedly in their interviews that they had never missed a day's work in many years of practice, a likely defense mechanism that reflected their inner denial of death. Arendt (1958) says that "unlike pain, there is one aspect of death in which it is as though death appears among the living, and that is in old age" (Woodward 1983). For the therapist, the older person can represent parental figures against whom they may have some unresolved problem. A gerontologic patient may seem to be of low status; they are often poor and do not fit into the YAVIS profile (young, articulate, verbal, intelligent and suave). Unfortunately, there are still few available courses in gerontology in colleges and graduate schools and only a few analytic supervisors are experienced in working with older people. Moreover, many people, particularly in urban areas, have become accustomed to ignoring and overlooking the homeless, the old and the frail. But for therapists and other helping professionals, when they are in the office, sitting face-to-face with an elderly person, they are suddenly obliged to take the person seriously. In fact, a therapist's attitude toward an elderly person who has come to him for help can literally be a matter of life and death for that person. This is the same patient that some therapists and a good portion of society want to separate themselves from, because they want reassurance that it is the elderly person who is hopeless, inept and frail, not themselves. There are only a few good older mentors and role models left. Even therapists with older relatives may see their own family as a different, special group whose longevity, by virtue of DNA, fortunately protects them from an early demise. Since the elderly differ from each other more than any other age group, the clinician must possess flexibility and a freedom from orthodoxy.

Aging itself does not prevent psychoanalytic or psychotherapeutic work; the old most definitely have the capacity for transference, insight, self-observation and the ability to work on dreams and unconscious material. As a plus, they are aware that there are time limitations, and this seems to mobilize their energies and speed up their motivation for change. The goals of therapy are to make the patient more alert to the real self so that he may enhance his present existence and further his chances for future creativity and pleasure, no matter what his age. For an activity-oriented therapist the fact that elderly patients often have no sense of the future and are not able to plan for later goals and positive actions can be very threatening. Perhaps there is a gender difference here, as Kurt Eissler has suggested; that women analysts are more able to accept passivity in patients than men are. When the patient wishes to self-destruct in a passive manner by refusing medication or by smoking, abusing alcohol and the like, the therapist's rejection of passive wishes may be exacerbated.

The older suicidal patient evokes many possibilities for countertransference to occur. The current era of more liberal thinking about euthanasia, living wills and assisted suicides may confuse therapists even further, for they desperately do not want their patients to kill themselves. An additional complication is the factor of possible litigation should the patient commit suicide. Everyone, especially the therapist, *must* recognize the signs of countertransference: withdrawal, changing or shortening appointments, passivity and anxiety. These reactions often occur when the older patient is covertly suicidal or closer to committing suicide than the therapist realized.

One frequent countertransferential response to the repeated appearance of apathy, discouragement, rage, fear, hopelessness and helplessness experienced in a suicidal patient is for the therapist to begin to hate the patient. The therapist may even wish to kill the patient, falling into the psychological trap of becoming the inflicter of punishment, the murderer.

The therapist can project feelings of aggression onto the patient, taking on a masochistic role and inviting the patient to be the sadist. Or the therapist's narcissistic response may be a frank aversion to the patient, translated by acting out. This countertransferential hate may also be a reaction to fear and a wish that the patient will actually injure herself, and that she will commit suicide. Patients seem to be able to bear sado-masochistic tendencies in their therapist more easily than deprivation of the therapist's social support. Aversion, of course, connotes rejection. The therapist may suggest rationalized, misplaced, premature termination of treatment or a turning to other modalities such as drugs and possibly electroconvulsive therapy, or calling friends or relatives to intervene, or sometimes even the police. These suggested termination threats or punitive ultimatums also appear when the patient is making ambivalently tinged suicidal attempts. (These attempts are actually less frequent with older persons who generally use far more lethal weapons and therefore more often complete suicide.)

Issuing any ultimatum, no matter what the age of the patient, suggests that the therapist's anxiety has soared to an intolerable level. The therapist is really declining to continue analyzing and shifting the blame onto the patient. (This is similar to a therapist telling an obese patient to stop overeating or he will discontinue work.) In this circumstance, undesirable, unacknowledged parts of the self have escaped repressive control and the therapist needs to talk to colleagues or supervisors. The therapist's dislike may show itself as outright indignation or as indirect attempts to manipulate, castigate, challenge or dare the patient. Others lecture, browbeat and raise guilt. For therapists who harbor rescue fantasies (directed originally perhaps toward a depressed parent), the patient's continued wish to die or to commit suicide may lead to more perilous, intense, negative countertransference feelings. It is one thing to be concerned with a patient's welfare, but quite another to act out the need to be the over-protective parent, offering quasi-supports rather than continuing the search for some healthy remnant that the therapist can bind into a working alliance. By acting out, the therapist, now thwarted, becomes more angry, despairing and resentful. Glover's famous dictum is right on target: "Your cooperation or your life!"

Preferably, we will utilize clinical data to reach decisions about suicidal patients. We cannot rely too much on our preconscious or unconscious to assess the danger of suicide, especially when dealing with schizophrenic or borderline patients. Brie and Maltsberger (1983) note that the subjective experiences of these patients are so different from ours that there is a generous margin for empathic failures. In other words, most therapists have not experienced the same type of profound aloneness or the devastating worthlessness that their clients have experienced. If they have, they may be more than amenable to disavowing those parts of themselves or isolating and even repressing the experience. It is also possible that therapists may be extraordinarily attuned to such feelings. Others believe that therapists must rely on their gut feelings (Litman 1959; Motto 1965). But patients are able to conceal from the wisest clinicians their deepest wounds and preoccupations. The therapist needs to detect when that bottom line of unbearability has been reached, but one should never rely solely on clinical intuition (Mann 1985).

From the patient's frame of reference there are also erroneous (or rather ignorant) beliefs that may eventuate in suicide. It is difficult to estimate the severity of suicidal attempts if the therapist and the patient disagree about external observable facts. Maltsberger and Brie cite the example of Valium or aspirin, which the patients often assume they can use to kill themselves. In contrast, wrist-cutting, often intended solely as a gesture, may actually result in lethal hemorrhage. A common misbelief is that those who talk about or threaten suicide, never do so. What does the patient imagine it would be like to be dead? Who (if anyone) in the patient's past has wished the him dead? Hidden illusions or secret delusions must be exposed, albeit many of these fantasies are often on a preconscious or unconscious level. As already mentioned, many patients fantasize a reunion with a dead loved one.

Another incorrect belief or hypothesis may be noted in therapists after repeated minor abortive suicide attempts are made by the same patient. It is imperative for the therapist to examine the life circumstances that may turn a spiteful, common overdose, for example, into a lethal dose the next time. Some patients consistently desire to be seen as desperate, while others are in fact genuinely suicidal; it is imperative that the therapist differentiate between these two types of persons. We cannot accept a suicidal person's estimate of himself, but neither can we ignore his threats. The threats are usually an attempt to establish a relationship with the therapist or a cry for help.

Many older isolated patients thrive in a hospital setting after a suicidal attempt, where the warmth and care that are often provided can allow for optimistic outpatient planning. Therapists have to be careful when the patient has to leave this environment. As well, when the therapist is on vacation, it can be a very difficult time for the patient. Therapists must alert their patients to other resources and should try to make sure that they will use them if they get in trouble. It is imperative to correctly assess the amount of available emotional support and determine whether or not the patient is able to accept the support. The therapist is in a precarious position when working by himself in a private setting. Therapeutic sessions are, after all, only a small fraction of the patient's life.

The interplay between the various caring disciplines may vitiate good therapy. The therapist may choose to ignore the advice of others, but the patient may discern this dissension, causing an increase in anxiety, a lack of holding support and a lack of the important support the therapist provides in stressful times.

These countertransferential errors are only a sampling. Almost all therapists have some patients who make them feel great, others who annoy them and some they are indifferent to. It is particularly vital to identify how the older suicidal patient makes the therapist feel and to utilize these feelings constructively. Therapists often mirror the lack of caring feelings for the patient, her family and her friends.

An important caveat is for therapists not to concur with the patient's fatalism and sense of hopelessness. They should never permit flight from important issues and should try to keep the working alliance going. On a final note, it is important for therapists to admit their errors, which has the added benefit of making the patient feel less "crazy" and more human.

The therapist must take all suicidal threats seriously. The question is not whether a nonpsychotic patient really wants to kill herself, but whether or not there is a real chance that a suicide attempt will be made (Zinberg 1964). People kill themselves even when they are under constant scrutiny in hospitals (Kahne 1968). Therefore, hospitalization may not be the answer even if the patient is about to commit suicide. It is important for therapists not to yield to a patient's despair and not to dissociate themselves from the patient. This can often encourage suicide.

THE EFFECT OF A PATIENT'S SUICIDE UPON THE THERAPIST

We have not discussed the impact on the therapist of a patient's death by suicide. The therapist, unlike other mourners, is quite alone and may often even be blamed by the family as the cause for suicide. Therapists should talk to supportive colleagues, to supervisors and other therapists who have experienced suicides. Young therapists react to suicide more strongly than older therapists, experiencing a sense of guilt, inadequacy and responsibility. However, if a therapist accepts suicidal patients, suicide by some of them is inevitable. The literature on this topic is sparse, but two studies (Rosen 1974; Litman 1964) show a high incidence of suicide in psychiatric training centers. The therapists, unable to really prepare themselves for these events, experienced feelings of disbelief and betrayal, shaken self-confidence, accident proneness and a lot of anger directed toward supervisors or the patients themselves.

Collegial consultation (Kolodny et al. 1979) can help the therapist work through this "unofficial" mourning. Many solve this problem instead by avoiding the treatment of suicidal patients in the future as much as possible. Others focus on the decay, frailty and age of the patient to assuage feelings of responsibility and guilt.

REFERENCES

Arendt, H. 1958. *The Human Condition.* Chicago: University of Chicago Press.

Blau, D. and M.A. Berezin. 1982. Neuroses and character disorders. *Journal of Geriatric Psychiatry* 15:55-95.

Blum, J. and M. Tallmer. 1977. The therapist vis-à-vis the older patient. *Psychotherapy* 14:361-367.

Brie, D. and J.T. Maltsberger. 1983. *The Practical Formulation of Suicide Risk.* Cambridge, MA: Firefly Press.

De Beauvoir, S. 1973. *The Coming of Age.* New York: Warner Books.

Grotjahn, M. 1955. Analytical psychotherapy with the elderly. *Psychoanalytic Review* 42:419-427.

Grotjahn, M. 1978. Group Communication and Group Therapy with the Aged: A Promising Project. In L.F. Jarvik, ed., *Aging into the Twenty-first Century: Middle-Agers Today.* New York: Gardner Press.

Havens, L.L. 1967. Recognition of suicidal risks through the psychologic examination. *New England Journal of Medicine* 276:210-215.

Kahne, M.J. 1968. Suicide among patients in mental hospitals. *Psychiatry* 31:32-43.

King, P. 1980. The life cycle as indicated by the nature of the transference in the psychoanalysis of the middle-aged and the elderly. *International Journal of Psychoanalysis* 51:153-160.

Kolodny, S., R.L. Binder and A.A. Bronstein. 1979. The working through of patients' suicides by four therapists. *Suicide and Life-Threatening Behavior* 9:33-46.

Krassner, J. 1977. Treatment of the Elder Persons. In F. Frabricant, J. Barron and J. Krasner, eds., *To Enjoy is to Live.* Chicago: Nelson Hall.

Lazarus, L.W., N. Newton, B. Cohler, et al. 1987. Frequency and presentation of depressive symptoms in patients with primary degenerative dementia. *American Journal of Psychiatry* 144:41-45.

Linden, M.E. 1957. The Promise of Therapy in the Emotional Problems of Aging. Paper presented at the Fourth Congress of the International Association of Gerontology, Merano, Italy.

Litman, R.E. 1959. Immobilization response to suicidal behavior. *Archives of General Psychiatry* 81:360-364.

Litman, R.E. 1964. When patients commit suicide. *American Journal of Psychotherapy* 19:570-576.

Maltsberger, J.T. 1988. Suicide danger: clinical estimation and decision. *Suicide and Life-Threatening Behavior* 18:47-54.

Mann, C. 1985. Aging: a developmental reality ignored by psychoanalytic theory. *Journal of the American Academy of Psychoanalysis* 13:481-487.

Meerloo, J.A.M. 1955. Transference and resistance in geriatrics psychotherapy. *Psychoanalytic Review* 42:72-82.

Motto, J.A. 1965. Suicide attempts. *Archives of General Psychiatry* 13:916-920.

Nunberg, H. 1948. Will to Recovery. In H. Nunberg, ed., *Practice and Theory of Psychoanalysis.* New York: International Universities Press.

Peniazek, Z. 1982. The experience of time and hope in the elderly. *Contemporary Psychoanalysis* 18:635-644.

Rangell, L. 1988. The decision to terminate one's life. *Suicide and Life-Threatening Behavior* 18:28-46.

Rosen, D.H. 1974. Mental Stresses in Residency Training and Opportunities for Prevention. Paper presented to the American Psychiatric Association, Detroit.

Roth, M. 1955. The natural history of mental disorders in old age. *Journal of Mental Science* 102:281-301.

Shneidman, E.S. 1981. Psychotherapy with suicide patients. *Suicide and Life-Threatening Behavior* 11:341-347.

Van der Kolk, A. 1983. The idealizing transference and group psychother-
    apy with elderly patients. *Journal of Geriatric Psychiatry* 16:99-103.
Woodward, K. 1983. Instant repulsion. *Kenyon Review* 5(4):43-66.
Woodward, K. 1986. Reminiscence and the Life Review. In T.R. Cole and
    S.A. Gadow, eds., *What Does it Mean to Grow Old?* Durham, NC: Duke
    University Press.
Zinberg, N. 1964. Psychoanalytic considerations of aging. *Journal of the
    American Psychoanalytic Association* 12:151-159.

6

Family Therapy for the Suicidal Elderly

Joseph Richman, PhD

Elderly suicide is preventable and treatable, but few people are aware of this. Even fewer realize the positive influence that the family of the potential suicide can offer. Therefore, suicidologists need to know much more about families, family therapists need to know much more about suicide, and both need to know much more about gerontology. All three areas are inextricably tied together; the suicide rate of the elderly is higher than any other age group and the family of the potential suicide is almost always involved.

The family can be a source of the tension that actually instigates the suicidal act, but they can also play a very important role in helping the potential suicide. Family therapy conducted by properly trained therapists is, in the author's opinion, the treatment of choice for suicidal patients. The discussion in this chapter—family treatment of the suicidal elderly—can also apply to people of all ages, for what is good therapy for an older suicidal person is usually good therapy for the younger suicidal person too.

Family therapy is a very powerful treatment tool, and as such some risks are always involved. More suicides have occurred during family treatment because of the dangers of *success* than because of feelings of disappointment of the treatment not working out. In this chapter I hope to make the reasons for these feelings clear. Training and experience of the therapist, the family and perhaps the patient can reduce risks and help the suicidal person and his family resume normal life. To this end, this chapter will describe the procedures and methods for the effective assessment and treatment of suicidal persons from a family therapy perspective.

The five goals of this chapter are to (1) evaluate the risk of suicide and its multidetermined foundations; (2) reduce the stress and tensions in the family that are contributing to the risk; (3) help the therapist be prepared for the conflicts and anxieties that are aroused during the treatment process; (4) learn how to anticipate and be prepared for crises and how to turn a negative interaction into a positive one; and finally, (5) know how to manage the stress that is inevitably aroused in the therapist.

Suicide based on false diagnoses occurs frequently, whether by a physician or by the suicidal person himself. Sometimes a suicidal person's diagnoses are delusional. Slaby (1992), for example, presented the case of a 90-year-old lady with the fixed belief she had AIDS. She had no other psychiatric symptoms, but was suffering from a monosymptomatic depression that was successfully treated with electroconvulsive therapy.

However, it is not often recognized that these delusions are often shared beliefs, a kind of folie à deux, that have more deadly strength because they are shared. On February 20, 1992, the television program *A Current Affair* presented an account of a man who helped his mother commit suicide because she thought she had cancer. It turned out that she did not have cancer. Nevertheless, her son proudly declared that he would do the same thing were the situation to be repeated.

Events such as these that lead to suicide occur frequently, but are rarely publicized. The lesson to be learned is that all those treating suicidal people must learn to work with the family, to educate them to recognize danger signs of depression and suicide in a family member and where and how to go for help. Finally it is important to erase erroneous beliefs and thinking that might cause suicide.

All of those who work with suicidal people must learn how to communicate with the suicidal person's family. As early as 1947, Bowlby reported that the true origin of a suicidal state often emerges only when the suicidal person's family is seen by the therapist. Unfortunately, there is often no family intervention when it is clearly called for. A recent example of this concerns Bruno Bettelheim, the famous psychoanalyst. When he was in his eighties, he suffered a stroke and some time later, committed suicide. In most of the published comments, including those by fellow analysts, Dr. Bettelheim's age and biological condition were presented as sufficient reason for his suicide, often with an attitude of unabashed approval and admiration. The rest of his life situation including his current relationships were not considered. However, in the obituary written for the *New York Times*, Dan Goleman explained that Dr. Bettelheim was involved in some sort of conflict with one of his daughters. He had just moved from a beautiful home in California to a senior residence in Maryland to be near another daughter. He was not adjusting well to the move and combined with the stress and worry about his medical problems, he soon became seriously depressed. He killed himself while in this depressed state and in the throes of a complex and unresolved life crisis.

As Dr. Bettelheim's case illustrates, the effects of having a serious illness cannot be considered apart from a person's entire psychosocial and family picture. Biological factors alone are not sufficient reason for suicide in the elderly, or for anyone else for that matter. The elderly suffer more losses, more life crises, more blows to their self-esteem and in general more of the events statistically associated with suicide than any other group. There is no reason to ignore these conditions and to deal exclusively with illness, as is too frequently the case. In particular, social supports, especially in the family, must be understood, evaluated and made a part of the therapeutic program.

Many of the elderly suicidal patients I have seen in a geriatric clinic and in my private practice had suffered multiple blows and many life crises. By and large, these patients were treated successfully; they not only survived, but ended up leading richer and more satisfactory lives.

It is unfortunate, therefore, that Dr. Bettelheim obtained no such care. One account described a conversation he had had with a man at a party. The man asked him how he felt and Dr. Bettelheim said he was depressed. The man's response was, "Have you heard of The Hemlock Society?" Dr. Bettelheim not only had heard of The Hemlock Society, but he was a member. Perhaps his involvement with this group contributed to his decision to commit suicide instead of trying to confront and resolve the crisis he was in.

We have found that suicide in the elderly (Bettelheim is a typical example) is very treatable, especially when the specific problem causing pain is emphasized during the treatment program. Many of those who work with people who are full of great despair and hopelessness have recognized the therapeutic role of the family. We do not need politicians who are running for office to affirm the value of the family. Family therapists have always recognized the potential value of the family.

In 1990, Elie Wiesel wrote a tribute to the musical play, *The Rothschilds*, and discussed its touching depiction of a loving, loyal close-knit family. He wisely observed that these qualities are universal. "The most moving aspect of this play comes when we realize that we have been present at a true celebration of the family, any family, irrespective of its ethnic origins."

Family therapists have also found that these constructive features are even present in families whose members may be destructive toward each other. Artists and writers, such as Elizabeth Swados (1991), have reached similar insights. Swados worked with troubled children who were in the cast of her play, *Runaways*. She saw that their self-destructive behavior represented a misguided effort to save and protect loved ones in their families who needed help. "Kids were loyal and loving to the most awful characters," she wrote, "simply because it was dictated by love." It is these forces of love, loyalty and the wish to heal that is behind the efficacy of family therapy, even with families that appear "rotten" and cruel. The therapist's task is to bring out and strengthen these potentials. These constructive and positive forces can be found in all family structures, not only in traditional two-parent families; they are present in families where old and young members are suicidal, where there is one parent, and in families that are dysfunctional.

As already noted, family conflicts are present in suicidal people of all ages. For example, I compared the precipitants and background of suicide attempts in younger and older patients who were seen for suicidal behavior or impulses (Richman 1975). Most of the younger persons (under 40) were responding to events such as problems in school or work and such potentially reversible losses as the breakup of a love affair. More of the over-40 subjects (many of whom were over 60) were responding to such events as a serious mental or physical illness and to irreversible losses, such as the death of a spouse. In other words, their suicidal reactions were related to age-associated problems. But family tensions and conflicts were present in over 90 percent of the younger and 70 percent of the older subjects.

Family problems are frequently compounded for the suicidal elderly when old, unfinished business between the older person and the other family members is brought up. I also found that more than one generation could become suicidal. Frequently, in fact very frequently, unresolved conflicts between parents and *their* parents were the cause of their children's suicides. They were caught in the middle of the conflicts of the two older generations. Suicide is often a family-determined reaction that may sometimes require three generations to develop.

A typical example was a mother who was involved in a conflict with her parents. This woman's daughter was assigned the impossible task of being the mediator between her mother and grandparents. Caught in the middle and pushed to take sides, she finally made a major suicide attempt. Her mother had done the same many years ago.

Suicide can also be an inherited behavior. A good example of this was the suicide of an elderly man who was terminally ill with cancer. He shot himself in the head and killed himself. Two months later, the newspaper reported the suicide of his 16-year-old grandson, who shot himself in the head with the same gun.

Despairing persons, such as the terminally ill grandfather, can be treated with medication, supportive psychotherapy, and especially with the help of their families. A comprehensive treatment program including family therapy with the terminally ill grandfather might also have prevented the suicide of the young grandson.

Unfortunately, family-oriented treatment has been generally recommended only for younger suicidal patients. For example, Mitchell and Rosenthal (1992) strongly recommend family therapy for suicidal children and adolescents, but neither they nor anyone else, aside from myself, make the same recommendations for the suicidal elderly. Both the clinical success of family therapy and the importance of a family evaluation for risk assessment highlight the need for more knowledge about how to work with the family of the suicidal elderly. This chapter summarizes the basic principles and procedures for the family assessment and therapy of suicidal patients in later life.

Family therapy and assessment are best understood within a comprehensive, multidetermined theoretical framework. Suicide is a biopsychosocial event, not a purely biophysical state, or a psychological reaction, or the result of social influences alone. Basic contributions to the understanding of suicide come from many disciplines.

In 1957, Freud covered individual, instinctual and dynamic interpersonal components. Erikson (1950) expanded the psychoanalytic theories of human development to encompass the entire life span from birth to death. Durkheim (1951) emphasized social integration and its breakdown in the etiology of suicide. Most family therapists and many suicidologists concur that both the individual and society—the "I" and the "we"—develop within the family where they either thrive or fail to mature. (Richman [1993] presents a fuller account of the theoretical basis for a multidetermined, family-oriented therapy of the suicidal elderly.)

ASSESSMENT

No matter what the treatment modality, the assessment must be as complete as possible. Even when family therapy is the treatment of choice, it is rarely the only treatment. Consequently, a competent and thorough individual assessment that is followed by a family evaluation is absolutely necessary.

The most important and frequent demographic, epidemiologic and recognition signs that are statistically and clinically associated with serious suicidal behavior (both attempted and completed) can be classified into the following five areas:

1. *Ego-Weakening Factors.* These include mental and physical illnesses, pain and other symptoms and the unremitting symptoms that do not respond to treatment.
2. *Social Factors.* For example, suicide in the elderly is often associated with living alone, living in the inner city and other variables associated with social isolation and alienation.
3. *Psychodynamic Factors.* These include a current and past history of major losses and separations, a history of suicide attempts, a family history of suicide and a variety of social and personal crises.
4. *Other Danger Signs and Communication Factors.* Included are the rejection of help, changes in mood and behavior, giving away precious possessions and other verbal and nonverbal suicidal communications.
5. *Recovery Factors.* These involve the personal strengths, defenses and abilities of the suicidal individual and the social resources in the family and social network that the therapist works with.

The above summary is incomplete because it deals primarily with the suicidal individual. However, the context is an essential component of the suicidal condition, especially the family context. I have devoted over a quarter of a century to the treatment and study of the family during a suicidal state and have written many volumes on the family and suicide. To briefly summarize my findings, the family context of a suicidal state can be seen as a process starting with a family history of separation anxiety (and therefore change anxiety), which in turn leads to a number of maladaptive family patterns, such as a closed family system. These are designed to protect what are perceived as threats to the family and a variety of role and behavior disturbances such as double-bind communications and scapegoating. These individual and family dynamics are behind an accumulation of unresolved crises, each one adding to a state of unbearable stress and distress. There is a direct line from the initial separation anxiety to the final crisis, which is seen as the last straw, ending in an attempted or successful suicide.

David Clark and his associates (1992) studied the development of suicide in a large number of elderly men and women in the Chicago area. They also described a series of attitudes and events that culminated in a suicidal act. Their data were derived from psychological autopsies of elderly completed suicides, while my formulations were based upon interviews and therapy with hundreds of living suicidal persons and their families of all ages. Nevertheless, I believe that our two sets of results complemented each other—the same kind of life histories looked at from different perspectives. The combination of clinical and research work can be very valuable.

The above-mentioned family features are not present in every family, but they are when suicide is an issue. Consequently, for an assessment to be adequate, both the individual and the family components must be evaluated. The greater the number of individual, family and social danger signs, the greater the suicidal risk. Some indicators, however, are more powerful than others. For example, the family factors associated with separation, loss and mourning are of particular importance because suicide often results from a crisis related to loss, which in turn precipitates a crisis in those involved. Similarly, in the suicidal individual the presence of a psychiatric illness, especially an affective disorder, is a major danger sign.

On the other hand, any one of these is best understood and interpreted in the context of the other signs. For example, an individual with a mental illness is more likely to be suicidal in a family with a history of suicide; or a patient may be vulnerable to being a scapegoat or is inducted into the suicidal role in other ways; or a patient may be from a family that exhibits a great deal of emotion, which often means that the family is critical, hostile and emotionally overinvolved with the patient. The emotional factors that involve other people are part of the distressed state which culminates in a suicide. Another example is the social isolation that is often associated with suicide. Social isolation does not occur in a social or family vacuum and there are many people who adjust well and are comfortable with isolation. There are two factors involved when the isolation is suicidogenic. First, those who are isolated and become suicidal have a great need, even a craving, for social contact and cohesion. Second, the isolation in those who are suicidal is dynamically associated with family conflicts, alienation and lack of support.

It is evident from the above examples that individual and family factors are intertwined, with each adding to the understanding of the other. The general public also needs to be educated in recognizing and responding to both the individual and family components of suicide. The problem is that the family members are often too involved to respond objectively and they all need help. All it takes is one perceptive and caring individual who can see that there is trouble; he can take the steps that might save lives.

There can be danger when the assessment results and recommendations are related to the patient and his family; suicides have been precipitated by diagnosis, treatment recommendations and by the unexamined meaning of these to the patient and family—unexamined, that is, by the therapist. The meaning of a diagnosis or recommendation is part of the assessment process and it must be explored. I even know of suicides that were precipitated by the recommendation of medication. To some patients and their families, mental illness means the end of the road. They respond to a mental illness diagnosis with feelings of terror, helplessness, hopelessness and despair and this in turn can precipitate a suicidal act. In some cases the result is a covert and implacable resistance to treatment. Such fear is sometimes compounded by "the myth of exclusiveness"; in other words, the belief that a close relationship, such as the one between a therapist and patient, can take place only by destroying a previous close relationship, such as the relationship between a mother and child. Suicidal patients may then receive the covert and often unconscious message not to succeed in treatment. Rather than establishing a therapeutic alliance with the therapist or hospital, they resist, fail to respond to the treatment program, and finally kill themselves. In these cases the family often attributes the suicide to the unrelenting nature of their relative's symptoms and the failure of the hospital or therapist to take sufficient precautions.

When suicide is the end result of such resistance, it only emphasizes the importance of broadening the therapeutic scope to include the role of others, especially the family. The closed-family system is where the rejection of needed help is frequent, and the help system is seen as an enemy. Failure in treatment sometimes occurs when patients are trying to be "loyal" to their family and to preserve a family in trouble. The resulting litigation may serve to deny and conceal the true situation.

ASSESSMENT AS THERAPY

When a therapist conducts an evaluation with a therapeutic attitude, the assessment itself can be part of the therapy treatment. However, the therapeutic uses of assessment require greater skill to achieve than assessment or therapy alone requires. In order to accomplish this task, the interviewer must first assume an accepting and interested attitude toward the patient. The feedback of the results of the assessment to the patient and family is also of great value. When properly conducted it can reduce tension and advance the healing process.

THE EVALUATION AND ALLEVIATION OF BURDENS

Virtually all of the suicidal persons that I have seen while I have been in practice have said that the major reason for their suicidal intent was that they felt they were a burden to others. This belief cuts across all age and cultural barriers. A recent (unpublished) paper about suicide among the elderly in Japan notes that a large majority of suicidal Japanese feel that they are a burden to someone else.

When this is the case, there is often a high degree of stress in another person to whom the suicidal person feels he is being a burden, and who is usually a relative. This, in turn, causes depression, suicidal thoughts and mental or physical distress of a significant other. It is a vicious circle. These feelings contribute greatly to the exhaustion of resources for both the suicidal individual and his family.

An example of this is a 60-year-old woman who was treated for depression, but who could not seem to maintain any sort of improvement. Her husband reacted to this by developing chest pains and her son reacted by developing symptoms of a stomach ulcer. "I am hurting everyone I love," the woman said; and as a result she committed suicide (Richman 1986).

Unusual or uncharacteristic behavior by a significant other or a bad turn of events is another cause of stress and burden. Derek Humphry (1978), for example, reported that he reacted to news that his first wife, Jean, had breast cancer by going out and having sex with another woman. Family therapy would have been a better choice.

THE POSITIVE USES OF DEATH WISHES

Death wishes have been theoretically considered to be a major component of the suicidal act. Death wishes are frequently reported by relatives in confidence during their interviews. In subsequent family meetings, I was surprised at first at how often the death wishes were also expressed directly to the suicidal person (literally, "You are causing us so much grief, we wish you would kill yourself"). Later, I began to ask relatives about possible death wishes when they did not verbalize them. This often led to statements such as "I want my son to be dead—it would be better than seeing him this way." I also discovered that statements such as these had already been made at home.

Finally, I learned that when a person expressed *during the session* the wish that the other would die, it could sometimes be the beginning of a cure. The meaning of the death wish is very different in a therapeutic situation than it is in the home. At some level, those involved in a family therapy session express rage and death wishes for a therapeutic intent in order to make things better and as part of a healing process. That is why the presence of death wishes is such a valuable part of the monitoring of suicidal risk.

Death wishes are part of a pervasive preoccupation with death that appears in suicidal persons, often—but not only—as a reaction to crises. An example was an 80-year-old woman who made a serious suicide attempt following the death of her 48-year-old daughter. She responded well to treatment but was preoccupied with the fear of becoming helpless and frequently expressed the thought that she would want to die before that occurred.

In one session with her 45-year-old son she repeated these thoughts, especially related to her fear of having to be dependent on someone else to care for her. "I would rather be dead," she repeated. I asked her son how he would feel about having to care for an aged and helpless mother. He agreed that he would rather that she be dead. I accepted their views and explained how they could obtain a living will which would help solve the problem. At the end of the session I also commented to the son that he was very young and that when he and his mother became older, he might feel differently. He agreed, adding that in reality he had never been faced with a situation such as this. At the end of the session, they left, but the mother lagged behind and said to me, "I have such a feeling of well-being."

The death theme expresses an effort to cope with basic situations that have to do with life and relationships. They touch upon people's need for each other, fear of abandonment and the reassurance that the forces of love and loyalty will always be there.

THE CLINICAL ASSESSMENT INTERVIEW

Information is not enough for an accurate assessment of the elderly. All of the data have to be understood and integrated by someone skilled in interviewing, therapy, gerontology and suicidology. The clinical process requires individual interviews both with the suicidal person and with relatives, followed by a diagnostic family interview.

I strongly recommend that both the individual and family interviews be conducted by the same person. In settings where one person sees the individual patient and another person sees the family, the result is often fragmented rather than providing a complete picture. In some settings, the family interviews are considered peripheral or irrelevant. My view is the opposite; the family interview is the central procedure. When this is not recognized the results can be most unfortunate.

One 78-year-old man was hospitalized on the psychiatric ward of a hospital because of uncontrollable anxiety reactions and suicidal ideation. He suffered from a severe heart ailment and attributed his suicidal reactions entirely to his physical state, but he said he would not act on these thoughts. His therapist agreed with the man's formulation and made no effort to inquire into the nonbiological aspects of his life situation.

The patient was also seen in family meetings by a social worker who discovered that the man had a bad marital situation. His wife found the patient's physical condition difficult to deal with. She felt burdened and began developing more independent activities, especially during his hospitalizations. One Friday, the patient was given a weekend pass. On Saturday, he went to the roof of their apartment house and jumped to his death. The entire hospital staff was extremely shocked, with the exception perhaps of the social worker who saw both the husband and wife together. She also saw the wife after the suicide; she confided that she had not wanted her husband to come home.

The rich marital material obtained by the social worker had been ignored or was unknown to the treatment team. Even in a postmortem conference, the information she provided was still basically ignored. This sort of terrible oversight is far less likely to happen when the same interviewer sees the family and the suicidal individual. The individual and family interviews are not separate; they form a dynamic integrated unit.

Through the assessment interviews, the interviewer can obtain a profile of the people that make up the family; this illuminates all information that is already known about the suicidal condition of the patient. Often the experience is a very intense and emotional one, with an arousal of primitive and violent emotions, which can be very trying, especially to the inexperienced therapist. Nevertheless, this sort of reaction is a desirable development, because no seriously suicidal state occurs without an underlying turmoil of rage and pain in which the family is often centrally involved. When such an eruption and intense interchanges occur during therapy, I know that the patient is going to get better.

MONITORING

The monitoring of depression and suicidal impulses, as well as death wishes and other significant events in the families of suicidal people, is an intrinsic part of the diagnostic interview. One of the basic principles in conducting such an inquiry is a positive attitude by the therapist. For example, when there has been a savage and seemingly destructive interchange, the therapist should commend the patients for being so open. Another principle is a gradually increasing intervention by the therapist through the monitoring of depression, suicide, death wishes and other relevant reactions, followed by such procedures as relabeling. For example, the therapist may point out that the death wish for a family member is a way of stating that the relatives feel completely exasperated, at their wit's end and that they do not know what to do about the situation. I have often experienced virtually total agreement by the family regarding the validity of these interpretations. The purpose of the family session is to reduce tensions, to provide an understanding of the rage and death wishes, to evaluate the family's ability to be part of the healing process, and of course to determine the disposition of the patient and the nature of the treatment plan. Thus, assessment and treatment are not rigidly demarcated activities; one shades into the other.

FROM ASSESSMENT TO CRISIS INTERVENTION

All treatment of suicide begins with crisis intervention and crisis intervention begins with the establishment of rapport, then pinpointing the degree of suicidal intent and identification of the major crisis of the moment. That is also true of assessment, which is why assessment and therapy are inseparable.

The elderly are subject to more crises than any other group. The message is clear—more crisis intervention is needed with the suicidal elderly. That message is pretty well ignored by supporters of euthanasia for the ill or unhappy elderly and by the recommendations that care for the elderly be decreased or discontinued by former Governor Lamm of Colorado and others (Callahan 1987).

For crisis intervention, the role of the family in the development of the suicidal state and the healing power of the family must both be understood. Consequently, everyone involved with suicidal persons should be familiar with family crisis intervention. If the stress in the entire family is not relieved, their separation and death anxieties not decreased and their fears that treatment will culminate in a loss not alleviated, then the treatment of the suicidal patient is much less likely to succeed.

One major question concerning those who are suicidal is whether or not they should be hospitalized. Langsley and co-workers (1968) performed an invaluable service to the mental health field in general, and the field of clinical suicidology in particular, in their description of family crisis intervention as an alternative to hospitalization. Nevertheless, hospitalization is sometimes necessary and, with the right timing and preparation, has saved many lives.

Suicides also occur in hospitals and cannot always be prevented. However, hospitalization itself can be considered as an effective form of crisis intervention which can relieve stress in both the patient and the family. As part of their outpatient family crisis intervention, Langsley and his colleagues occasionally kept a patient in the emergency room overnight in order to afford a temporary respite for the family.

COMMONALITIES IN TREATMENT

There are principles that are valid for all treatment of the suicidal elderly. They comprise three major aspects: the doctor-patient relationship, the presence of themes or content in common, and the personal qualities of the therapist.

1. A positive doctor-patient relationship is a prerequisite for all treatment of the suicidal, with the recognition that in the course of treatment the relationship may become strained and subject to many ups and downs. The ability of the therapist to maintain a hopeful attitude is a prerequisite. The availability of the therapist in time of need is part of this therapeutic relationship. Continuity of care is part of this availability.
2. The central problems of the suicidal person revolve around separation and loss. In the suicidal separation, death anxiety is one. For these reasons, the therapist must be prepared to deal with problems ranging from marital separations to vacations and termination that inevitably arise during treatment.
3. The availability of supports outside the dyadic doctor-patient relationship, notably in the family and social network support systems, is an important component of treatment. The therapist works with these resources and does not place himself in an adversarial position.
4. The qualities of the therapist who can work successfully with suicidal patients include warmth, accurate empathy, an acceptance of the person and family as they are, without demanding that they think and feel differently, and genuineness.

These are universal aspects of all effective mental health professionals as well as all caring people. There are two other requirements for working with suicidal people. First, therapists must have worked out their own destructive and self-destructive wishes, in other words, their own attitude toward death and suicide. Second, the therapist, whether a male or a female, must have a mothering quality because the trauma and the needs behind the inability to tolerate separation, loss and death go very deep. They touch upon the earliest experiences of the infant-mother relationship. Consequently, the therapist must be the "good mother" who will symbolically feed and love the patients and help them grow, mature and develop.

The need for mothering and the other basic needs and conflicts of the suicidal person apply to the entire family. That is why the therapist must be empathic toward all relatives, should not take sides and should be equally committed and caring to all family members. The families of suicidal persons are not simply bystanders. That is why family therapy is so important and is, in my opinion, the treatment of choice, providing the greatest promise for healing.

Therapists who treat suicidal people must be trained in suicidology. If the therapists are trainees or inexperienced, then they must be supervised, with consultation quickly available. Simply being a professional does not qualify someone to work with suicidal patients. There must be training with such a population, and I firmly believe that family therapy must be part of that training.

CONCLUSION

Because of the amount of loss and separation throughout their lives, the suicidal person and family have experienced many traumatic episodes of disruption or discontinuity. Therefore, change has become associated with loss, death, the dissolution or disorganization of the family structure and other traumatic or unbearable events. Consequently change, even positive change, poses a threat. That is why a positive experience in treatment can result in the seeming paradox of a negative therapeutic reaction.

I emphasize the family with the belief that family therapy for suicidal people rests upon two foundations: (1) the potential presence of love and of growth and healing forces in the family, even when they are not present at the time of the suicidal crisis and (2) the presence of a therapist who can help potentiate these loving and positive resources.

The therapist provides an opportunity for contact with the constructive and often creative powers that can overcome the destructive ones. The greater the destructive forces, the greater may be the strength of the constructive forces. It has been a privilege, therefore, to help restore meaning and a sense of community and family in the despairing, suicidal elderly.

REFERENCES

Alger, I. 1986. In J. Richman, ed., *Family Therapy for Suicidal People*. New York: Springer.

Bowlby, J. 1949. The study and reduction of group tensions in the family. *Human Relations* 2:123-128.

Callahan, D. 1987. *Setting Limits*. New York: Simon & Schuster.

Clark, D. 1992. Narcissistic Crises of Aging and Elderly Suicide. Presidential address presented at the 25th Annual Conference of the American Association of Suicidology, Chicago, IL.

Durkheim, E. 1951. *Suicide.* New York: The Free Press (originally published in 1897).

Erikson, E. 1950. *Childhood and Society.* New York: W.W. Norton.

Ferguson, J.H. 1991. Charge to the Panel. Consensus Development Conference on the Diagnosis and Treatment of Depression in Late Life, Bethesda, MD.

Freud, S. 1957. *Mourning and Melancholia.* In J. Strachey, ed., *Standard Edition of the Complete Psychological Works of Sigmund Freud,* Vol. 14. London: Hogarth Press (original work published 1917).

Humphry, D. 1978. *Jean's Way.* Eugene, OR: The Hemlock Society.

Langsley, D.G. and D.M. Kaplan. 1968. *The Treatment of Families in Crisis.* New York: Grune & Stratton.

Leenaars, A.A., R.W. Maris, J.L. McIntosh and J. Richman. 1992. *Suicide and the Older Adult.* New York: Guilford.

Mitchell, M.G. and D.M. Rosenthal. 1992. Suicidal adolescents: Family dynamics and the effects of lethality and hopelessness. *Journal of Youth and Adolescence* 21:23-033.

Richman, J. 1993. *Preventing Elderly Suicide: Overcoming Personal Despair, Professional Indifference and Social Bias.* New York: Springer.

Slaby, A. 1992. The Differential Diagnosis and Diagnostic Specific Management of Suicidal Behavior. Paper presented at the Middletown Psychiatric Center, Middletown, NY.

Swados, E. 1991. *The Four of Us.* New York: Farrar, Straus & Giroux.

Wiesel, E. 1990. Treasured family is the secret wealth of the Rothschilds. *New York Times,* September 23, E5-6.

7

Gender Issues in Counseling the Suicidal Elderly

Silvia Sara Canetto, PhD[*]

In the literature on treatment of suicidal elderly there is a notable absence of any discussion of the impact of gender on the counseling process. Interventions with the suicidal elderly are typically formulated in terms of a gender-neutral elderly person (for example, De Leo and Diekstra 1990; Foster and Burke 1985; Osgood and Thielman 1990; Stenback 1980; Templer and Cappelletty 1986) or in terms of elderly males (for example, Miller 1979; Wolff 1971). The implicit assumption in the first case is that counseling dynamics transcend gender issues. In the second case, the assumption is that whatever applies to men also applies to women. But these assumptions should be reexamined. First, patterns of suicidal behavior in late life vary by gender (see Canetto 1992 for a review). Second, some experiences of aging are different in women and men (see Ory and Warner 1990; Troll and Turner 1979; Hess 1990). Third, gender issues have an impact on the counseling process (Bograd 1990; Brown 1986; Kaplan 1987; Lerner 1984; Mintz and O'Neil 1990; Sherman 1980; Turner and Troll 1982).

This chapter focuses on gender issues bearing upon the initiation, process and goals of counseling the suicidal elderly. Gender patterns of suicidal behavior in the elderly will be reviewed first. Gender differences

---

[*]The author is especially grateful to her collegues and friends Julie Beyers, Jeremy Gersovitz and David Wohl for their helpful comments and suggestions on an earlier version of this chapter.

and similarities in the experience of aging will be discussed next. Lastly, potential gender biases in the counseling process will be addressed.

Since the literature on suicide and the elderly has assumed that gender issues do not influence the counseling process, this chapter will focus more on the differences than on the similarities between older women and men. It is important to remember, however, that older women and men also share many experiences and that in various situations, such as the need for self-expression through relationships and employment, the differences across gender may be less significant than the differences among individuals within each gender.

GENDER AND SUICIDAL BEHAVIOR IN THE ELDERLY

Patterns of elderly suicidal behavior by gender are difficult to determine because of limitations and omissions in the data sources (Canetto 1992). The two main sources of information on suicidal deaths—national official suicide statistics and local epidemiological surveys—do not systematically categorize the information by both gender and age. Official mortality statistics are geographically comprehensive, but limited in content, as they do not include information on occupation, socioeconomic status, or living circumstances (McIntosh 1989). Local epidemiological surveys typically cover a broad range of variables, but may be less representative of national trends. A more serious limitation on available data may be the underreporting of women's deaths by suicide (Kushner 1985). The available information on non-fatal suicidal behavior is even more limited than that on suicidal deaths, as there is no national comprehensive record of non-fatal suicidal behavior.

According to the available evidence, older women in the United States are less likely to kill themselves than older men. For white women, rates of fatal suicidal behavior tend to peak around age 50 (Humphrey and Palmer 1990-91; Manton et al. 1987). For non-white women, rates of death by suicide remain low throughout adulthood and late life. Middle-aged women who kill themselves are often married. Men aged 60 and over have the highest rates of suicide. For white males, the peak suicide years are ages 45 to 50 and age 80. A large increase in death by suicide in older non-white men has recently been reported. Older men who kill themselves often live alone, are unmarried (whether single, separated, divorced, or widowed), and are socially isolated, unemployed, or retired (Canetto 1992; Kirsling 1986; Lyons 1984; Stenback 1980).

According to the available evidence, rates of non-fatal suicidal behavior (suicide attempts) diminish with age in both women and men (Wilson 1981). Studies of gender patterns of non-fatal suicidal behavior have, however, produced inconsistent results. A British study (Pierce 1987) reported that rates of deliberate self-harm were equal in older men and older women; a Canadian study (Jarvis et al. 1976) and a United States study (O'Neal et al. 1956) found that older men outnumbered older women in rates of non-fatal suicidal acts; while other British and Canadian studies (Sendbuehler and Goldstein 1977; Upadhyaya et al. 1989) found that older individuals who engaged in non-fatal, deliberate self-harm were predominantly women. The question of gender and non-fatal suicidal behavior is not clarified when overt versus covert suicidal behavior are examined separately. One study of institutionalized elderly reported a greater frequency among male residents of covert, indirect suicidal be-havior, such as refusing food or medication, than among female residents (Kastenbaum and Mishara 1971). And yet another study of institutional-ized elderly found that older women were more likely to engage in covert life-threatening behavior and older men were more likely to display overt suicidal behavior, such as wrist slashing (Osgood et al. 1988-89).

GENDER AND THE EXPERIENCE OF AGING

The experience of aging involves changes and transitions, some of which are the same for women and men, and some of which are quite different. In this section the similarities and differences in the experience of aging for women and men in the United States will be reviewed and the implications for counseling will be discussed.

Life Expectancy

Women have a 7-year advantage over men in life expectancy (Ory and Warner 1990; Smith 1990). According to Smith, "the male mortality rates are greater for each of the 10 major causes of death in America today, although the difference in rates varies from close to 1.0 for diabetes and stroke to about 1.8 for heart disease, to 3.0 and more from death due to accidents, suicides and homicides." According to several researchers, gender differences in mortality are only partially explained by biological, hormonal or genetic factors (Ory and Warner 1990; Smith 1990). Far more important appear to be acquired risk and health habits, some of which are related to feminine and masculine socialization. For example, women have lower rates of death by accident, suicide and homicide. Women also have lower rates of tobacco, alcohol and illicit substance use and consequently lower rates of death due to lung cancer, chronic liver diseases and illicit drug overdose (Canetto 1991; Smith 1990). Older women are more likely to utilize ambulatory care than older men; older men use more inpatient hospital care than older women (Thomas and Kelman 1990). According to Ory and Warner (1990), a narrowing of the gender gap in mortality may most likely result from the "reductions in males' exposure to risk behavior and their increased health-promoting activities" (for example, cholesterol reduction, exercise, no smoking), rather than from increases in mortality in women who enter traditional male roles and activities, as was originally assumed.

Women live longer than men, therefore they outnumber men in late life. According to a review by Ory and Warner (1990), there are three older women for every two older men. One important implication of this life-expectancy trend is the issue of outreach. Older men are more likely to engage in risk-taking, life-threatening behavior, but are less likely to use care services than are older women. However, the care services older women tend to use are outpatient physician services, not mental health services. Therefore, counselors need to take a particularly active role in identifying and engaging older women who may be at risk for suicidal behavior.

Morbidity

Women have more incidents of physical illness and disability than men and are more likely than men to suffer from acute illnesses and non-fatal conditions, such as rheumatoid arthritis and osteoporosis; because their lives are longer, these conditions tend to turn into chronic disabilities. Men have higher rates of the leading causes of death than women. According to Verbrugge (1990), the excess incidence of many diseases in women is driven by social factors, such as less employment, higher stress and insufficient physical activity.

Many older women are in poor health and tend to utilize outpatient health services. Their poor health is also a key reason for their high utilization of legal prescriptions and non-prescription drugs. Another reason is the attitudes of most physicians toward women; according to a review by Verbrugge (1990), "physicians tend to prescribe more drugs to women for virtually all kinds of health problems, even after medical factors (such as patient age and seriousness) are controlled."

Information is limited regarding the incidence of mental disorders in late life, especially data on gender patterns of mental disorders (George 1990). People age 65 and older are less likely to be diagnosed with non-organic mental disorders than those who are younger. However, according to George, reports of lower rates of mental disorders in late life may simply reflect the inadequacy of diagnostic criteria of adult patterns.

The mental disorders most commonly associated with suicidal behavior are depression and alcohol abuse and dependence (Stenback 1980). Gender patterns of depression in late life have not been firmly ascertained. According to one review of the literature (George 1990), rates of affective disorders are similar for women and men in late life, presumably because of declining rates of affective disorders in older women, rather than increasing rates in older men. It appears, however, that older women and men are vulnerable to depression for different reasons and circumstances. Women seem be most vulnerable to depression when their health is poor (Thomas and Kelman 1990) and men when they become widowed (Siegel and Kuykendall 1990). Thomas and Kelman's study (1990) of gender and health service use among elderly persons found higher rates of depression in older women than in older men and linked women's depression to their poor health. In contrast, a study of widowhood among the elderly found that depression was more common among widowers, especially those who were isolated, than among widows (Siegel and Kuykendall 1990). With regard to the course of depression, several studies have shown that older men are less likely than older women to recover from depression within 1 year of diagnosis (Murphy 1983; Baldwin and Jolley 1986). However, another study found that adequate social support increased the likelihood of recovery from depression only among older men (George 1989).

Another condition often associated with suicidal behavior is alcohol abuse and dependence. Chronic alcohol abuse is typically associated with non-lethal suicidal behavior and this is especially true for males over 65 of age. In general, however, chronic alcoholism is more common in suicidal persons under age 65 (Stenback 1980). According to a study of middle-aged and older individuals, men (especially isolated, older men) are less likely to recover from alcoholism than women (Helzer et al. 1984).

The implications of the morbidity trends presented above for counseling the suicidal elderly are manifold. First, traditional definitions of depression may not fit patterns of depression in late life; consequently, counselors must become acquainted with the different manifestations of depression in older adults. Counselors should also recognize and remember that older women tend to be particularly vulnerable to depression when they are in poor health and that men tend to be susceptible to depression when they lose their wives. Counselors should also be aware that many older women are overmedicated and that they are likely to have access to many potentially lethal prescription and over-the-counter drugs. When counseling older men, counselors should carefully assess the possibility of alcohol abuse and dependence.

Living and Family Arrangements

In the United States, females aged 65 and over are 3.5 times more likely to be widowed than their male peers, and older widows are less likely to remarry than older widowers (Hess 1990). Studies of bereavement and mental health indicate that widows report fewer mental health problems than widowers. For example, Siegel and Kuykendall (1990) found that widows were at a lower risk for depression and suicidal behavior than widowers (Bock and Webber 1972; MacMahon and Pugh 1965).

Older women are much more likely to live alone than older men. According to a review of the literature by Hess (1990), there are 6.5 million women aged 65 and over who live alone, compared to less than 2 million men who live alone. Females aged 65 and over are also almost half as likely as their male age peers to be married.

Disabled older women are at a higher risk of being institutionalized than disabled older men (Hess 1990). Only 18 percent of disabled women are cared for by their spouses, in contrast to 55 percent of disabled men whose wives do care for them. Those who are institutionalized often display high rates of indirect suicidal behavior, such as refusing food or medication. The percentages of older individuals engaged in indirect suicidal behavior vary from 22 percent to 88 percent, depending on the study (Kastenbaum and Mishara 1971; Nelson and Farberow 1982; Osgood, Brant and Lipman 1988-89).

To summarize, different family and living arrangements appear to have a unique impact on the differences of well-being in older women and men. Counselors should be aware that bereaved older men who live alone and are socially isolated are at a higher risk for suicidal behavior than older women in similar living situations and that older persons, especially disabled, institutionalized, older persons, are likely to engage in indirect suicidal behavior.

Economic Resources

In the United States, older women have more limited financial resources than older men (Hess 1990). Eighty percent of women aged 65 and older have yearly incomes of under $13,000; women age 65 and older who live alone have a median income of only $8000; slightly higher if they are white and only $5000 if they are African American. By contrast, married couples who are older and white have a median income of $21,000.

Households headed by older women are almost twice as likely as those headed by older men to have incomes below the poverty level of $5500 for a single person over 65 and $6900 for a two-person household.

According to Hess (1990), these figures underestimate true poverty of older women because many poor older women live with an adult child or they become homeless.

The fact that women are more vulnerable to chronic illnesses may place further strain on their limited financial resources; they are less likely than older men to have private insurance coverage (Hess 1990) and are more likely than older men to exhaust their financial resources because of having to pay for the care of their more prolonged illnesses. Higher numbers of women compared to men depend on government programs such as Medicaid.

Gender differences in economic resources may also have an impact on the process of counseling. For women, lower incomes and lower rates of private insurance coverage may be a deterrent to seeking or continuing counseling. On the other hand, more women receive Medicaid and this may be a factor in their high rate of utilization of health services.

Socialization, Family and Employment

"Learning to be a 'psychological' male or female is one of the earliest and most pervasive tasks imposed upon the individual by his culture" (Kaplan 1979). For women and men, the process of socialization involves pressure to develop the feelings, behaviors, sense of self and life style considered by society to be appropriate to one's gender within one's culture (Albee et al. 1991). In the United States, women are socialized to be accommodating and nurturing and are supposed to vicariously satisfy their own needs for achievement through identification with men's achievements (Kaplan 1979; Mintz and O'Neil 1990). Women are expected to put their family first, in other words, to be responsible for the well-being of others and of family relationships (Canetto 1992; Troll and Turner 1979). Men are socialized to be assertive, aggressive, self-centered and to delegate social, family and emotional tasks to women (Mintz and O'Neil, 1990; Pasick et al. 1990). Gainful, income-earning work is expected to come first in men's lives (Canetto 1993; O'Neil 1981; Pasick, et al., 1990). As summarized by Kaplan (1987), we "live in a highly gendered society, with strong norms about appropriate modes of being for men and women…regardless of the extent to which we consciously accept or reject these norms, we act in some relation to them and are experienced by others in relation to them."

Considering the pressure on women and men to follow different gender-specific life paths, it is not surprising that the life-situations of many older women and men are different. A majority of women who are now elderly spent a lifetime organizing their lives around their families

(Troll 1977). For many of these women, this investment in the family may often continue throughout their later years, from the raising of their children's children to caring for disabled aged parents and other relatives. Women outnumber men in all caregiving categories: more mothers than fathers care for children (Silverstein 1991); more wives than husbands care for disabled spouses; more daughters than sons care for older parents; and more women than men assist other relatives and friends with their illnesses and problems (Montgomery et al. 1990). As well, because the employment histories of many older women were usually brief and often discontinuous—as employment was traditionally supposed to come secondary to family—through this exclusive commitment to their family, many women enter late life with unique strengths and weaknesses that men often do not possess. They may be highly skilled at initiating and maintaining relationships and at providing for their own and others' personal care (Canetto 1992; Troll and Turner 1979). Of course, a negative result of this is that they may have limited experience with and lack seniority in employment, a condition that most probably contributes to their economic vulnerability following divorce and widowhood (Canetto 1992; Holt and Datan 1984; Russell et al. 1990). Conversely, a majority of men who are now elderly invested their time and energy in their careers (Pasick et al. 1990) and this investment in extra-domestic work and activities may have extended through their lifespans, from commitment to employment during their early and middle adulthood years to investment in community activities after retirement. As well, their family contributions may often have been superficial and discontinuous, as their family took a back seat to their career (Canetto 1992; Troll and Turner 1979). Because of this exclusive commitment to their careers, in late life many men develop a different set of unique strengths and also various weaknesses that are different from those that women have. They may have become skilled at taking care of themselves and others financially: however, they have limited experience taking care of their own and others' social and emotional needs, a condition that may contribute to their emotional vulnerability to depression and suicide following divorce or widowhood.

Despite the many differences in socialization and life situations, women and men appear to have many similar psychological needs. For both, employment and family seem to make an independent and important contribution to their health and sense of well-being. For example, despite the common assumption that employment is more important to men than to women, the majority of empirical evidence suggests that employment does, indeed, benefit women's health (Verbrugge 1990; Kritz-Silverstein et al. 1992). As discussed in the conclusion of a study of middle-aged women by McKinlay and associates (1990), "rather than increasing role demand or constraining role obligations, work may actually alleviate the stress of nurturing and thus prevent morbidity."

The findings regarding retirement and health in women support the findings on employment and health. According to a review by Troll and Turner (1979), retirement from employment can be stressful for both women and men, even though some of the reasons for retirement can be different for women and men. For example, for many older men a unique stressor may be role ambiguity (Lyons 1984); some older men may not see family and domestic activities as a proper or comfortable outlet for self-expression. For many older women, retirement may be especially difficult if they have had interrupted careers. According to Atchley and Corbett (1977), the assumption that older women can easily refocus their energy on domestic and familial roles ignores the fact that it was partly because of the loss of familial roles at middle age that caused some women to start working in the first place. Most older women who are retired have no children who live at home and 30 percent of elderly women are widows. It is, therefore, not surprising that "older women take longer than older men to adapt to retirement." Similarly, despite the common assumption that family relationships have more important implications for women's than for men's health, more and more evidence indicates that marriage benefits men more than women (McKinlay et al. 1990; Canetto 1993). Consistent with findings on health and marriage are the findings on health and widowhood that suggest that widowhood increases the risk for mental distress more for men than for women (Canetto 1993). Furthermore, according to Ory and Warner (1990), global negative explanations regarding the effect of retirement and widowhood may be inadequate, as the outcome of these transitions may depend on specific intervening processes "such as coping style, or affective ties toward the particular spouse or the particular job that has been lost."

Gender-specific experiences of socialization may also influence perceptions of the acceptability of different kinds of suicidal behavior and, therefore, the risk for suicide (Canetto 1991). Studies of attitudes toward suicidal behavior suggest that males may be encouraged to kill themselves by cultural norms that define death by suicide as a masculine gesture (Linehan 1973; White and Stillion 1988). Stillion says "attempted suicide by troubled males may be viewed by other males as violations of the sex-role messages of strength, decisiveness, success and inexpressiveness." For elderly females, the social norms regarding suicidal behavior appear to be complex and contradictory. While non-fatal suicidal behavior is usually considered feminine (Linehan 1973), older women's non-fatal suicidal behavior may not be considered worthy of sympathy (Stillion et al. 1989).

In summary, gender differences in socialization influence the timing and meaning of life transitions, as well as perceptions of the acceptability of different kinds of suicidal behavior. At the same time, the similarities in psychological needs in women and men—such as the need to love and the need to work—may, in some ways, counteract the effects of gender socialization.

Counselors should take into account how gender differences caused by socialization and life experiences may influence the tendency toward suicidal behavior as well as toward the counseling process. For women, especially married women, the highest risk for suicide is at mid-life, between the ages of 40 and 60 (Humphrey and Palmer 1990-91). Counselors should explore how shifts in family and employment roles may contribute to women in mid-life committing suicide. Given current patterns of socialization, the combination of unending expectations of care for family and friends and frustrated career aspirations may be a significant source of stress and conflict for women who are in mid-life.

Older men are most likely to kill themselves when they are isolated, perhaps owing to the socialization that encourages their dependence on women for social and emotional needs. Counselors should be aware of how socialization into masculinity may restrict a man's likelihood of survival from suicide since attempting (as opposed to completing) suicide is considered as feminine behavior by most of society.

An assessment of gender-role identifications, attitudes and conflicts—the degree to which a client adopts, endorses and is affected by societal gender expectations—may help counselors to determine a client's risk of suicide. Counselors should be open-minded enough to recognize the similarities in women's and men's psychological needs and should be aware that career and family make a unique and independent contribution to well-being in both women and men.

GENDER AND THE COUNSELING PROCESS

Gender and Definitions of Mental Health

Definitions of mental health and abnormality are culturally and historically based (Albee et al. 1991; Canetto 1991; Counts 1987; Kushner 1985; Schur 1984). Cultural definitions of gender include gender-appropriate deviance and mental health (Canetto 1991). Counselors, like all other people, absorb cultural definitions of femininity and masculinity and may uncritically use these definitions to determine what is healthy or "natural" for women and men. As noted by Turner and Troll (1982), the "goals of treatment are, of course, inseparable from norms of appropriate sex-role behavior, which are tied to age."

Uncritical adoption of these gender stereotypes may lead to a failure on the part of counselors to discuss with their clients the defensive and maladaptive determinants underlying their choice to conform to culturally prescribed notions of masculine and feminine behavior. For example, counselors may not recognize or question intense self-absorption, stoicism, overachievement or disengagement from family responsibilities in suicidal male clients, since these behaviors may strike them as quite natural in males.

Counselors who explicitly label, or even privately conceptualize certain wishes, strivings and behavior as unfeminine or unmasculine may exacerbate their clients' conflicts and inhibitions for assuming a broader and more flexible gender identity instead of promoting more options. Older suicidal women may be at a disadvantage in therapy when counselors ignore their strivings for autonomy and mastery or label these strivings as dysfunctional behavior. As discussed by Steuer (1982), negative labels like controlling, domineering, difficult and aggressive are words that are frequently used "to describe elderly women patients who want things their way...despite research indicating that assertiveness and autonomy have survival value for the elderly."

Older women may be harmed by counseling if their suicidal behavior is defined by the counselor as manipulative (see, for example, Stengel 1964) or hysterical (for example, see Wold 1971). The label "manipulative" fails to recognize that individuals who are powerless may need to resort to indirect forms of influence, because direct forms of influence are not available or permissible to them (Albee et al. 1991). Research studies of suicidal people's interpersonal relationships (Canetto et al. 1989; Kirsch 1982), as well as clinical studies (Sefa-Dedeh et al. 1992) and anthropological studies (Counts 1987) of suicidal women's relationships suggest that suicidal persons, and in particular suicidal women, often find themselves in relationships where their ability to negotiate is increasingly restricted, until suicide becomes the only culturally sanctioned move possible.

Cultural definitions of abnormality also include gender-appropriate kinds of suicidal behavior. Counselors who uncritically adopt the gender stereotype that non-fatal suicidal behavior is unmasculine (Linehan 1973; White and Stillion 1988) may inadvertently reinforce the lethal intent of their suicidal male clients.

Gender and Causes of Suicidal Behavior

Gender stereotyping can affect the interpretation of the causes of suicidal behavior, as well as the options for treatment and prevention. For suicidal women, the most common diagnostic bias is the assumption of the primacy of interpersonal needs and motivations (Kushner 1985; Canetto 1993). This bias is quite prevalent in the suicide literature, where women's suicidal behavior is typically associated with problems and losses in relationships (Breed 1972; McIntosh et al. 1981; Simpson 1976). For example, in a case study reported by McIntosh and associates (1981), suicidal behavior in an older woman is linked to the death of her husband and her son's impending relocation, despite the fact that this woman had a history of chronic suicidal behavior. Furthermore, women's relationship problems and suicidal behavior are often seen as the consequence of irrational thinking and inadequate—dependent, borderline or hysterical—emotional functioning (Birtchnell 1981; Simpson 1976; Wold 1971). Factors other than internal, individual, psychological disabilities are typically not given prominence in theories of women's suicidal behavior, despite evidence suggesting that unemployment may play a significant role (Canetto 1993).

Consistent with these diagnostic biases, interventions for suicidal women often focus on personal change through individual psychotherapy (see Simpson 1976). These diagnostic and intervention biases can have negative consequences in counseling suicidal women. First, by obscuring the role of external factors, these biases may reinforce women's often highly developed inward focus and self-critical attitude and ultimately may amplify rather than diminish depression (Nolen-Hoeksema 1987). Second, they may foster in suicidal women a sense of uniqueness, shame and isolation. Third, they may limit the range of options for intervention and prevention. It is unlikely that mental health professionals will direct a suicidal woman to reach out for educational or employment opportunities if they believe that a woman's relationship needs ultimately override all other needs.

In fact, even when the link between suicidal behavior in women and diminished employment is recognized, suicidologists often fail to recommend that they pursue employment as a suicide prevention measure. For example, in a study of patterns of suicide by gender, age and marital status by Humphrey and Palmer (1990-91) the authors conclude that married women's exclusive dedication to their families may contribute to their high rates of death by suicide at mid-life: "without a worthwhile career to sustain them, the future of middle-aged women may appear bleak."

Curiously, however, they do not recommend that, as a preventive measure, married women should be encouraged to cultivate independent careers.

For suicidal men, the most common gender bias is the assumption that impersonal needs are most relevant to their mental health (Kushner 1985; Canetto 1993). This bias is quite prevalent in the suicide literature, where men's suicidal behavior is typically associated with problems related to income, employment and health (for example, Breed 1963, 1972; McIntosh et al. 1981; McCall 1991). For example, in a case study described by McIntosh and co-workers (1981), the suicidal death of an elderly man who experienced both severe illness and widowhood is interpreted as a rational response to his illness, but not to the loss of the wife. Factors other than external, economic or physical adversities are typically not given prominence in theories of men's suicidal behavior, despite evidence suggesting that social isolation may play a role (Canetto 1993). Consistent with these diagnostic biases, intervention and prevention strategies for suicidal men often emphasize external changes that the suicidal person has no ability to change, such as eliminating the mandatory age for retirement (Lyons 1984; Osgood 1982).

These diagnostic and intervention biases can have negative consequences in counseling suicidal men. First, by diminishing the role of personal and interpersonal factors, these biases may make it difficult for suicidal men to voice their need for connectedness in counseling. A focus on impersonal factors may reinforce men's already highly developed outward focus and emotional detachment (Mintz and O'Neil 1990; O'Neil 1981; Pasick et al. 1990) and ultimately amplify rather than diminish their emotional constriction and isolation. Second, these biases may foster reliance on external solutions and thus discourage personal change. Furthermore, some of these external solutions, such as regaining health and employment, are often simply unfeasible. Third, they may limit the scope of intervention and prevention options. It is unlikely that mental health professionals will encourage suicidal men to invest in their emotional growth and in their personal relationships if they believe that emotional and interpersonal needs are not very salient for men.

Interestingly, even when the link between suicidal behavior and interpersonal disengagement is recognized (Stenback 1980; Osgood 1982), it is rarely suggested that men should invest more time and energy in their personal relationships.

SUMMARY

Culturally prescribed gender role experiences have a profound effect on the way individuals think, feel and act (Brown 1986; Kaplan 1979; Mintz and O'Neil 1990; Steuer 1982). These gender role experiences have an impact on both clients and counselors, both outside and within the counseling setting. Competent and effective counseling should include consideration of gender issues.

For counselors of the suicidal elderly, consideration of outside counseling gender issues can be enhanced by knowledge of gender differences and similarities in adult development and aging. Counselors must be aware of the differences in the developmental experiences of women and men and how these differences may influence the resilience to suicidal behavior in late life. As Hess (1990) put it, "women and men enter old age with vastly different personal and social resources as a result of life course experiences within social structures influenced by gender." At the same time, counselors should be aware of gender similarities and support the common need in women and men for self-expression in work and personal relationships. Sensitivity to gender issues within the counseling relationship may be enhanced by awareness of potential gender biases in definitions of mental health, diagnostic preferences and recommendations for intervention and prevention.

REFERENCES

Albee, G.W., S.S. Canetto and A. Sefa-Dedeh. 1991. Naming a syndrome is the first step. *Canadian Psychology* 32:154-160.

Atchley, R.C. and S.L. Corbett. 1977. Older Women and Jobs. In L. Troll, J. Israel and K. Israel, eds., *Looking Ahead*. Englewood Cliffs, NJ: Prentice-Hall.

Baldwin, R.C. and D.J. Jolley. 1986. The prognosis of depression in old age. *British Journal of Psychiatry* 149:574-583.

Birtchnell, J. 1981. Some familial and clinical characteristics of female suicidal psychiatric patients. *British Journal of Psychiatry* 138:381-390.

Bock, E.W. and I.L. Webber. 1972. Social status and the relational system of elderly suicides. *Life-Threatening Behavior* 2:145-159.

Bograd, M. 1990. Women treating men. *The Family Therapy Networker*, May/June.

Breed, W. 1963. Occupational mobility and suicide among white males. *American Sociological Review* 28:179-188.

Breed, W. 1972. Five components of a basic suicide syndrome. *Life-Threatening Behavior* 2:3-18.

Brown, L.S. 1986. Gender-role analysis. *Psychotherapy* 23:243-248.

Canetto, S.S. 1991. Gender roles, suicide attempts and substance abuse. *Journal of Psychology* 125:605-620.

Canetto, S.S. 1992. Gender and suicide in the elderly. *Suicide and Life-Threatening Behavior* 22:80-97.

Canetto, S.S. 1993. She died for love and he for glory: gender myths of suicidal behavior. *Omega* 26:1-17.

Canetto, S.S., L.B. Feldman and R.A. Lupei. 1989. Suicidal persons and their partners. *Suicide and Life-Threatening Behavior* 19:237-248.

Counts, D.A. 1987. Female suicide and wife abuse. *Suicide and Life-Threatening Behavior* 17:194-204.

De Leo, D. and R.F.W. Diekstra. 1990. *Depression and Suicide in Late Life.* Toronto: Hogrefe & Huber.

Foster, B.G. and W.J. Burke. 1985. Assessing and treating the suicidal elderly. *Family Practice Recertification* 7:33-45.

George, L.K. 1990. Gender, age and psychiatric disorders *Generations* 14:22-27. George, L.K., Blazer, D.G. and D.C. Hughes. 1989. Social support and the outcome of major depression. *British Journal of Psychiatry* 154:478-485.

Helzer, J.E., Carey, K.E. and R.H. Miller. 1984. Predictors and Correlates of Recovery in Older versus Younger Alcoholics. In G.L. Maddox, L.N. Robins and N. Rosenberg, eds., *Nature and Extent of Alcohol Problems among the Elderly.* Rockville, MD: National Institute on Alcohol Abuse and Alcoholism.

Hess, B.H. 1990. The demographic parameters of gender and aging. *Generations* 14:12-16.

Holt, L. and N. Datan. 1984. Senescence, Sex Roles and Stress. In C.S. Widom, ed., *Sex Roles and Psychopathology.* New York: Plenum.

Humphrey, J.A. and S. Palmer. 1990-91. The effects of race, gender and marital status on suicides among young adults, middle-aged adults and older adults. *Omega* 22:277-285.

Jarvis, J.K., R.G. Ferrence, et al. 1976. Sex and age patterns in self-injury. *Journal of Health and Social Behavior* 17:145-154.

Kaplan, A.G. 1979. Toward an analysis of sex-role related issues in the therapeutic relationship. *Psychiatry* 42:112-120.

Kaplan, A.G. 1987. Reflections on Gender and Psychotherapy. In M. Braude, ed., *Women, Power and Therapy.* Binghamton, NY: Haworth Press.

Kastenbaum, R. and B.L. Mishara. 1971. Premature death and self-injurious behavior in old age. *Geriatrics* 26:71-81.

Kirsch, N.L. 1982. Attempted suicide and restrictions in the eligibility to negotiate personal characteristics. *Advances in Descriptive Psychology* 2:249-274.

Kirsling, R.A. 1986. Review of suicide among elderly persons. *Psychological Reports* 59:359-366.

Kritz-Silverstein, D., D.L. Wingard, et al. 1992. Employment status and heart disease risk factors in middle-aged women. *American Journal of Public Health* 82:215-219.

Kushner, H.I. 1985. Women and suicide in historical perspective. *Signs* 10:537-552.

Lerner, H.E. 1984. Special Issues for Women in Psychotherapy. In P. Perry Rieker and E.H. Carmen, eds., *The Gender Gap in Psychotherapy*. New York: Plenum.

Linehan, M.M. 1973. Suicide and attempted suicide. *Perceptual and Motor Skills* 37:31-34.

Lyons, M.J. 1984. Suicide in later life. *Journal of Community Psychology* 12:379-388.

MacMahon, B. and T.F. Pugh. 1965. Suicide in the widowed. *American Journal of Epidemiology* 81:23-31.

Manton, K.G., D.G. Blazer, et al. 1987. Suicide in middle age and later life. *Journal of Gerontology* 42:219-227.

McCall, P.L. 1991. Adolescent and elderly white male suicide trends. *Journal of Gerontology* 46:S43-S51.

McKinlay, S.M., R.S. Triant, et al. 1990. Multiple Roles for Middle-Aged Women and their Impact on Health. In M.G. Ory and H.R. Warner, eds., *Gender, Health and Longevity*. New York: Springer.

McIntosh, J.L. 1989. Official U.S. elderly suicide data bases. *Omega* 19:337-350.

McIntosh, J.L., R.W. Hubbard, et al. 1981. Suicide among the elderly. *Journal of Gerontological Social Work* 4:63-74.

Miller, M. 1979. *Suicide After Sixty*. New York: Springer.

Mintz, L.B. and J.M. O'Neil. 1990. Gender roles, sex, and the process of psychotherapy. *Journal of Counseling and Development* 68:381-387.

Montgomery, R.J.V. and M. McGlinn Datwyler. 1990. Women and men in the caregiving role. *Generations* 14:34-38.

Murphy, E. 1983. The prognosis of depression in old age. *British Journal of Psychiatry* 142:111-119.

Nelson, F.L. and N.L. Farberow. 1977. Indirect Suicide in the Elderly, Chronically Ill Patient. In K. Achté and J. Lonnqvist, eds., *Suicide Research*. Helsinki: Psychiatrica Fennica.

Nolen-Hoeksema, S. 1987. Sex differences in unipolar depression. *Psychological Bulletin* 101:259-282.

O'Neil, J.M. 1981. Patterns of gender role conflict and strain. *Personnel and Guidance Journal* 60:203-210.

O'Neil, J. 1990. Assessing Men's Gender Role Conflict. In D. Moore and F. Leafgren, eds., *Men in Conflict*. Alexandria, VA: American Association of Counseling and Development.

O'Neil, P., E. Robins and E.H. Schmidt. 1956. A psychiatric study of attempted suicide in persons over sixty years of age. *Archives of Neurology and Psychiatry* 75:275-284.

Ory, M.G. and H.R. Warner. 1990. Introduction: Gender, Health and Aging: Not Just a Women's Issue. In M.G. Ory and H.R. Warner, eds., *Gender, Health and Longevity*. New York: Springer.

Osgood, N.J. 1982. Suicide in the elderly. *Post-Graduate Medicine* 72:123-130.

Osgood, N.J., et al. 1988-89. Patterns of suicidal behavior in long-term care facilities. *Omega* 19:69-78.

Osgood, N.J. and S. Thielman. 1990. Geriatric Suicidal Behavior: Assessment and Treatment. In S.J. Blumenthal and D.J. Kupfer, eds., *Suicide Over the Life Cycle*. Washington, DC: American Psychiatric Press.

Pasick, R.R., S. Gordon and R.L. Meth. 1990. Helping Men Understand Themselves. In R.L. Meth and R. S. Pasick, eds., *Men in Therapy*. New York: Guilford Press.

Pierce, D. 1987. Deliberate self-harm in the elderly. *International Journal of Geriatric Psychiatry* 2:105-110.

Russell Hatch, L. 1990. Gender and work at midlife and beyond. *Generations* 14:48-52.

Schur, E.M. 1984. *Labeling Women Deviant*. Philadelphia: Temple University Press.

Sefa-Dedeh, A. and S.S. Canetto. 1992. Women, Family and Suicidal Behavior in Ghana. In U.W. Gielen, et al., eds., *Psychology in International Perspective*. Amsterdam: Swets & Zeitlinger.

Sendbuehler, J.M. and S. Goldstein. 1977. Attempted suicide among the aged. *Journal of the American Geriatric Society* 25:245-248.

Sherman, J.A. 1980. Therapist Attitudes and Sex-role Stereotyping. In A. Brodsky and R. Hare-Mustin, eds., *Women and Psychotherapy*. New York: Guilford Press.

Silverstein, L.B. 1991. Transforming the debate about child care and maternal employment. *American Psychologist* 46:1025-1032.

Siegel, J.M. and D.H. Kuykendall. 1990. Loss, widowhood, and psychological distress among the elderly. *Journal of Consulting and Clinical Psychology* 58:519-524.

Simpson, M.A. 1976. Self-Mutilation and Suicide. In E.S. Shneidman ed., *Suicidology*. New York: Grune & Stratton.

Smith, D.E.E., 1990. The biology of gender and aging. *Generations* 14:7-11.

Stengel, E. 1964. *Suicide and Attempted Suicide*. Harmondsworth, England: Penguin Books.

Stenback, A. 1980. Depression and Suicidal Behavior in Old Age. In J.E. Birren and B. Sloane, eds., *Handbook of Mental Health and Aging*. Englewood Cliffs, NJ: Prentice-Hall.

Stillion, J.M., H. White, P.J. Edwards, et al. 1989. Ageism and sexism in suicide attitudes. *Death Studies* 13:247-261.

Steuer, J.L. 1982. Psychotherapy with older women. *Psychotherapy* 19:429-436.

Templer, D.I. and G.G. Cappelletty. 1986. Suicide in the elderly. *Clinical Gerontologist* 5:475-487.

Thomas, C. and H.R. Kelman. 1990. Gender and the Use of Health Services Among Elderly Persons. In M.G. Ory and H.R. Warner, eds., *Gender, Health and Longevity*. New York: Springer.

Troll, L.E. 1977. Poor, Dumb and Ugly. In L.E. Troll, et al., eds., *Looking Ahead*. Englewood Cliffs, NJ: Prentice-Hall.

Troll, L.E. and B.F. Turner. 1979. Sex Differences in Problems of Aging. In E.S. Gomberg and V. Franks, eds., *Gender and Disordered Behavior*. New York: Brunner/Mazel.

Turner, B.F. and L. Troll. 1982. Sex differences in psychotherapy with older people. *Psychotherapy* 19:419-428.

Upadhyaya, A.K., H. Warburton and J.C. Jenkins. 1989. Psychiatric correlates of non-fatal deliberate self harm in the elderly. *Journal of Clinical Experimental Gerontology* 11:131-143.

Verbrugge, L.M. 1990. The Twain Meet: Empirical Explanations for Sex Differences in Health and Mortality. In M.G. Ory and H.R. Warner, eds., *Gender, Health and Longevity*. New York: Springer.

White, H. and J.M. Stillion. 1988. Sex differences in attitudes toward suicide: Do males stigmatize males? *Psychology of Women Quarterly* 12:357-272.

Wilson, M. 1981. Suicidal behavior. *Suicide and Life-Threatening Behavior* 11:131-139.

Wold, C.I. 1971. Subgroupings of suicidal people. *Omega* 2:19-29.

Wolff, K. 1971. The treatment of the depressed and suicidal geriatric patient. *Geriatrics* 26(7):65-69.

8

Psychiatric Management of the Suicidal Elderly

Henry P. Rosenvinge, MD

Studies of the clinical and social aspects of people who have committed suicide agree that this group shows a high prevalence of psychiatric illness, particularly depression (Robins et al. 1959; Dorpat and Ridley 1960; Barraclough et al. 1974). Of the population of elderly suicides, nearly four out of five exhibited depressive symptoms prior to death (Cattell 1988).

The suicide rate in the elderly rises with increasing age, especially in men. This is true despite the fact that there is probably a tendency to underreport suicide, particularly the cases of possible overdose where death from natural causes could be identified. Elderly men are more likely to commit suicide by violent means. Analgesics and anti-inflammatory medication are the drugs of choice for fatal overdose for men.

In analyzing coroners' reports and interviewing nearest relatives, Barraclough (1971) found that 59 of his series of 100 suicide completers had seen their doctor within one month, and 40 of them within 7 days. This suggests that the family doctor can play a key role in the prevention of suicide. MacDonald (1986) reported that the identification of depression in the elderly by general practitioners was adequate, but he suspected that the illness was insufficiently treated judging by the small number of patients who were receiving antidepressant medication and because of the low referral rate for specialist help.

The purposes of this chapter are to identify how a suicidal person might present his symptoms and to discuss the management of these symptoms once they have been established.

RECOGNIZING THE SUICIDAL PERSON

It is common for elderly people to express a willingness or a desire to die as a result of life review. In fact, many elderly face death without anxiety and often welcome the prospect of not waking on the morrow. This behavior is clearly in stark contrast to those who carefully plan their suicides, who are depressed and have feelings of guilt and of being a burden to others.

Case 1

A 73-year-old man was referred after taking an overdose. Widowed within the year of a stroke which had impaired his speech and hand movements, he was no longer able to carve wood, a hobby that he had previously greatly enjoyed. Although tearful and distressed, he would not admit to being depressed and refused to make follow-up appointments. Six months later he was referred again with a 2-week history of inappropriate behavior. He was telling his neighbors that he was going on a long vacation. Access was gained to his house and he was found unconscious in his bath having taken an overdose of aspirin. A live bare electric wire was suspended above the slowly rising bath-water level. For the 2 weeks prior to this he had been putting his affairs in order and had left notes for his family indicating his feelings of hopelessness. He had even written a letter to a coroner in which he exonerated everyone from being blamed for his behavior. When he recovered, he finally consented to treatment for his depression.

Thirty-four of Barraclough's (1974) series had made unequivocal statements about suicide and many of the alcoholics gave very stark warnings. The proportion of elderly suicides that have given very direct indications that they plan to kill themselves is not known. Some patients make more passive and less discernible attempts at suicide, either by fasting or exhibiting careless behavior (for example, not paying attention while driving or crossing roads without looking). Others may try to avoid investigation by refusing to take necessary medication, with the hope that this will cause them to die. Also, it is believed that many deaths caused by suicide are often included among deaths that are recorded as due to uncertain or accidental causes. Patients may also avoid investigation of physical illness or withhold taking their medication in the hope that they might die from natural causes. The prevalence of psychiatric illness among these groups is quite similar.

Case 2

A 70-year-old Polish immigrant had been suffering from depression for the last 2 years following the breakup of his marriage to a woman who was 20 years younger than he. A known hypertensive, he had stopped his diuretics with the hope that he would have a stroke and die. He said he would not contemplate taking an overdose because it conflicted with his devout Roman Catholic beliefs.

In some cases a person's presentation of severe depressive symptoms may be masked behind the concern shown for the partner's welfare, wrongfooting the clinician who may then become puzzled by the patient's lack of response to treatment or the patient's exaggeration of the partner's symptoms. This occurs among depressed caretakers of patients with dementia who may seek seemingly excessive support or reassurance. Unless the focus is drawn away from the needs of the dementia sufferer to the welfare of the depressed caretaker, much inappropriate and often totally unnecessary provision will result. One case in our unit killed himself and then his wife because no one would listen to his protestations about the severity of her illness. (She had mild dementia.) Tragically, we missed his real despair and offered to admit the wrong patient.

Patients suffering from delusions of either physical illness or guilt represent an important and often covert risk of suicide (Roose et al. 1983). Severely depressed elderly patients often make instances of personal failure or past wrong-doings the central themes of their present depressive preoccupations. For example, past extramarital relationships are looked at in a renewed light or they might think that they had a venereal disease at one point in life (reality is not an issue here), which they think they may have passed on to their marriage partner. Long-forgotten, now-taken-care-of skirmishes with the Internal Revenue Service (no matter how minor) sometimes suddenly take on current importance, causing the patient to believe that he is a thief, a shameful member of society or, more especially, a disgrace to his own family. From this mire of despondency the notion of suicide seems a welcome relief for the wretched patient and, in his view, for his long-suffering family as well.

There is a seemingly contradictory tendency for hypochondriacal patients to commit suicide. The feeling that some incurable illness has befallen them, coupled with fear of the inevitable oncoming suffering and pain, often prompts depressed elderly patients to kill themselves. This tends to occur at a point when the physical diagnoses reported to patients are negative, but for some reason they do not listen to this and still feel fear and hopelessness. In the series of Barraclough and co-workers

(1974), terminal disease played only a negligible part in causing suicidal behavior and the severity of physical disease was the same as in the control groups (although there was a greater preponderance of sufferers in the suicide group who suffered from gastrointestinal symptoms, but this may possibly have been related to their excessive alcohol consumption). In Cattell's (1988) study of elderly suicides there were physical abnormalities detected at autopsy in 63 percent of the sample. Restricted to coroners' reports, it is not known how many of the people in this series believed they had incurable illness.

Some despairing elderly patients do not consider suicide as an option because of fear of failure rather than of genuine desire to remain living.

Case 3

A 76-year-old spinster, who lived an increasingly isolated life complicated by reduced hearing and ulcerations on her feet, had been suffering a depressive illness for about 2 years. She was referred by her general practitioner after developing acute agitation associated with a sudden onset of temporary blindness, probably of cerebrovascular origin. Asking to be "put down," she said she had not tried to kill herself because she knew she would make a mess of it and end up "like a cabbage" in a mental home.

Indeed, it is often the forethought and planning that prevents retarded depressed patients from killing themselves. The suicidal act can be simplified if the person lives near something that will aid him in his attempt— a tall bridge without an adequate guard rail or an easily accessible electrified railway line—and this does increase the possibility of suicide. Surtees (1982) analyzed deaths at Beachy Head (chalk cliffs on England's south coast) and commented on its attraction as a place to commit suicide because so little preparation was required. As one patient reported, "all you need to do is keep walking."

In assessing the suicidal thinking of patients it is important to recognize that they may frequently change their outlook, particularly if aroused and agitated; when seen in the morning they may be optimistic and hopeful, but at night, if they are despairing of recovery and alone in the darkness while their spouse is fast asleep upstairs, a sudden change in thinking may occur. It is well known that suicide may take place during recovery, particularly in the retarded depressed patient who is demonstrating improvement in coping mechanisms without coexistent improvement in outlook.

SPECIFIC RISK FACTORS

In clinical work most attention is paid to the identification of short-term
risk factors for suicidal patients, with concentration on what symptoms
and signs predict high risk in individual patients. Most research has,
however, concentrated on long-term risk factors expressed in
demographical profiles and these are not of great benefit to the clinician
in the management of patients. A measure of bias in long-term predic-
tions may have occurred because many suicides occur despite treatment
(Hawton 1987).

It is useful to consider specific risk factors in individual patients, the
combination of past events, physical health and current symptomatology
as a whole, because it is the sum of the factors that is the measure of the
total risk of suicide.

Previous Suicide Attempts

The more a suicide attempter's demographic and clinical characteristics
resemble those of actual completed suicides, the greater the risk of eventual
suicide (Tuckman and Youngman 1963, 1968). Medical seriousness of the
attempt does not correlate with psychiatric seriousness (Rosen 1970), but
there is evidence that, if the extent of the danger is known to the patient,
the correlation is high with suicide intent and eventual suicide (Beck et al.
1975a). The elderly are as yet a largely unsophisticated and ill-informed
group of users of medication and may therefore have little knowledge of
the type and quantities of medication that could prove fatal in overdose.
One patient, an 86-year-old widow, took six aspirin tablets with the firm
belief that it would kill her. Intention scales (Beck et al. 1974) have a useful
place in research for suicide and clinical practice, particularly for teaching
of suicide risk. It is our practice, though, to regard all parasuicides as failed
suicides in the assessment and treat all suicide attempters as severely
depressed people unless proven otherwise. It is important to remain
watchful of a repeated attempt in the elderly overdose patient who is
temporarily relieved of his distress, and also of distressed relatives who
attempt to minimize the seriousness of this type of situation.

Family History of Suicide

Patients with a family history of suicide have an increased risk of suicide
themselves (Roy 1982). It is not clear whether this is due to an inherited
predisposition or whether it is a result of models of behavior that influence patients when they are distressed. The discovery of a family history

of suicide is important and the patient's view in this can be a useful guide during interview.

Bereavement

Bunch (1972) found that in all age groups the risk of suicide was raised for 5 years following bereavement and that this was true especially during the first 2 years. Cattell (1988) found that bereavement was the main precipitant to suicide in 14 percent of his elderly suicides. The quality of the bereaved relationship may influence the survivor's response; those with high levels of disorganization may well be at a greater degree of risk for also committing suicide. When assessing patients, careful examination of their feelings about their loss, their views of the future and their perceived abilities to cope alone are essential to investigate. There might be signs that the patient views the loss as a temporary phenomenon and he may also indicate a wish to join the dead loved one.

Alcoholism

The majority of alcoholics who kill themselves are also depressed (Pitts and Winokur 1966). Many of the other social and clinical factors associated with suicide may have alcoholism as a common theme: divorce, separation or a previous poor work record. Motto (1980) found also that poor physical health and a previous suicide attempt were important in determining suicides among elderly alcoholics. The use of alcohol as an intoxicating agent during the suicide act is common in all age groups.

Physical Illness

In Dorpat and Ripley's (1960) study at least half of the suicides had a relatively serious physical disorder, and this was most marked in elderly men. In Cattell's (1988) study of elderly suicides, 63 percent showed evidence of physical abnormality, the most frequent of which was cardiac disease. Fifty-six percent were reported by their family practitioners as having health problems that were severe enough to interfere with daily life and one-fifth complained of pain. Barraclough and co-workers (1974) compared the prevalence of terminal disease in their series of 100 suicides with that of 150 age-matched controls with no disease and found no increase in suicide. It is not certain whether the knowledge of impending death will promote or reduce suicidal thinking in individual patients. The association between suicide and physical illness is surely enhanced by the high risk of depressive illness common to both.

Personality Disorders

Stress factors such as physical illness, bereavement, divorce and isolation have different effects on different individuals. No two people react in the same way, but most elderly persons experience some of these stress factors at some time without developing psychiatric illness. This suggests that personality resilience may be absent in those who become ill. Elderly patients most at risk are those who tend to alienate themselves. While there is debate about this regarding the elderly, these people often harbor a significant degree of anger and their moods are sometimes impulsive and labile. Many suicides are colored by hostility and may occur in impulsive individuals unable to utilize offers of support. Alcohol can increase the risk in such individuals.

Depressive Illnesses

It is necessary to identify the characteristics of depressed patients most at risk because those with depressive illnesses as a whole constitute the most common group of patients that are referred (apart from those with dementia) and yet only a small minority of this group commits suicide. Barraclough and Pallis (1975) identified that suicide was more common in men, in older women and those who were single than it was in the only-depressed control group. They also found that insomnia, self-neglect and impaired memory were common symptoms. Also important was a past history of attempted suicide (seven times more frequent than in the controls). We have already confirmed the presence of delusions as a key factor in the assessment of risk in the suicidal patient. Neurotic illness with the absence of major depression in old age is rarely associated with suicide or suicide attempt. Coryell's (1981) 40-year mortality follow-up supported earlier conclusions that patients with obsessive-compulsive disorder tend to have a low risk of suicide.

Schizophrenia

It is difficult to estimate the risk of suicide in this group because of varying diagnostic criteria, though suicides have been shown to occur in younger patients at a relatively nonpsychotic phase of their illness (Drake et al. 1984). Figures for elderly schizophrenics are not available. In clinical practice one might suspect that it is the depressed schizophrenic who is most at risk for suicide, sometimes as a result of treatment for delusions.

Case 4

A 72-year-old widow who believed that a champion snooker player was communicating with her through her TV screen, experienced tactile hallucinations of being controlled by her sexual organs. She was treated with phenothiazine and this removed most of these symptoms. The patient then became profoundly depressed and exhibited suicidal ideas that were so intense that she required hospitalization and antidepressant therapy to feel better.

Dementia

When depression is absent, suicide among dementia sufferers is rare, although the mood disturbance that is often present early in the course of this illness may be profound. We do not know the proportion of patients who are aware of their own failing intellectual function or other problems caused by the dementia, who kill themselves during the prodromal phase of dementia when depression, agitation, sleep problems and confusion are present. The sedative action of antidepressants will promote sleep. Electroconvulsive therapy has been described as being beneficial in some dementia cases (McAllister and Price 1982).

Hopelessness

The common theme linking the risk factors considered here is a feeling of hopelessness or negative expectations about the future. Beck and co-workers (1975b) have suggested that hopelessness may be the main symptom preceding suicide, proposing that it might be of greater importance than depression. A pessimistic outlook may be the key item in depressive rating scales in the prediction of suicide. In the assessment of the depressed patient, questions about outlook often precede questions about suicidal intentions. When a more general exploration about negativism is followed, it may allow the patient to express specific thoughts about suicide, although if this does not occur, more direct questions may be required.

Biological Factors

Some explanation for the increased incidence of depression in old age may be found in the aging process itself. Several methods of measuring this process are being developed. It is known that the levels of monoamine oxidase in the brain rise with age, particularly in women. Abnormalities on CT scans, in particular an increase in ventricular size and reduction in brain density, have also been shown in elderly depressed patients (Jacoby et al. 1983). Advancing techniques in brain imagery will further define the structural abnormalities seen in these patients. Several studies have revealed abnormally low serotonin concentrations in the brain and cerebrospinal fluid (CSF) of suicide subjects (Asberg et al. 1976). This suggests that serotonin levels might be used as an indication of patients at high suicidal risk. It is tempting to surmise that the boundary between functional illness in old age and dementia has become increasingly less distinct.

DIFFERENTIAL DIAGNOSIS OF THE SUICIDAL OLDER PERSON

Most elderly patients who present with suicidal thinking suffer from a major depressive disorder. There will be some who despite thorough assessment, present neither the history nor the signs of psychiatric illness and one must conclude that these particular people wish to die as a consequence of reasoned judgment, possibly because of a severe debilitating physical illness. It is unlikely that such a person will wait to present for psychiatric assessment. Such patients may feel psychiatric consultation is an insult. One way that they might come to the attention of officials is if their family practitioner or hospital specialist is seeking help because of the person's request for euthanasia.

The correct diagnosis of the type of psychiatric illness a person has is easier to achieve than is the assessment of a person's degree of suicidal risk, for even in severe depression there may be more than one reason why a patient is threatening self-harm. Correct treatment matched to the severity of the underlying illness will help illuminate suicidal threats, real or otherwise.

The distinction between the patient suffering from major depression and the one suffering from schizophrenia may be difficult to make when he is suffering from a severe delusional illness. Schizophrenic patients may be at risk of accidental death as a result of their delusions. Essentially the distinction between these two groups is that those who are depressed experience either pronounced feelings of guilt or their delusions have a depressed content.

MANAGEMENT OF THE SUICIDAL ELDERLY PERSON

Whenever possible, management of the suicidal elderly person should be conducted in a safe place, such as a hospital. There the person's needs can be assessed and a care plan can be outlined. It is important not to assume that because patients are old they do not want to know what is going on; they should be included in the plan of care. Close supervision of suicidal elderly patients may be needed for their own safety. A patient's needs should be constantly reassessed. The idea is to help patients feel that their situation is not hopeless and that caring professionals will take responsibility for helping them to feel better. Elderly suicidal patients may need sedation to reduce agitation and distress. Thioridazine, Haloperidol or depoflupenthixol may be required and during this time antidepressant therapy may be started.

Antidepressant Drugs

No satisfactory alternative to the monoamine theory of depression devised in the 1960s has yet been found. The second generation of antidepressants, with their sharper profile of action as inhibitors of reuptake of monoamines, have shown little or no advantage over the efficacy levels of their first- generation tricyclic cousins. However, the increasing awareness of the subtypes of depression, each with a different biochemical foundation, will be matched by an increasing diversity of pharmacologic agents designed to treat them. There has been great improvement in the control of side effects and toxicity, for example, a reduction in the anticholinergic effects of tricyclics and also a reduction in tyramine potentiation in monoamine oxidase inhibitors. By decreasing the side effects of drugs, the possibility of reaching therapeutic drug levels in elderly persons with the newer antidepressants is now possible; although newer antidepressants are not as powerful, their end result may have a greater therapeutic effect.

Concern has been expressed that the developmental costs of these newer antidepressants have resulted in a much more expensive product. In times of limited spending on drug budgets, prescribers will first turn to the older, effective, but potentially more toxic agents. The emergence of an indisputably more effective antidepressant, if similar in cost, will have major implications for resource management.

It has been well established that tricyclic antidepressants have an advantage over placebo treatment (Morris and Beck 1974) and this superiority is so evident that drug trials conducted in the elderly should no longer require a placebo group for control. Almost two-thirds of depressed elderly respond well to tricyclics and the dose is usually one-third to one-half less than the dose that is required for younger patients. The onset of significant improvement often occurs as early as 2 weeks after treatment, although clinicians can sometimes detect a response that will predict a favorable outcome within 1 week. The main problems arise from the inhibition of alpha$_1$ adrenergic, muscarinic and histamine H1 receptors (Tang and Seeman 1980; Shein and Smith 1978; Richelson and Nelson 1984), resulting in dry mouth, blurred vision, sweating, constipation and urinary flow obstruction. Other side effects that put the patient at risk may include falls associated with postural hypotension and changes in cardiac rhythm, both of which can be quite sudden. The risk from overdose of tricyclics is of vital consideration in the suicidal patient and prescription should be conducted only under close supervision. It is, however, important to strike a sense of balance in the assessment of the role of tricyclics. They are an extremely valuable, effective and well-understood group of drugs that are commonly prescribed in the United States and England. More patients kill themselves for the want of an effective antidepressant than those who die because of them.

Although a diverse group, the newer antidepressants have a more limited field of reuptake inhibition. Considerable interest has been shown in the serotonin reuptake blockers including fluvoxamine, fluoxetine and paroxetine. This development followed studies in which the chemical transmission system played the key part in the etiology of depression. Possibly though, a balance between simultaneously active noradrenaline and serotonin systems may be important (Van Praag 1982).

Demonstrations that suicidal acts were associated with decreased 5-hydroxytryptamine and 5-hydroxyindoleacetic acid levels in cerebrospinal fluid (Asberg et al. 1975) and a decrease in serotonin-2 binding sites in the cortex of patients who commit suicide (Arora and Meltzer 1989) support the use of serotonin agonists in the treatment of depressed suicidal patients, although there have been reports of fluoxetin triggering agitation and suicide attempts (Teicher et al. 1990).

Common unavoidable side effects of serotonin reuptake blockers include nausea, vomiting and other gastrointestinal disturbances. Milder symptoms may be weight loss due to anorexia, which may occur even when there is an overall improvement in mood. The prolonged half-life of the active metabolite of fluoxetine increases the washout period, particularly if other antidepressants such as lithium and monoamine oxidase inhibitors are contemplated. Antidepressants that have a long delay in onset of action have little place in the treatment of an acute and distressing depressive illness.

One group of drugs that has enjoyed the peaks and troughs of therapeutic popularity is monoamine oxidase (MAO) inhibitors. Theories of their action, particularly in the elderly, are based on the increase in MAO activity in old age. Their potential use was recognized before the introduction of tricyclics but was not supported by the findings that they were less effective than imipramine, electroconvulsive therapy (ECT) and even placebos (Medical Research Council 1965), though the trial has been criticized for using ineffective doses.

The dietary restrictions necessary when taking MAOs, such as avoiding foods containing large amounts of tyramine, have given these drugs much notoriety. Elderly people sometimes depend on cheese as their major source of protein and fat in their diet because it is easy to keep, does not need cooking and most like the taste. In my practice, the use of tricyclics has helped patients with long-term recovery when more conventional treatments have failed.

Case 5

A 65-year-old lady presented a 30-year history of hypochondriasis, fluctuating agitation and depression, and she had made a number of suicidal attempts. The onset of the original illness appeared to be triggered by the death of her mother on whom she depended despite her own supportive marriage. Repeated admissions to the local psychiatric hospital where multiple changes of psychotropic medication and courses of ECT and psychotherapy, both individual and marital, failed to result in any lasting improvement of her distress. It was the addition of phenelzine and amitriptyline that finally resulted in her improvement which has now lasted over 10 years, barring one subsequent brief relapse 4 years ago when lithium was added.

The development of the selective type-A and type-B MAO inhibitors whose actions are reversible has been welcomed, particularly as dietary restrictions are not necessary. Their role may useful alternatives to traditional MAO inhibitors in the treatment of tricyclic-antidepressant-resistant depressives. However, their onset of action is no quicker than the older MAO inhibitors, taking up to 4 to 6 weeks. Tranylcypramine, a first-generation MAO inhibitor, may have an unusually swift onset of action in some patients, reflecting its amphetamine-like properties as well as monoamine oxidase inhibition. In some cases there may be a worrying tolerance to this drug. There is also concern over the efficacy of the reversible type-A MAO inhibitors being sustainable in long-term treatment (Udabe et al. 1989; Laux et al. 1989).

Recent evidence for the use of lithium for its antidepressant potentiating effect is promising (Austin et al. 1991) but its narrow therapeutic/toxic dose ratio plus its risk of toxicity in patients taking thiazide diuretics or nonsteroidal anti-inflammatory drugs means that close monitoring of serum levels is essential. The role of lithium as prophylaxis is more widely used and, when added to the treatment regimen of the treated suicidal patient, may significantly lower the risk of relapse. The role of lithium as prophylaxis is little understood by patients (Rosenvinge et al. 1990). One welcome consequence of this is that lithium is rarely used as a overdose drug, which would be extremely dangerous.

Electroconvulsive Therapy

Where the patient constitutes a major suicidal risk and where a rapid improvement in symptoms is demanded, electroconvulsive therapy (ECT) is the treatment of choice and may in fact be safer in patients where there is coexistent cardiovascular disease that makes antidepressants toxic. A recent survey of psychiatrists who care for the elderly (Benbow 1991) found that 95 percent were in favor of ECT in appropriate patients. Elderly depressed patients, especially with "endogenous" type symptoms, respond well (Benbow 1989). Patients with delusional depression may require ECT as the treatment of choice (Kantor and Glassman 1977; Baldwin 1988). Elderly people with anxiety and agitation have also responded well to ECT (Fraser and Glass 1980; Salzman 1982).

Debate has occurred over whether unilateral or bilateral application is preferable in the elderly. The former is promoted for the restriction of cognitive impairment, the latter for its greater speed of response and consequent shortening of treatment course. There is a tendency for treatment course to be longer in the elderly (Godber et al. 1987). If the diagnosis is confident, treatment should continue until full recovery. Response to ECT may often be dramatic and life-saving, such as in the case of the retarded depressed patient not maintaining adequate fluids and solid food intake.

Many patients offered ECT, particularly those indicating suicidal preoccupations, may agree to it as an extension of their death wish or to abdicate responsibility for themselves to the clinician in the hope that some catastrophe might occur during the treatment. In others, refusal to accept ECT treatment may be based on ignorance, bad publicity or poor knowledge about the actual treatment procedure itself (Rosenvinge 1991). In our unit a video of a patient having ECT is shown to doubting patients and relatives and a bimonthly ECT group is conducted to discuss concerns about the ECT procedure. Nevertheless the suicidal patient reluctant to have ECT presents a difficult management problem where recourse to compulsory detention and a second opinion provided by the Mental Health Commission will be considered. This is, however, rarely done; suicidal patients needing ECT can usually be persuaded to accept treatment once they have agreed to enter the hospital.

There is no upper-age limit in suitability of patients for ECT. Many authors (O'Shea et al. 1987; Abrams 1988; Kendell 1981) report its value in the very old. This is reassuring considering the recent rise in the suicide rate in the elderly.

No treatment procedure mentioned so far can be seen in isolation from other forms of therapy considered in the management program for the patient. Physical forms of treatment such as antidepressants or ECT do not take the place of psychotherapeutic techniques and psychological approaches. A patient may well benefit from an antidepressant, relaxation therapy and marital therapy all at the same time. Cognitive therapy in elderly suicidal patients involving brief problem-solving interventions may be helpful. One study has reported a decrease in the frequency of suicidal attempts following cognitive behavior therapy (Salkovskies et al. 1986).

There is no doubt that a number of suicidal patients will be unaltered by treatment even if it is comprehensive. This may be because the original diagnosis of depressive illness was erroneous or because the situation in which the patient finds himself is so stressful and hopeless that there is no prospect of change. Provided that all other possible causes have been excluded—for example, hidden depression in a partner or existence of covert concerns or guilt feelings—frank discussion and acceptance of the suicide risk with both the patient and the relatives may be required and may have the beneficial effect of reducing any associated anger experienced by the patient. In cases where suicide occurs in a patient known to the service, considerable counseling may be required with both family members and involved staff.

The practice of auditing the management of patients who kill themselves, coupled with the necessary support of involved staff members, is an essential part of the improvement of the treatment process and maintenance of staff morale. Our role in the management of the suicidal elderly person is the recognition and positive treatment of the underlying psychiatric illness. The prognosis for the active treatment of depressive illness in old age is very good.

REFERENCES

Abrams, R. 1988. *Medical Considerations: The High Risk Patient in Electroconvulsive Therapy*. Oxford: Oxford University Press.

Arora, R.C. and H.Y. Meltzer. 1989. Serotonergic measures in the brains of suicide victims. *American Journal of Psychiatry* 146:730-736.

Asberg, M., L. Traskman and P. Thorn. 1976. 5-HIAA in the cerebrospinal fluid as a biological suicide predictor. *Archives of General Psychiatry* 33:1193-1197.

Austin, M.P., F.M.G. Souza and G.M. Goodwin. 1991. Lithium augmenta-
tion in antidepressant resistant patients. *British Journal of Psychiatry*
159:510-514.

Baldwin, R.C. 1988. Delusional and nondelusional depression in late life.
British Journal of Psychiatry 152:39-44.

Barraclough, B.M. 1971. Suicide in the Elderly. In D.W. Kay and A. Walk,
eds., *Recent Developments in Psychogeriatrics*. Kent, England: Royal
Medico-Psychological Association.

Barraclough, B.M., J. Bunch, B. Nelson, et al. 1974. A hundred cases of
suicide. *British Journal of Psychiatry* 125:355-373.

Barraclough, B.M. and J. Pallis. 1975. Depression followed by suicide.
Psychological Medicine 5:55-61.

Beck, A.T., R. Beck and M. Kovacs. 1975a. Classification of suicidal
behaviors. *American Journal of Psychiatry* 132:285-287.

Beck, A.T., M. Kovacs and A. Weissman. 1975b. Hopelessness and suicidal
behavior. *Journal of the American Medical Association* 234:1146-1149.

Benbow, S.M. 1989. The role of electroconvulsive therapy in the treatment
of depressive illness in old age. *British Journal of Psychiatry* 155:147-
152.

Benbow, S.M. 1991. Old age psychiatrists' views on the use of ECT.
International Journal of Geriatric Psychiatry 6:317-322.

Bunch, J. 1972. Recent bereavement in relation to suicide. *Journal of
Psychosomatic Research* 16:361-366.

Cattell, H.R. 1988. Elderly suicide in London. *International Journal of
Geriatric Psychiatry* 3:251-261.

Coryell, W. 1981. Obsessive compulsive disorder and primary unipolar
depression. *Journal of Nervous and Mental Disease* 169:220-224.

Dorpat, T. and H.A. Ripley. 1960. A study of suicide in the Seattle area.
Comprehensive Psychiatry 1:349-359.

Drake, R.E. and J. Erlich. 1985. Suicide attempts associated with aka-
thisia. *American Journal of Psychiatry* 142:499-501.

Fraser, R.M. and I.B. Glass. 1980. Unilateral and bilateral ECT in elderly
patients. *Acta Psychiatrica Scandinavica* 62:13-31.

Godber, C., H. Rosenvinge, D. Wilkinson, et al. 1987. Depression in old
age. *International Journal of Geriatric Psychiatry* 2:19-24.

Hawton, K. 1987. Assessment of suicide risk. *British Journal of Psychiatry*
150:145-153.

Jacoby, R.J., R. Dolan, R. Levy, et al. 1983. Quantitative computed tomog-
raphy in elderly depressed patients. *British Journal of Psychiatry*
143:124-127.

Kantor, S.J. and A.H. Glassman. 1977. Delusional depressions. *British
Journal of Psychiatry* 131:351-360.

Kendell, R.E. 1981. The present status of electroconvulsive therapy. *British
Journal of Psychiatry* 139:265-283.

Laux, G., T. Becker and W. Classen. 1989. Clinical and Biochemical Findings with New MAO-A Inhibitors in Major Depressive Disorders. In C.N. Stefanis, C.R. Soldatos and A.D. Rabavilas, eds., *Psychiatry Today: Accomplishments and Promises*. New York: Excerpta Medica.

McAllister, T.W. and T.R.P. Price. 1982. Severe depressive pseudodementia with and without dementia. *American Journal of Psychiatry* 139:626-629.

MacDonald, A. 1986. Do GPs miss depression in the elderly patient? *British Medical Journal* 282:1365.

Medical Research Council. 1965. Clinical trial of the treatment of depressive illness. *British Medical Journal* 1:881-886.

Morris, J.B. and A.T. Beck. 1974. The efficacy of antidepressant drugs. *Archives of General Psychiatry* 130:1022-1024.

Motto, J.A. 1980. Suicide risk factors in alcohol abuse. *Suicide and Life-Threatening Behavior* 10:230-238.

Office of Population Censuses and Surveys (Medical Statistics Division). 1990. *Annual Report*. London: Her Majesty's Stationary Office.

Office of Population Censuses and Surveys. 1991. *Mortality Statistics, Cause 1990, Series DH2, No. 17*. London: Her Majesty's Stationary Office

O'Shea, B., T. Lynch, J. Falvey, et al. 1987. Electroconvulsive therapy and cognitive improvement in a very elderly depressed patient. *British Journal of Psychiatry* 150:255-257.

Pitts, F.N. and G. Winokur. 1966. Affective disorder. *Journal of Psychiatric Research* 4:37-50.

Richelson, E. and A. Nelson. 1984. Antagonism by antidepressants of neurotransmitter receptors of normal human brain in vitro. *Journal of Pharmacology and Experimental Therapeutics* 239:94-102.

Robins, E., G.E. Murphy, R.H. Wilkinson, et al. 1959. Some clinical considerations in the prevention of suicide based on a study of 134 successful suicides. *American Journal of Public Health* 49:888-898.

Roose, S.P., A.H. Glassman, B.T. Walsh, et al. 1983. Depression, delusions and suicide. *American Journal of Psychiatry* 140:1159-1162.

Rosen, D.H. 1970. The serious suicide attempt. *American Journal of Psychiatry* 127:764-770.

Rosenvinge, H.P. 1991. The real value of electroconvulsive therapy in the elderly. *Dementia* 2:225-228.

Rosenvinge, H.P., E.P. Groarke and J.W.S. Bradshaw. 1990. Drug compliance amongst psychiatric day hospital attenders. *Age and Aging* 19:191-194.

Roy, A. 1982. Risk factors for suicide in psychiatric patients. *Archives of General Psychiatry* 39:1089-1095.

Salkovski, P.M. and H.M. Warwick. 1986. Morbid preoccupations, health anxiety and reassurance. *Behavior Research and Therapy* 24:597-602.

Salzman, C. 1982. Electroconvulsive therapy in the elderly patient. *Psychiatric Clinics of North America* 5:191-197.

Shein, K. and S.E. Smith. 1978. Structure activity relationships for the anticholinoceptor action of tricyclic antidepressants. *British Journal of Pharmacology* 62:567-571.

Surtees, S.J. 1982. Suicide and accidental death at Beachy Head. *British Medical Journal* 284:321-324.

Tang, S.W. and P. Seeman. 1980. Effect of antidepressant drugs on serotonergic and adrenergic receptors. *Naunyn-Schmiedeberg's Archives of Pharmacology* 311:255-261.

Teicher, M.H., C. Glod and J.O. Cole. 1990. Emergence of intense suicidal preoccupation during fluoxetine treatment. *American Journal of Psychiatry* 147:207-210.

Tuckman, J. and W.F. Youngman. 1963. Identifying suicide risk groups among attempted suicides. *Public Health Reports* 78:763-766.

Tuckman, J. and W.F.A. Youngman. 1968. A scale for assessing suicide risk of attempted suicides. *Journal of Clinical Psychology* 24:17-19.

Udabe, R.U., C.A. Marquez, C.A. Traballi, et al. 1989. Double-Blind Comparison of Moclobemide, Imipramine and Placebo in Depressive Patients. In C.N. Stefanis, C.R. Soldatos and A.D. Rabavilas, eds., *Psychiatry Today: Accomplishments and Promises*. New York: Excerpta Medica.

Van Praag, H.M. 1982. Neurotransmitters and CNS disease. *Lancet* 2:1259-1264.

9

Suicidal Elders in Long-Term Care Facilities: Preventive Approaches and Management*

Nancy J. Osgood, PhD and Nancy R. Covey, MS, RN

I'm no good to anybody. I can't drive. They took all of my money for this place. I can't even go fishing with my boy, and fishing was the only thing I really loved after Martha died. I wish I could just sneak out of this place one time and get my pole and tackle and get in the boat and fish all day long. But, I can't even drive and they sold my boat, too. I took the operation on my legs a few years ago cause they gave me a 90 percent chance of dying. Well, that's why I took the blame thing. And wouldn't you know it's my luck. I didn't die and here I am. I'm no use to anybody. I can't do nothing now but just sit and stare out the window. I'd be a whole lot better off if I was to die. (A 75-year-old nursing home resident who attempted suicide, from Osgood, Brant and Lipman 1991.)

Residents of nursing homes and other long-term care facilities represent a large and growing population of people who are at high risk for depression and suicide. Expressions of suicidal ideation and intent like the one shown above are not uncommon among nursing home residents. Until very recently the mental health needs and vulnerabilities of this group have been virtually ignored.

Statistics released in 1990 showed that in the United States approxi-

---

*Portions of this chapter have been adapted from Osgood, Brant and Lipman, *Suicide Among the Elderly in Long-Term Care Facilities* and from Osgood, *Suicide in Late Life*.

mately 1,553,000 people resided in 25,646 nursing homes. The institutionalized elderly represent a rapidly growing segment of the 65 and older age group. Forty-three percent of all persons who entered the 65 and over age bracket in 1990 will eventually reside for some time in a nursing home (Kemper and Murtaugh 1991).

Older residents of nursing homes and other members of long-term care facilities face unique challenges not encountered by elders living in the community, particularly their high risk of suicide and depression. Osgood, Brant and Lipman (1991) recently conducted a national study on the nature and extent of suicide in long-term care facilities. Based on responses to questionnaires mailed to a national random sample of over 1000 long-term care institutions, Osgood and colleagues found that of the 463 facilities that returned completed questionnaires, 84 had experienced at least one suicidal act (19 percent); 11 facilities had experienced nine or more instances of suicidal behavior; and the rate of overt suicides was 15.8 per 100,000. The suicide rate from deaths caused by overt suicide and by intentional life-threatening behaviors (ILTBs), such as refusing to eat or drink, was 94.9 per 100,000. In a study of nursing home patients (conducted in New York City between 1980 and 1986) who were 70 years of age and older, Abrams and associates (1988) reported an overt suicide rate of 19.7 per 100,000.

This chapter focuses on the institutionalized elderly and their special problems and concerns. We will examine some of the factors that contribute to suicide in this population and consider various ways to improve their lives thereby reducing their risk of suicide.

FACTORS CONTRIBUTING TO SUICIDE

The Process of Institutionalization

Nursing homes usually represent the last resort for those who can no longer help themselves, who have no friends or loved ones to care for them at home. For most residents, institutionalization represents rejection. Nursing homes are one type of "total institution," a phrase defined by Erving Goffman (1960) in his classic work on mental institutions as "social hybrids, part residential community, part formal organization. These establishments are the forcing homes for changing persons in our society. Each is a natural experiment, typically harsh, on what can be done to the self." Total institutions have the following characteristics in common:

> First, all activities are conducted in the same place and under the same authority. Second, each phase of the resident's daily activity is carried on

in the immediate company of a large group of others, all of whom are treated alike, and are required to do the same thing together. Third, all phases of the day's activities are tightly scheduled, with one activity leading from a prearranged time into the next, and the whole sequence of activities is imposed from above by a body of officials. Fourth, the various enforced activities are brought together into a single plan, purportedly designed to fulfill the official aims of the institution (Goffman 1960).

Goffman further suggests that people who enter a total institution undergo both a "stripping" and self-mortification process; they are stripped of property, personal possessions, pets, and as a result, they lose their personal identity. Life-long habits and styles must be abandoned for a scheduled and routinized existence dictated by strangers. The stigma of occupying a devalued state is known as a "spoiled identity" (Goffman 1963).

One consequence of institutional totality of the type that Goffman describes may be the eventual loss of self-determination in nursing home residents. Reduced self-determination, freedom, functional capacity and competence often accompany living in a nursing home or institutional setting. Lack of choice and loss of control lead to psychologically debilitating feelings of helplessness.

Negative effects of institutional care have been classified into four general areas by Sommer and Osmond (1960):

- Deindividuation, or a reduced capacity for thought and action, resulting from dependence learned in the institution.
- Disculturation, which occurs when persons are stripped of the stable social arrangements of their home and forced to accept a different set of values and attitudes (the institutions). Due to loss of status and security and feelings of estrangement, residents undergo emotional, social and physical damage.
- Isolation through loss of stimulation and contacts with family, friends, neighbors, church and the outside world.
- Deprivation and deadening of the senses.

Residents of long-term care facilities suffer from depersonalization, dehumanization and deprivation. Depersonalization is caused by being treated as an object rather than as a person. For example, when a nurse enters a resident's room and takes his pulse and blood pressure or empties the bedpan before even saying hello, understandably the resident will soon begin to feel more like an object than a human being. Older adults in nursing homes and other long-term care institutions experience a feeling of unreality and in turn an absence of self-image. Finding themselves in a strange and unfamiliar environment further increases their feelings of depersonalization. Institutionalized elders often become confused about where they are, who they are and their value as people.

Dehumanization, or divesting a person of human qualities and attributes, occurs quite frequently in institutions. When, for example, a nurse feeds a resident without even looking or talking to him, this greatly contributes to the dehumanization process. Staff who refer to residents as "old fossils" or "vegetables" certainly add to the problem. It is humiliating and dehumanizing enough when a person is no longer able to dress, bathe and use the toilet without assistance and the situation should not be exacerbated by behavior of this sort by staff.

Sensory deprivation is caused by a reduction in the amount and intensity of the sensory input. When an older person moves into a nursing home or other long-term care facility, all of the familiar sights, sounds and smells from home are suddenly gone. As well, friends, relatives and neighbors are no longer present to provide various forms of sensory stimulation. Residents of long-term care institutions are also subject to physical, social, emotional and spiritual deprivation (Stotsky and Dominick 1969). Deprivation is related to a lack of stimulation, recreational and occupational opportunities, adequate walking space inside and outside of the facility and a lack of space for social activities. In these situations, it is not hard to understand how elderly residents can easily become disoriented, disorganized, less alert, helpless, out of control, lonely, or depressed. These attitudes readily cause feelings of rejection, abandonment and the belief that they are now unwanted and unloved.

Institutionalization also often represents a loss of freedom. In their study of freedom and alienation in homes for the aged, Dudley and Hillary (1977) found that "conditional freedom" (a form of deprivation of freedom) was greatest in nursing homes and similar organizations that employ a rigorous institutionalized structure and was closely related to alienation (normlessness, powerlessness and isolation). Conditional freedom is defined by the authors as the recognition that a person's choices are prescribed by the social milieu in which they are operating, and are not solely a result of aging (Dudley and Hillary 1977).

Adaptation to institutional living is impeded by the emotional impact of separation and estrangement from family, friends, relatives and the outside world. The serenity and protection often provided by members of the family no longer exist. Another factor (cited by Bennett in Shuttlesworth et al. 1982) is that privacy and freedom of movement tend to become lost and interaction with friends and relatives often becomes strained and superficial in the institutional environment. As one older woman put it, "This is not really my place. I can't fix a friend or neighbor a cup of tea when they drop by and just chat."

One of the most traumatic losses is the loss of one's home (Hirst and Metcalf 1984). For some people, entering an institution means having to give up one's home and this truly reinforces the reality that the ability to control one's life has been threatened and this causes feelings of abandonment, anxiety, loneliness, grief, anger and despair. In his 1984 study of the emotional impact of possession loss, McCracken-Knight reported the responses and feelings of a woman who had given up her possessions when she moved into a long-term care residence: "You close your eyes, it's got to go." McCracken-Knight concluded that the loss of possessions accompanied by relocation adds significantly to the difficulty of the move, accentuating the loss of life's continuity as well as the loss of self-identity. People who have always maintained control over their lives—who have, as Weber (1980) terms it, "called their own shots—want control to the end, even to dying on their own terms." Perceived or actual inability to maintain control over one's life, compounded by a diminished self-esteem, a sense of helplessness, hopelessness and loss of power and decision-making about one's life in the present and future, makes a person vulnerable and depressed. This in turn puts a person at high risk for suicide.

Based on their study of several institutions for the aged, Tobin and Lieberman (1976) described institutionalization in these words: "The meaning of losses connected with giving up independent living is separation; the experience is that of abandonment, and reaction to it is extreme. Increasingly, the person becomes cognitively constricted, apathetic, unhappy, hopeless, depressed, anxious, and less dominant in relationships with others."

Nursing homes, which were initially intended to enhance socialization and solidarity of residents, may in fact contribute to feelings of personal isolation and alienation. In 1979 Shomaker wrote:

> Nursing home existence was intended to translate collective lives into social solidarity, but fails to achieve such an end because survival and sociability grate against one another creating isolation. Therefore, the positive and identifiable ties that bind these people together are also the shadowy areas that divide them. There are those who argue that a nursing home was never intended to become a place where solidarity exists. If this is so, then the name becomes a paradox. "Home" then takes on the connotation that because one is incapacitated...the remainder of one's life...must be "lived" at "home" as a nonhuman with few shared values or sociability.

When elderly persons move into an institution they must suddenly live their lives very publicly; they must share places that not only once belonged to them, but were also private. Bathrooms, bedrooms and dining rooms are now shared with persons they have never met before. Not only does one usually have one or two roommates, but staff have ready, often unannounced access to the one place that is probably the closest to ones own space. It is rare to be able to choose one's own seat in the dining room; residents are usually assigned by the nursing or dietary staff to eat with people they barely know, with whom they have little in common and whose mannerisms and eating habits may be offensive. After looking at a sea of faces in the communal dining room, one female resident stated in exasperation to a nursing assistant, "This is not my dining room!"

It is not hard to understand how the process of institutionalization contributes to residents' depression. Even when elders have actively made the choice to be in a nursing home and believe that it is in their best interest, adjusting to such a dramatic change is often difficult and sometimes impossible.

Depression

As we have discussed, depression is all too common among residents of nursing homes and other long-term care facilities. Several studies of the prevalence of mental illness in nursing homes have indicated that more than half the residents suffer from mental disorders of one type or another. In his 1986 study, Rovner and colleagues found that 80 percent of the 454 new admissions to eight nursing homes had major mental illnesses. Approximately one in five residents has a primary diagnosis of mental illness, and depression is the most common ailment (Harper 1986). We also know that for the elderly, depression is the most common precipitant to suicide.

Depression in elderly people has been linked to several consequences of aging, some of which are: degenerative changes within the brain and nervous system; biological and genetic variables; life changes that emphasize the impact of stress on both body and mind; and behavioral responses and cognitive coping styles. Late-life depression is most likely related to the changes that occur as a person gets older. As individuals age, they experience a deficiency of catecholamines (especially norepinephrine) at important receptor sites. Aging also results in decreases in certain adrenergic neurotransmitters in the brain, notably serotonin and dopamine. Age-related changes in the endocrine system that increase the risk of late-life depression include diminished thyroid function, decreased hypothalamic function and diminished hypothalamic releasing response of the pituitary gland. These organic changes place the older adult at increased risk of suffering a major depression.

Drug abuse in late life is also common. Certain medications, many of which are used to treat chronic diseases, are responsible for causing depression in older adults. The following are known offenders: anti-hypertensives, anti-inflammatory agents, anti-parkinsonian drugs and chemotherapeutic drugs are just a few. Additionally, depression in the elderly may be caused by illnesses such as stroke, arthritis, chronic lung disease, Parkinsonism, pernicious anemia and cancer. In fact, that technology allows people to live longer with terminal diseases automatically places the elderly at a higher risk for depression and therefore for suicide.

Depression in the institutionalized elderly is also related to the losses that are commonly caused by aging and institutionalization. Many older residents who suffer from depression have experienced multiple losses, such as the loss of a spouse, children, close friends and pets. Loss of cognitive function is also understandably a major cause of depression. When it becomes a struggle to remember people, places and dates, when misplacing items becomes a regular event, most people find it unusually hard to cope.

Moving to a nursing home or other long-term facility from the house where one's children were born and reared and where one's whole life was lived means leaving the very familiar for the totally unfamiliar. The move is usually terribly traumatic, because it often signals the beginning of the end. Loss of control of one's own money, house, car, land and other possessions results in feelings of powerlessness and a lack of independence. These losses strip people of their self-esteem, status and dignity and with each new deprivation the loss of continuity with life as they knew it before the nursing home increases.

In summation, for most people, becoming institutionalized typically and frequently represents a loss of independence, freedom, privacy, personal autonomy, control and choice. Depersonalization, dehumanization and deprivation fostered in institutions contribute to a person's loss of self-esteem, loneliness, isolation and feelings of helplessness, hopelessness, depression and despair. How people cope with these major changes is often related to their cognitive appraisal of their circumstances and the level of their ability to adapt.

Hallie is a typical example. Widowed for 40 years, Hallie had many years to learn to cope well by herself. She was extremely independent and often voiced with pride that she was well equipped to take care of herself. Following her retirement at age 72, she moved to a small town near the farm where she and her husband had raised their children. Her new house was within sight of the home of her only son. Her other family members lived over an hour away.

After the sudden death of her son, her remaining daughters encouraged her to sell her home and move back to the city to be near them. Hallie did not drive and was therefore dependent on neighbors to drive her to the market and to the doctors. They also assisted her other activities of daily living. Her daughter-in-law was devastated at the death of her husband, was in poor physical health and had to work in order to support herself. Hallie moved into a small apartment in a retirement community. There she was able to have assistance 24 hours a day and they also served one meal daily. She did not like living in a high-rise building, even though she herself had chosen this facility. After several months she announced she "hated the place" and began to spend a lot of her time in bed complaining of various physical ailments. A physical evaluation found no significant problems and she was placed on a mild antidepressant. Within 3 months she contacted one of her grandchildren and arranged a "visit" to the small town in which she lived. When she returned, she announced to her daughters that she had found and already signed a lease on a new apartment near her grandchild. She was 82 at the time.

For about 2 years after the move Hallie managed to function quite well with the assistance of her grandchildren and neighbors. She could easily walk the 3 blocks to the center of town by herself and shop at the local grocery store. Frequently she ate at a small restaurant. During the third year, economic hard times led to the closure of the both the grocery and the restaurant. Gradually many of her friends and neighbors died and her family, involved with their own lives, had not maintained close contact with her over the years. Hallie began to spend a lot of time in bed, ate poorly, complained of physical ailments and went to the doctor whenever she could find someone to take her. She also began to wander around the town. When friends would find her, they would take her home, but before long she would leave home and wander again. She began to have difficulty keeping her finances in order. When her family did visit, they often found spoiled food in her refrigerator. She would often lose things—her pocketbook, dentures and keys—and once she was robbed. The townspeople warned her family that Hallie needed more supervision.

Her family then decided to move Hallie into a board-and-care facility. This depressed her and her life began to go downhill. She fell several times, was hospitalized once for elevated blood sugar and again for an irregular heartbeat. She was discharged from the hospital with prescriptions for seven different medications that she was told to take for her various ailments.

After her return to the home, Hallie began to complain of nausea, dizziness and headaches. She refused to eat or drink and would often spit out her medications after the staff left. She experienced rapid weight loss and it became very hard for her to walk. She began to complain that she was tired of living; she looked sad and very rarely expressed any sort of joy. She was no longer her feisty self and she abandoned her lifelong need to control the events of her life. Her daughters agreed that at age 87, Hallie should have no further medical intervention, but be allowed to die naturally, a request she herself had frequently made.

Hallie was suffering from depression. Her granddaughter, after much objection from Hallie, insisted that a psychiatric evaluation be made. In her healthy state, Hallie had always expressed a strong will to live. The psychiatric evaluation resulted in a 3-week stay in a geropsychiatric unit. On admission, the psychiatrist indicated that all of the medications that she was taking should be terminated. Electroconvulsive therapy was discussed, but not administered. After the elimination of all medications except digoxin, which was regulated carefully by blood value tests, Hallie once again returned to being her usual jovial self. She continues to live in a sheltered environment and has recently celebrated her 91st birthday.

TREATMENT AND MANAGEMENT OF
INSTITUTIONALIZED SUICIDAL RESIDENTS

Depressed, suicidal elders in institutions share certain basic characteristics. It is important for staff to be aware of these characteristics and be able to recognize them. Depressed, suicidal residents of long-term care institutions can indeed be effectively treated and their risk of suicide reduced, but there must first be an accurate diagnosis and prompt treatment of depression. Physicians, nurses and other staff members can manage and treat depressed, suicidal elders using a variety of techniques and therapies. In addition to the more frequently used medication and psychotherapeutic interventions, newer techniques have been found to be effective: the use of humor therapy, therapeutic touch, caring communication and other effective therapies will be discussed in the following pages. Environmental changes, which can improve the quality of life of nursing home residents, will also be highlighted.

Common Characteristics

The following characteristics distinguish depressed, suicidal institutionalized residents:

- The occurrence of multiple serious losses (for example, physical

faculties and ability, deaths of loved ones, financial status) in rapid
  succession
- Lack of family, friends and other significant others, who provide
  emotional and social support and affection and sensory stimulation
- Significant loss of personal control
- Psychological exhaustion (tired of living, tired of life and no energy
  to carry on)
- Lack of meaning and purpose to life

Older suicidal persons often have no family or friends left. They
express intense feelings of loneliness and an inability to find meaning in
the institutional environment in which they now live. Older individuals
who experience multiple losses, in particular physical losses and loss of
mental function in a short period of time, often become clinically depressed. Depression is usually present when a person speaks in a flat,
monotone voice, shows a lack of facial expression, expresses no joy in
describing things that previously brought pleasure and ruminates about
losses in every conversation.

People who have had a life filled with meaningful family relationships
and friends may not be able to develop significant attachments in the
long-term care facility. Burnside (1981) has noted that one of the most
important elements in keeping a suicidal individual alive is the presence of
a dedicated, responsible person with whom the person may develop a close
relationship. Burnside points to the findings of Jerome Motto who concluded
that most completed suicides that take place after hospitalization occur among
individuals who have no close relationships or follow-up from staff.

As we have discussed, personal control is often lost in the long-term
care setting. A resident in one facility complained that he had been given
just one small closet in which to place a lifetime of memories and articles
that helped him maintain his sense of who he was. He became furious
one day when a nurse decided to "organize his belongings to reduce the
clutter and fire hazard." He complained that people always told him what
to do, when and how to do it, and the pain that this violation of his private
sanctum had caused him. Even though he was allowed to vent his anger,
the incident resulted in a depression that lasted for days.

Living takes energy. When people are depressed, they often have little
or no desire or energy to engage in activities. It is often painful to be
around people, particularly people who are happy. The energy needed
to participate in activities is often overwhelming. Nursing staff should
carefully develop a gradual regime of participation. The following suggestions are offered in this regard. Begin by positioning the depressed person

on the fringes of activity where he can see and hear what is going on, but does not directly feel pressure to be involved. Tell the resident in a matter-of-fact way that being in an environment with others is part of the treatment program. If he asks to be taken back to the solitude of his room, by all means follow through with the request. Gradually increase the frequency and duration of observing group activity. Look for nonverbal cues of changes in affect such as a hint of a smile or lip movement with the words to a song. Geropsychiatric staff will feel greatly rewarded when a patient is slowly able to tolerate group activity and, finally, laughter.

Suicide notes of older people often reflect the agony of being "too tired to continue." When an individual expresses this kind of tiredness or the feeling of being "all used up," staff should be particularly attentive to signs of life-threatening behavior. Many suicidal elders say things such as, "I am tired of living" or "I just can't go on anymore." Some of them feel that their lives are worthless and meaningless and that even if they killed themselves it would not cause anyone significant pain and that it may even go unnoticed. They see no purpose for living. Helplessness and hopelessness, loss of meaning and purpose in life and the hope that it will improve are attitudes that are frequently found together.

Kierkegaard (1941) referred to such despair as "sickness unto death." Miller (1979) describes crossing the "line of unbearability" as the primary factor in elderly suicide:

> Lying dormant within all of us is an extremely personal equation which determines the point at which the quality of our lives would be so pathetically poor that we would no longer wish to live. This "line of unbearability," as it might be called, usually exists only subconsciously and we are therefore not normally cognizant of it. However, when we actually find ourselves in an intolerable situation, even for the first time in our lives, we become conscious of our "line of vulnerability." Once that line is crossed, a crisis is triggered. Those who still maintain hope cry out for help. Those who don't kill themselves quickly and with determination.

According to Himmelhoch (1988), "successful treatment of suicidal patients...requires greater attention to detail, greater interpersonal contact, greater general knowledge and greater clinical wisdom than any other psychotherapeutic task."

Treating Depression

Management of the clinical symptoms of late-life depression should be coordinated by a physician trained to assess and recognize the unique needs of the elderly. All physicians, nurses, nursing assistants and other staff of long-term care facilities should be trained to recognize late-life depression. Staff should remain constantly alert to changes in mood or behavior and other signs and symptoms of depression and they should be instructed to report any suspicion of depression to the physician.

Major signs and symptoms of depression include: change in mood (feeling sad, gloomy, having the "blues"); loss of appetite and rapid weight loss; change in sleeping patterns, particularly insomnia and early morning wakening; constant and unexplainable fatigue; withdrawal from family, friends, social groups and activities; apathy; somatic complaints (for example, constipation, racing heart, neck ache, backache, etc.); and thoughts, dreams, ideation, or actual threats of suicide. Suicidal threats in the elderly require careful and immediate intervention. Older persons talk about their intent less frequently, but those who do communicate their suicidal intent are much more likely to complete the act.

A number of different psychotropic medications are available to treat late-life depression, particularly when severity and duration of signs and symptoms are accompanied by compromised functional ability. These include antidepressants, lithium, minor tranquilizers and stimulants. Dramatic improvements in cognitive function can result when appropriate drugs are used in correct geriatric doses. Physicians who prescribe these medications to the elderly must be aware of the special problems associated with each drug. A pharmacist can help monitor compliance and drug interactions.

Despite adverse publicity, electroconvulsive therapy remains one of the most effective treatments in the psychiatric armamentarium, provided it is used to treat appropriate disorders and in appropriate conditions. When electroconvulsive therapy is used to treat major depression, it results in more rapid improvement and shorter hospital stays than tricyclic antidepressant therapy (Markowitz, Brown et al. 1987). For the suicidal elderly patient with melancholia or psychotic depression, electroconvulsive therapy may well be the treatment of choice. For older patients, as for younger patients, unilateral electroconvulsive therapy with brief pulse wave stimulus is preferred because it tends to produce substantially less cognitive memory impairment than bilateral electroconvulsive therapy (Weiner, Rogers et al. 1984).

In addition to these medical treatments, various psychosocial therapies are also effective. Psychotherapy, reminiscence and life review therapy, creative arts therapy and support group therapy all are potentially useful treatments. For a complete review of these therapies, refer to Osgood (1985). The remainder of this chapter is devoted to less well known methods of treatment.

Humor Therapy

The merits of laughter and a good sense of humor have been extolled throughout history. The Old Testament says that "a merry heart doeth good like a medicine" (Proverbs 17:22). The medieval practice of keeping court jesters attests to the value placed on humor by royalty. In his work, *The Anatomy of Melancholy*, Robert Burton, an English scholar who wrote 400 years ago, attributed curative properties to mirth. Mirth was recognized as the most effective method for alleviating melancholia. Many Native American tribes had ceremonial clowns to entertain them. Sigmund Freud considered humor as the highest-level defense mechanism and linked humor with the will to live. He asserted that laughter saves psychic energy that would otherwise be needed to suppress unacceptable sexual and hostile feelings. The German philosopher Friedrich Nietzsche recognized the value of laughter when he wrote: "Man alone suffers so excruciatingly in the world that he was compelled to invent laughter."

Norman Cousins (1979), former editor of *The Saturday Review*, popularized the benefits of humor and laughter in fighting disease and illness. Upon his return from an exhausting trip to Russia in 1964, Cousins was diagnosed with a serious collagen disease that caused the connective tissue in his spine and joints to disintegrate and this produced excruciating pain throughout his body. He was given a very slim chance of recovering, but Cousins refused to accept the prognosis and, with the help of his physician, took charge of his own recovery program. His first move was to check out of the hospital and move into a motel. He ate a very healthy diet, took large doses of vitamin C intramuscularly and put himself on a program of "humor therapy," watching *Candid Camera* episodes and old Marx Brothers films, reading jokes and humorous books and stories. He laughed a lot. He found that the laughter had an anesthetic effect that allowed him to sleep without pain. Pain was reduced as humor and laughter stimulated the production of endorphins, natural opiates. Slowly, the connective tissue in his joints regenerated and he actually was able to recover. He attributed his recovery to his self-designed humor therapy. He was convinced that his focus on positive images and his immersion in humor and laughter had a positive effect on his immune system, which was then able to fight the progressive disease.

Older adults, like people of all ages, can derive many psychological and physiological benefits from humor and laughter. A good deal of anecdotal evidence exists suggesting that clowns have a therapeutic effect on hospital patients of all ages. Not only do clowns lift the spirits and produce laughter with their antics, but also they can be the stimulus for recovery from serious physical illnesses. Extensive examples of this effect are provided by Moody (1978). Siegel (1986) also found that cancer patients who are willing to laugh at themselves, make mistakes and are not afraid of looking foolish have survivor personalities.

Humor and laughter also have many physiological benefits. Cousins said that laughter was able to "jog the innards." Hearty laughter actually exercises the heart, lungs and other vital organs. Laughter also increases the flow of air through the lungs and increases the level of oxygen in the blood. Laugher also increases the production of catecholamines, which stimulate the production of endorphins that enhance feelings of well-being and increase pain tolerance. In addition, laughter relieves pain resulting from muscle tension, increases the heart and respiration rate, enhances metabolism, improves muscle tone and stimulates the immune system and this indirectly increases resistance to disease. For all of these reasons it is worthwhile to encourage humor and laughter in the depressed elderly.

Laughter and humor also provide many psychological benefits and can alleviate depression in older individuals. Laughter is one of the best ways to release anger, tension and anxiety, reduce stress and promote relaxation. Humor is related to positive self-concept and self-esteem. People who feel good about themselves can laugh at themselves. Laughter and humor can lift the spirits and liberate older people from their troubles and depression. Laughter provides simple distraction, a means of escape. Individuals who can laugh and see the humor in life events, in their own and other's mistakes and shortcomings, have a more realistic appreciation of the imperfect world in which we live and the imperfect people with whom we share it. Laughter is a mechanism to express joy and pleasure. Humor lightens the burdens of living a little and enables one to be less serious and less somber. Humor also brings people together and serves as a very positive means of communication.

It has been said that a smile is the shortest distance between two people. Humor brings a bond of fellowship between the one who laughs and all of those in his presence. Laughter really is contagious. It provides relief and delight, reduces social distance and increases social communication and social cohesion.

Humor and laughter stimulate institutionalized elders. Smiling and laughing, like touch, are powerful forms of nonverbal communication. Humor can provide a link with the past, an affirmation of present life and hope for the future. It can also provide perspective. To appreciate humor, one must separate, if only briefly, from the real, hard reality of life and assume a perspective broader than the actual circumstances.

The psychological value of systematically using humor as a therapeutic technique with older adults has been well documented empirically. McQuire and associates (1990) conducted a study of the effectiveness of humor in improving the quality of life of institutionalized residents. Thirty residents from eight different institutions were randomly assigned to a humor, a non-humor, or a control group. The humor group viewed funny movies; the non-humor group viewed serious films; and the control group didn't watch any films. The Affect Balance Scale and VIRO Scale were administered both prior to the start of the study and upon the completion of the study. Analysis of results provides strong support for the effectiveness of humor therapy with institutionalized elders. Watching humorous films had a significant positive effect on the mood and affect of residents. Those who viewed funny films felt better about their lives than those who watched serious films or no films at all. Similarly Simon (1988), in an earlier study with 24 adults who were older than 61 years, found a positive relationship between humor and morale. Napora (1984) conducted a program of humorous activity with 60 older adults for 6 weeks. Thirty elders participated in humorous activities and 30 served as controls. Analysis of mood levels of participants before and after the humor program was conducted; the results confirmed that participation in humorous activities has a major positive effect on mood. These as well as less controlled studies support the use of humor therapy with older adults.

Specifically, humor therapy for older adults utilizes humor and laughter in a systematic fashion to improve mood and quality of life. An important aim of this type of therapy is to create a climate that produces laughter, joy and happiness. Happiness can lift older people out of the depths of despair and can help them overcome sickness, boredom, loneliness, sadness and the feelings of injustice and imprisonment of being institutionalized. As Muller (1978), a former delegate to the United Nations said, "happiness is triumph of life; pessimism is its defeat." A group at Oregon Health Sciences University call themselves "Nurses for Laughter" and wear buttons that read: "Warning: Humor May Be Hazardous To Your Illness."

Humor therapy can be used successfully in long-term care institutions; it is relatively easy and inexpensive to implement such a program. One goal of a therapy program of this sort is to provide at lease a laugh a day. At the simplest level, humorous movies, films, videos and audiotapes can be played regularly. Humorous books are also useful and should be made available to residents or read to them by staff members. Following is a list of funny books, movies and videos that can be used to make people laugh.

Films and Videos

Marx Brothers films
Abbott and Costello films
Laurel and Hardy films
Buster Keaton films
Candid Camera videos
World's Funniest People videos
World's Funniest Home Videos
How to Marry a Millionaire (Marilyn Monroe)
I Love Lucy TV shows
The Keystone Cops
The Good Humor Man (Jack Carson)
The Making of the Stooges
The Return of the Pink Panther

Audio Cassettes, Records and Radio Programs

The Best of Bill Cosby; 200 M.P.H.; Wonderfulness (Bill Cosby)
The Works (Groucho Marx)
Ogden Nash Reads (Ogden Nash)
Crackin' Up (Ray Stevens)
George Burns and Gracie Allen radio programs

Books

Penguin Dreams (Berke Breathed)
You Can Fool All of the People All of the Time (Art Buchwald)
Dear George (George Burns)
How To Eat Like a Child and Other Lessons in Not Being Grown Up
    (Delia Ephron)
Please Don't Eat the Daisies (Jean Kerr)
It's Hard to Be Hip Over Thirty and Other Tragedies of Married Life
    (Judith Viorst)
Without Feathers (Woody Allen)
Murphy's Law (Arither Block)
Crackers (Roy Blount, Jr.)
Chocolate: The Consuming Passion (Sandra Boynton)

The following suggestions can help introduce humor, laughter and joy into an institution. Have a local scout troop, school class, or seniors' group prepare riddles and jokes, and then place one riddle or jokes on each dinner tray every evening. Put on funny plays and performances using scripts of amusing one-act plays with staff and residents as actors. Play different non-competitive games that encourage fun and laughter. Hire a clown to come to the facility regularly to give performances and also to visit residents in their rooms. Ask local comedians and magicians to come in and perform (they can be semi-professionals, staff members, or students from nearby schools or colleges).

Another valuable way to introduce humor therapy is to create a Laughing Room or a Humor Room—a place that encourages laughter. The room should be colorfully decorated with funny pictures on the walls and jokes and humorous sayings displayed in a variety of ways throughout the room. Joke books and other humorous materials such as amusing toys and gadgets should be readily available. Funny films and audio cassettes should be played at least once a day in the room. Daily or weekly humor sessions can be held in the room and should include both residents and staff.

Humor sessions are structured group sessions that attempt to stimulate and encourage laughter. Humor groups can be led by a staff member or resident with a good sense of humor. In the groups, jokes and funny stories can be told, puns shared and, if possible, short humorous plays can be performed. Residents should be challenged to come up with their own funny stories and to make up humorous captions to pictures, or to write down good jokes or funny stories they hear or read. Members of the group who are too shy to tell a joke, can be encouraged to share one funny thing or at least one joyful thing that happened during the week. Over time the group could create its own humor book composed of cartoons, jokes, witticisms and funny stories contributed by group members. Such a task not only encourages cooperation and a team effort by members, but it also preserves their humor in a tangible form for them to look at over time and to share with others.

Some residents will not be able to participate in the humor group. For non-ambulatory residents, a "laughter wagon" or "humor cart" containing all sorts of humorous materials such as joke books, comics, funny toys and gadgets and comical photos can be rolled into each room.

Two other wonderful sources of humor are pets and children; they are both often very amusing to watch and should be brought into the facility regularly. Children are pure and simple-hearted and their laughter is so honest and heart-felt; this is part of their magic and what makes them so enchanting and endearing to the elderly. Some of life's loveliest moments are provided by pets. The purring of a kitten curled up asleep in your lap, the head of a puppy snuggling under your hand and the sensation of a puppy licking your hand are warm and comforting experiences, especially for an older person who is no longer accustomed to having any sort of physical contact.

It is a good idea to determine which staff members have a sense of humor, laugh easily and smile often, to work with institutionalized elders. Nursing assistants and other staff members should be encouraged to let the cheerful and playful dimensions of their personalities emerge in their daily interaction with residents, even when they are performing mundane tasks such as changing the sheets. It is important to foster an awareness in staff and residents of why humor in this environment is so valuable and to encourage open laughter in both.

Sara, age 83, is a good example of how a problem can be solved using humor. Sara could not get in and out of the bathtub or shower without assistance. To make matters worse, her independent nature and pride prevented her from allowing staff to help. She was described as a "difficult" patient and true to the tag, she became increasingly problematic to deal with during other routines. Finally, one assistant was successful in her efforts when she was assigned to Sara. Sara stopped refusing to cooperate during her bath and even seemed to look forward to it. During a planning conference, the staff asked Millie, the nursing assistant, what she had done to make Sara so cooperative. Millie stated she looked for ways to allow Sara as much independence as possible. Because Sara preferred a night bath, she had accommodated this choice. She let Sara regulate the water temperature, select her nightgown and get her soap, deodorant, toothbrush and other equipment together by herself. During her bath, Millie encouraged Sara to bathe herself as much as possible. They talked about things such as bathing their children and funny stories about the past and present. Bath time became a fun time and the association with joking and laughter took away some of Sara's embarrassment and pain of needing assistance.[*]

Touch Therapy

Human beings have a biological need for touch, an actual skin hunger that can only be met in contact with another human being. Touch is the earliest sense that develops in the newborn infant. Infants who are deprived of physical contact may actually die. Touch is also a major form of communication. Through physical touching individuals develop a healthy sexual identity, a bond with others; they experience self-awareness

---

[*]A full program of humor, developed and instituted by the Ethel Percy Andrus Gerontology Center, was published in 1983 as a monograph entitled *Humor: The Tonic You Can Afford.*

and self-love, explore their environment, and experience pleasant sensations. The frequency of touch has a proven effect on metabolism, the endocrine and muscular systems and intestinal motility.

Touch can be therapeutic and has been used in various civilizations throughout the ages as a method of healing. The oldest documentation of the healing powers of touch is a classical work in internal medicine from the Orient, the *Huang Ti Nei Ching*, written 5000 years ago. The laying on of hands to heal is an ancient practice recorded in the hieroglyphics, cuneiform writings and pictographs of early cultures. Hippocrates also described the healing powers of touch in his medical writings. Faith healing, too, involves the laying on of hands.

Older people either gradually lose many of those who previously provided touch experiences—parents, spouse, children and close friends—or when they are institutionalized, these people are no longer around on a regular basis. The elderly also suffer from other sensory deprivation; they cannot hear, see or taste as well as they used to. Touch therefore assumes an even greater importance for them.

Unfortunately, many Americans are intolerant of the elderly. They do not want to touch an old, wrinkled body. The caregiver who withholds touch reinforces the resident's feeling of low self-worth by confirming that perhaps the person is unclean, unattractive, unlovable and, therefore, not worthy of touch. Those who are not touched and do not have the opportunity to touch have one of their senses shut off. The effect is to reduce their comprehension of reality. Words and verbal communication can never replace the richness and multidimensionality of the physical senses. Without touch the world is a strange and frightening and impoverished place that lacks color and character. Touch deprivation creates a sense of alienation from self and isolation from others. These feelings may be experienced as boredom or lack of energy and a feeling of being disconnected from people and the outside world. The poem *Minnie Remembers* by Donna Swanson (1977) poignantly expresses the older person's need for touch.

> God,
> My hands are old.
> I've never said that out loud before
> but they are.
> I was so proud of them once.
> They were soft
> like the velvet smoothness of a firm, ripe
> peach.
> Now the softness is more like worn-out sheets
> or withered leaves.
> When did these slender, graceful hands

become gnarled, shrunken claws?
When, God?
They lie here in my lap,
naked reminders of this worn-out
body that has served me too well!
How long has it been since someone touched me
Twenty years?
Twenty years I've been a widow.
Respected.
Smiled at.
But never touched.
Never held so close that loneliness
was blotted out.
I remember how my mother used to hold me,
God.
When I was hurt in spirit or flesh,
she would gather me close,
stroke my silky hair
and caress my back with her warm hands.
O God, I'm so lonely!
 I remember the first boy who ever kissed me.
We were both so new at that!
The taste of young lips and popcorn,
the feeling inside of mysteries to come.
I remember Hank and the babies.
How else can I remember them but together?
Out of the fumbling, awkward attempts of new
lovers came the babies.
And as they grew, so did our love.
And, God, Hank didn't seem to mind
if my body thickened and faded a little.
He still loved it. And touched it.
And we didn't mind if we were no longer beautiful.
And the children hugged me a lot.
O God, I'm lonely.
God, why didn't we raise the kids to be silly
and affectionate as well as
dignified and proper?
You see, they do their duty.
They drive up in their fine cars;
they come to my room to pay their respects.
They chatter brightly and reminisce.
But they don't touch me.
They call me "Mom" or "Mother"
or "Grandma."
Never Minnie.
My mother called me Minnie.
So did my friends.
Hank called me Minnie, too.
But they're gone.

And so is Minnie.
Only Grandma is here.
And God! She's lonely!

It is clear how and why touch is such an important nursing intervention; it should be used often when working with depressed elders in long-term care institutions. Vortherms (1991) says that patients perceive the nurse's role as a nurturing one and, therefore, allow them permission to provide intimate bodily care. Touch involves transmission and reception of a signal through a communication channel of the haptic system, a biologic system pertaining to tactile sensation in the body. Touch may help reawaken the older person's perceptual abilities and help orient the disoriented. It provides an effective way to wake up, stimulate and re-establish an elderly person's sense of reality—that they really are in the physical world.

We can channel the love in our hearts through our hands to relieve the pain and suffering of lonely, depressed elders. Touch is a gesture of positive regard for another and expresses that one perceives another as a valuable and acceptable person. This powerful nonverbal message can influence the older person's self-image. For those who hate the way they look and feel, touch and physical affection are the best way to communicate love and affection. Touch conveys love and acceptance, support and reassurance, empathy, understanding and personal commitment. A hand gently placed on a resident's arm or shoulder is a shelter against the darkness. A touch can combat the fear and loneliness and the isolation and pain experienced by a lonely, disoriented or dying resident. It is a form of interpersonal communication and bonding and helps promote trust and cooperation between residents and staff. Montague (1978) points out, "In the aged especially, the need for tactile stimulation is a hunger which has so often remained unsatisfied that, in their disappointment, its victims tend to become uncommunicative concerning their need for it." He further describes a caressing hand as "the only touch of love."

Watson (1975) defines a category of touch called expressive touch as "relatively spontaneous and affective contact which is not necessarily an essential component of a physical task." Gently holding a resident's hand or gently stroking her hair or shoulder are valuable forms of touch. A simple warm gesture like a hand on the shoulder may do more to help a depressed elder regain hope and a will to live than many other sophisticated interventions. Touch sends a "live" message, as well as a love message.

Touch is frequently used effectively as an intervention with older nursing home residents. Burnside (1973) reports on her work with six nursing home residents, suffering from chronic brain syndrome in whom touching was used as a nursing intervention. She found that it resulted in less babbling behavior, more eye contact and more sociability in residents. Copstead (1980), who examined the effects of touch on 33 permanently institutionalized residents, found a statistically significantly positive correlation between frequency of touch and positive self-appraisal by residents. Every nursing intervention with an older adult should be planned to include touch.

Nights and bedtime are often lonely, difficult times for the elderly. While less sleep is required and sleeping and waking patterns change with age, most institutions use set patterns and have uniform expectations for all residents at nighttime. Frequently, nursing staff will rush the residents to bed early so they have time for charting and other required duties they must fulfill before their shift ends. Their duties are frequently interrupted by patients who cannot sleep and who therefore make demands on staff members during a period when they are busy. This leads to anger and resentment on the part of staff.

The following case example utilized touch and allowed one nurse to find uninterrupted time for her work once the unit was quiet. Elizabeth was depressed. She exhibited her depression by constant somatic complaints and sleeping difficulties. During her hospitalization, she received various drugs to help her sleep, but none had worked successfully. The staff began to dread night routines because Elizabeth would follow the medicine cart from room to room, asking for her sleeping pill, and after taking it at 9:30 was awake by midnight, asking for a repeat dose. She never slept more than 2 hours at a time. She did not sleep during the day.

The night shift decided to alter Elizabeth's routine. At 9:00 Elizabeth was offered a bath and warm drink. Extra attention was offered to Elizabeth during these activities. She had developed a good relationship with several staff members and they would regularly oversee her care. At 10:00, Elizabeth was "put to bed" with a back rub. One of her caregivers began to hum a tune as she massaged Elizabeth's back. Elizabeth described how she liked that song because when she was young her mother had sung it to her when it was bedtime. They began to hum and sing together.

One night, the staff member spontaneously pulled the covers up and tucked them around Elizabeth, then gave her a hug and sat quietly on the bed, holding her hand for a few minutes. When she left, the nurse made sure a night light was on. In the past Elizabeth had asked for her sleeping pill moments after the staff left her room. On this particular night she did not ask for a sleeping pill and did not awaken until early morning. On awakening, she described having "a wonderful night's sleep." The hug became part of her bedtime routine.

Nurses, other care providers and family members should be sensitive to nonverbal requests for touching—such as back-scratching, assistance with dressing, reaching out and hand-holding—and should take the time to enjoy the mutual experience. Hand-holding, hand-patting, a hand gently placed on the arm or shoulder, stroking of head or hands and other forms of touch should be used frequently to stimulate, encourage, calm and comfort older residents in institutions. Nursing assistants should include touching while feeding, bathing and dressing residents. Touching the face of an older man after shaving him "to make sure it's rid of the whiskers" is non-threatening.

Each time staff enters a person's room they should use some form of touching. Touching should also be used when medications are given. Among the most comfortable places to be touched are the hand, arm and upper back. Should an individual withdraw, however, the caregiver should understand that people have different comfort levels with the invasion of personal space and withdrawal of any sort is an indicator of anxiety.

Two beneficial sources of touching are hugging and massage, both of which are particularly appreciated by the elderly. Massage can be done by another or by "self-massage." To administer self-massage, tennis balls can be rolled over various parts of the body, a rolling pin can be rolled under the feet, a brush can be used to stimulate the bottom of the feet, the head and other parts of the body. Back rubs and foot massages can be practiced with a partner and are particular favorites because they feel so good.

Older people love to be touched, but they also love to touch others. They like to touch clothing, jewelry and other people's hands and faces. Touch can help create a sense of "whole" image in one who has lost a significant degree of vision. This exercise should be encouraged. As mentioned earlier in this chapter, young children are usually warm and expressive and enjoy touching and being touched. Children should be brought into the institution regularly. They should be allowed to sit in the laps and on the beds of residents, touching them and being touched by them. Animals are warm, furry objects that lick and cuddle; and residents can pet and stroke them. Pet visitation programs offered by the SPCA or other volunteer groups in the community should be a part of the regular recreational programming at the facility.

Another important touching activity for residents is dancing. While dancing, individuals not only hold hands, but also make body contact in numerous other ways and therefore a variety of dancing opportunities should be provided. Staff can dance with residents; residents can dance with each other. High school or college students can come in and dance with residents or even have a "senior prom" inside or outside of the institution. In addition to ballroom dancing, line dances, circle dances and scarf dancing all encourage touching. Dancing offers many other benefits for residents including physiological benefits such as improved breathing, cardiovascular conditioning and weight control; a means of creative expression, personal growth and development; and a way to promote communication, socialization, friendship and, of course, fun.

Caring Communication

Communication is the cornerstone of all relationships. While we generally think of communication as being expressed through words, caring communication encompasses far more than this, including how and when we speak, as well as the way we emphasize our words with facial and body expression. Caring communication includes choice of words, voice intonation, frequency of talking and gestures. It imparts feeling and sets the tone for an empathetic relationship between individuals or groups. Caring radiates a sense of warmth.

The caring communication we normally experience is expressed in our social milieu with family, friends, neighbors, support groups and acquaintances. With age, changes occur in the patterns of interaction and caring communication may be lost.

Retirement from work represents a loss of communication with fellow workers as common interests no longer bond the relationship. While new friends may be made, for some people the closeness that comes from years of experience together is missing. With old age, many of the people who are important in caring relationships such as spouse, friends and family die; the circle of people to whom one can turn contracts.

Sensory loss may also become more apparent. It is difficult to talk to one who cannot hear well, or describe the meaning of visual experience to one who cannot see. Time and energy are required to paint a word picture or write a thought to share. Many in our culture tend to exclude those with disabilities rather than find clever ways to communicate with them. This is because they are essentially fearful and anxious about disability.

When a person must move into an institution, which is devoid of familiar sights, sounds, smells and comforts of home and family, the adjustment is usually extraordinarily stressful. Strangers often become the core of life. Below is a description of the reaction of a new patient as she was moving into a nursing home (Eliopoulous 1989):

Mrs. Evans encouraged her son to leave and assured him that she would be just fine. After he left, her confidence dwindled as she began to wonder how she would manage living in such a strange new environment. She wondered if she should ask staff members why they ignored a patient who had been screaming for help, make a special effort to introduce herself to staff and other patients, or explain her unique likes and dislikes. She feared her efforts would be resented, and, besides, she was not sure she had that kind of energy. She was not certain whether it was the fear of the unknown or the sadness and anger of spending her last days reduced to this form of living, but she felt a level of discontent never before experienced in her entire life.

Patients like Mrs. Evans may bring with them anger, fear, anxiety and depression and may regress to childlike coping patterns in their effort to adapt. This childlike behavior may be responsible for the all-too-frequent statement that older people should be "treated like children." Caring communication from staff in a strange new place can help ease the transition and preserve dignity.

For example, it is not unusual for a frightened elder to call out for "Mama" or scream in fear when restrained or left alone for long periods of time. Calling for "Mama" represents fear expressed in the only terms the demented brain can recall. Telling the person that you understand she may be frightened and lonely is much more helpful than reminding her that her mother is dead. An appropriate response from staff would include, if possible, talking to residents about their fears. If the resident is demented, speaking softly and quietly, holding her hand for a few moments and bringing her to a place where there is activity—such as near a nursing station—will help ease her panic of being alone. A person in an area of activity is less likely to feel abandoned. Keeping cages of colorful birds that sing and playing soft music are also soothing and bringing a person to this area can help with anxiety. Increasing the opportunities for staff-resident interactions and relationships can be a positive contribution to a resident's physical and psychosocial well-being, whatever the mental state of the resident.

Resident friendships are encouraged by the age-segregated environment. Residents may find common interests with their peers and their close physical proximity can often nurture strong relationships. For example, two residents who shared a room became extremely close. Both were from large families and were sole survivors. Both spoke English as a second language and each was conversant in the native language of the other. One was blind and the other deaf. They joked that together they made a "whole person." A nurse had noticed the similarities these two women shared and had suggested they room together. Hand in hand they went to meals and activities and walked about the grounds, describing the sights and sounds of life to each other. Each resident provided an opportunity to give and receive caring communication.

In an extensive analysis of communication and language in the institutionalized elderly, Nussbaum (1991) attempted to understand the social lives of elderly persons in nursing homes. He found that the architectural design of the home, the medical model of rules and policies and the individual disabilities brought unique obstacles to an active social environment. He concluded that the homogeneity of the environment, however, combined with involvement by staff, families and others from the outside presented a solid foundation for an active social life.

One of the most important contributions to caring communication that can be made by staff is the day-to-day conversation with the residents that they can provide. Topics of interest can be integrated into the individual nursing care plan so that staff can be more aware of individual needs and interests. The goal of each care plan will vary, but the actions to meet that goal should always include one-to-one relationships. Such nursing interventions will promote nurturance and warmth and provide meaningful relationships.

Nursing staff members should be encouraged to go out of their way to get to know each of the residents in the facility. It is of interest to note that Nussbaum (1991) has shown that residents do not feel they should initiate relationship-building actions, but will reciprocate overtures made by staff. Nursing staff who developed closeness with their patients reported more conversation on religion, community events, family events and personal problems. These topics have been considered taboo and not "professional behavior" in the past. Unfortunately, many nurses and other staff may have been warned to avoid "closeness in relationships with patients." Such an admonition, if taken to heart, diminishes caring communication and inhibits staff-resident relationships.

The Nussbaum study further indicates that nurse's aides viewed their interaction with residents as a time to achieve their tasks. Their primary focus was efficiency because of pressure from supervisors to get their jobs done. The elderly represented a task to be accomplished—a job—that would hopefully provide as little trouble as possible. Such an attitude will establish a barrier to positive resident-staff psychosocial interaction and quality communication. Penner, Ludenia and Mead (1984) point out that when nursing staff members simply meet a resident's basic physiologic needs, this may lead to burdensome requests for assistance; this is because residents have been socialized into a passive-dependent role. The simple dynamic of switching from using the word "patient" to "resident" will contribute significantly to a change in staff attitudes and perceptions of the caregiver role. Such a change promotes greater equality between residents and staff and makes sharing of ideas and information easier.

Elliott and Hybertson (1982) described negative feelings expressed by nursing assistants when caring for extremely debilitated and dependent elderly. They found independence in self-care elicited more positive feelings, and working with patients who were agitated, verbally abusive or manipulative produced negative feelings. "Difficult" patients were regarded as unpleasant and unrewarding. When "difficult" patients are recognized by staff as being lonely, anxious and unhappy people who have lost a zest for life, they will often become less difficult. When a relationship begins to develop in which the nursing assistant receives positive feedback from the "difficult" person, the entire unit is enriched by the experience. This process may take a long time, but it is very important.

The nursing assistant must be taught techniques of reaching the residents who have turned away from the world, though many employees have learned these methods from life experiences. They may simply need permission from supervisors to participate in such a valuable exercise. Elliot and Hybertson suggest an educational program to assist aides to articulate their feelings about caring for difficult residents and to develop interpersonal skills to understand, accept and cope with behaviors that are caused by illness and are inherent in some patient personality types.

The following case of Joe shows how a nursing assistant was able to improve a life through her use of caring communication. Joe was the victim of a stroke which resulted in left hemiplegia and depression. Formerly an active, outgoing person, he had progressed sufficiently to carry on some conversation, but normally he just stared at the walls wherever he was placed. One aide took a special interest in Joe and lingered over his care, encouraging him to help with his bath and feed himself. She was particularly conscious of his distress about his sloppiness when eating because he could no longer control the responses of his dominant hand. One day while eating, Joe seemed to be struggling especially hard. The aide quietly encouraged his efforts, making no comment but carefully brushing away the few crumbs that fell. As he finished his dinner, Joe looked at the assistant, smiled and said for the first time, "That was a really good dinner!"

Although relationships with staff are important, it is equally important to create an environment that encourages involvement with families and others from outside the facility. Examples of projects to enhance nursing home life include: developing an on-site child day care center; taking residents on outings, picnics and other ventures in small groups with staff and community volunteers; establishing a tea hour for socialization when all work stops and residents and staff can enjoy sharing drink, food and friendship; taking the residents who are able on trips to fairs, casinos or cultural events; and, when there is no family involvement, encouraging staff to "adopt" residents to take home with them for special events such as Thanksgiving, Christmas and birthdays. All of these strategies have been used in facilities with which the authors are familiar and all have promoted greater connectedness with the outside world. While some of these actions may seem more appropriate for residents with a higher functional level, with grit and determination, wheelchairs, catheter bags and oxygen can be brought along and some of these activities can be accomplished even by the fully debilitated.

The following is a representative reaction to residents' increased involvement with the outside world. After a picnic in a local park with a group of residents, the driver of the van took a wrong turn and, in doing so, provided an unexpected tour of town. During the time they drove around town, the group discussed areas they recognized and talked about other times in life when they had been "lost." When they finally returned to the facility an hour and a half late, one of the ladies admonished the administrator, "Don't you fuss at this driver. This is the first time I've felt like a real person since I moved into this place!" Some of the elements important to providing an environment that supports caring communication may require administrative initiatives or innovation. A supportive administrator is the key to bringing about these changes. Aguilar (1978) studied loneliness in nursing home residents and found that facilitating self-help, establishing and maintaining scheduled activities, assisting residents to keep a daily schedule, offering choices, providing clear feedback, providing privacy when giving personal care and listening were all essential to maintaining a relationship and decreasing loneliness.

Cox and his team (1991) designed an experimental trial to focus on the quality of life in long-term facilities. They found that when certain changes in routine were made measures of general well-being were improved, despite declining health and self-care capacity. The changes included permanent assignment of staff to residents; identification of individual case managers for each resident; shift-schedule alteration to accommodate individual residents' preferred waking and sleeping patterns; and ten 1-hour weekly educational sessions on strategies to emphasize resident control over choice. Additionally, daily team meetings were held to review and update staff on resident progress. This study demonstrates the importance of policies that foster concern and communication about the well-being of residents. In this project the effects of these interventions on administrator attitudes was overwhelmingly positive. Administrators expressed a commitment to resident-centered staffing after the experimental period was complete. Moreover, the experiment demonstrated that enhanced quality of life can be provided without additional cost to the institution or to the resident. Staff emphasis was changed from an orientation focused on procedures and tasks to a holistic concept of care. This is the kind of total care that many nurses learned to provide as students and which many of them yearn to provide to achieve greater job satisfaction.

Other ways in which administrators can provide resident-centered care include providing a child day care facility so that staff can bring their preschool children to work and residents will have the added pleasure of intergenerational experiences; avoiding the use of temporary personnel; increasing staff training opportunities with competency-based skill training in areas such as managing behavior, interpersonal relationships, ways to encourage and allow independence, sensitivity to sensory loss and its effect on the person; providing career ladders with increased responsibility; providing a break area that is comfortable, clean and pleasant for a short relaxation period; giving incentive awards to workers who are chosen by residents, such as scholarships and worker of the month awards and increased pay as a reward for outstanding work.

Caring communication is provided in many ways. It may be a smile or a touch on the shoulder with a quick hello while scurrying down a hallway. It may be sharing a hot dog at the county fair or writing down an involved plan of care that includes one-on-one interaction time to build a relationship. One thing is very clear: these gestures create an atmosphere that resembles a home more than an institution and allow staff members to provide the closeness normally associated with family relationships and friendships for which nursing home residents hunger. These measures contribute to building self-esteem and giving new meaning to life. They help provide new ways to combat depression—a disorder that all too often leads to suicide.

Stenback (1980) has noted that in addition to crisis therapy for the treatment of depression, goal-directed methods of therapy should also be used. He suggests techniques that can contribute to learning how to care for new things after a loss, relieving bitterness and low self-esteem and reducing feelings of hopelessness. Persons who feel they have been failures need to be assisted to stop ruminating over the past and focus on new goals that are both inspiring and realistic. Stenback concludes that most people need new interpersonal relationships and social activities in addition to any psychotherapeutic intervention.

Quoting Litman and Wold, Stenback reiterates, "extended personal relationships are the most potent of suicide remedies," and concludes by saying, "Failures and losses are burdens easier to bear when a friend is at hand." The way we interact with elders in nursing homes indicates how we care for and about them. Through caring communication, staff can become the friend that helps to bear the burdens inherent in late life.

Environmental Manipulation

According to Bengtson (1979), the three social-psychological needs of older people are: identity, connectedness and effectance. Identity is a personal sense of one's place in the world and of one's unique qualities as a human being. Connectedness refers to the need to be a part of the social setting and social group, the feeling of belonging. Effectance refers to a sense of control over one's life and one's environment and the ability to make choices and influence change. The environment in which the older individual lives largely determines to what extent these three needs are met and has a primary impact on physical and cognitive functioning. An individual's behavior is shaped, facilitated or constricted by the environment (Lawton 1980) which may either be conducive to challenge and stimulation or may promote relaxation.

The institutionalized elderly are particularly vulnerable due to extended longevity, functional deficits and lack of other social support. They are extremely dependent on their immediate environment (George 1980) and often have less control over their lives than do the elderly in the community.

The institutional environment should be designed to enhance competence, choice, independence, freedom and personal autonomy; to encourage continued responsibility and independent functioning; to compensate for sensory losses; and to facilitate creative living. Residents should be given a choice of what they want to eat, what activities they want to participate in and what time they want to go to sleep in the evening. Other ways of encouraging autonomy and responsibility are to give residents plants to care for and tasks to do. Resident councils that have a major role in policy decisions in the institution should give residents some control over their lives. The administrator and staff should make it clear to residents that their opinions matter and allow them to make suggestions for improvement. Their suggestions should be taken seriously and actual changes implemented when possible and appropriate.

An institution should not look, feel or smell like a hospital. There are many ways to achieve an aesthetically pleasing environment. Artwork, pictures, murals and wall hangings can be displayed. Cheerful, bright colors should be selected and there should be many different objects for residents to observe and touch. Music is always pleasant and residents should be able to listen to the type of music they like. Perhaps a room could be designated as a music room. Flowers and plants can be placed throughout the institution and outside landscaping can include gardens with flowers and comfortable places to sit in the sun or shade. It is important whenever possible to take residents outside often so that they get plenty of sunshine and fresh air. Trips away from the institution also provide sensory stimulation. College and high school students, church groups, seniors' groups and other community groups can be asked to come to the facility to provide various activities.

Privacy is essential to maintaining positive self-regard, self-reflection and autonomy, and to providing emotional release (Louis 1983; Tate 1980). Environmental manipulations can enhance privacy, such as the use of curtains between beds in multi-bed rooms to create physical boundaries and to assist residents to maintain their own private territory; small dining areas for a limited number of residents to reduce crowding and social overload; comfortable furniture for small casual groupings to facilitate social functioning; in-room bathrooms for privacy; knocking before entering a person's room; asking permission to enter the room before intruding on a resident's territory; and respecting the need of the resident for solitude and intimacy. These are the resident's basic rights and they should never be overlooked.

REFERENCES

Abrams, R.C., R.C. Young, et al. 1988. Suicide in New York City nursing homes. *American Journal of Psychiatry* 145:1487-1488.
Aguilar, V.B. 1978. Intervening on Loneliness in a Group of Nursing Home Residents. Unpublished master's thesis, School of Nursing, Virginia Commonwealth University, Richmond.
Bengtson, V.L. 1973. The Aged and Their Social Needs. In E. Seymour, ed., *Psychosocial Needs of the Aged.* Los Angeles: University of Southern California Press.
Burnside, I.M. 1973. *Psychosocial Nursing Care of the Aged.* New York: McGraw-Hill.
Burnside, I.M. 1981. Suicide in the Aged Person. In I.M. Burnside, ed., *Nursing and the Aged.* New York: McGraw-Hill.
Burton, R. 1927. *The Anatomy of Melancholy.* New York: Vintage Press.
Copstead, L.C. 1980. Effects of touch on self-appraisal and interaction appraisal for permanently institutionalized older adults. *Journal of Gerontological Nursing* 6:747-752.
Cousins, N. 1979. *Anatomy of an Illness.* New York: Bantam Books.
Cox, C.L., L. Kaeser, et al. 1991. Quality of life nursing care. *Journal of Gerontological Nursing* 17(4):6-11.
Dudley, C.J. and G.A. Hillary. 1977. Freedom and alienation in homes for the aged. *The Gerontologist* 17:140-145.

Eliopoulos, C. 1989. *Caring for the Nursing Home Patient.* Gaithersburg, MD: Aspen.

Elliott, B. and D. Hybertson. 1982. What is it about the elderly that elicits a negative response? *Journal of Gerontological Nursing* 8:568-571.

Ewers, M., S. Jacobson and V. Powers. 1983. *Humor: The Tonic You Can Afford.* Los Angeles: Andrus Gerontology Center.

George, L.K. 1980. *Role Transitions in Later Life.* Monterey, CA: Brooks/Cole.

Goffman, E. 1960. Characteristics of Total Institutions. In M.R. Stein, A.J. Vidich and D. M. White, eds., *Identity and Anxiety: Survival of the Person in Mass Society.* New York: Free Press.

Goffman, E. 1963. Stigma. Englewood Cliffs, NJ: Prentice-Hall.

Harper, M.S. 1986. Introduction. In M.S. Harper and B.D. Lebowitz, eds., *Mental Illness in Nursing Homes: Agenda for Research.* Washington, DC: U.S. Government Printing Office, DHHS Publication No. (ADM) 86-1459.

Himmelhoch, J.M. 1988. What destroys our restraints against suicide? *Journal of Clinical Psychiatry,* Suppl. 49 (September), 46-52.

Hirst, S.P. and B.J. Metcalf. 1991. Promoting self-esteem. *Journal of Gerontological Nursing* 10(2):72-77.

Kemper, P. and C. Murtaugh. 1991. Lifetime use of nursing home care. *New England Journal of Medicine* 324:595-600.

Kierkegaard, S. 1941. *The Sickness unto Death.* Princeton, NJ: Princeton University Press.

Lawton, M.P. 1980. Environmental Change: The Older Person as Initiator and Responder. In N. Datan and N. Lohmann, eds., *Transitions of Aging.* New York: Van Nostrand Reinhold.

Louis, M. 1983. Personal space boundary needs of elderly persons. *Journal of Gerontological Nursing* 7:395-400.

Markowitz, J., R. Brown, et al. 1987. Reduced length and cost of hospital stay for major depression in patients treated with ECT. *American Journal of Psychiatry* 144:1025-1029.

McCracken Knight, A.M. 1984. Teaching nursing homes. *Journal of Gerontological Nursing* 10(6):14-17.

McQuire, F.A., K.F. Backman and R. Boyd. 1990. The Efficacy of Humor in Improving the Quality of Life for Residents of Long-Term Care Facilities. Final report submitted to AARP Andrus Foundation, Washington, DC.

Miller, M. 1979. *Suicide after Sixty.* New York: Springer.

Montague, A. 1978. *Touching.* New York: Harper & Row.

Moody, R.A. 1978. *Laugh after Laugh.* Jacksonville, FL: Headwaters Press.

Muller, R. 1978. *Most of All, They Taught Me Happiness.* New York: Doubleday & Co.

Napora, J.P. 1984. A study of the effects of a program of humorous activity on the subjective well-being of senior adults. *Dissertation Abstracts International* 46: 276A.

Nussbaum, J.F. 1991. Communication, language and the institutionalized elderly. *Aging and Society* 11:149-165.

Osgood, N.J. 1985. *Suicide in the Elderly.* Rockville, MD: Aspen.

Osgood, N.J. 1992. *Suicide in Late Life.* New York: Lexington.

Osgood, N.J., B.A. Brant and A. Lipmann. 1991. *Suicide among the Elderly in Long-Term Care Facilities.* Westport, CT: Greenwood Press.

Penner, L.A., K. Ludenia and G. Mead. 1984. Staff attitudes: image or reality? *Journal of Gerontological Nursing* 10(3):110-117.

Rovner, B.W., S. Kafonek, et al. 1986. Prevalence of mental illness in a community nursing home. *American Journal of Psychiatry* 143:1446-1449.

Shomaker, D. 1979. Dialects of nursing homes and aging. *Journal of Gerontological Nursing* 5(5):45-48.

Shuttlesworth, G.E., A. Rubin and M. Duffy. 1982. Families versus institutions. *The Gerontologist* 22:200-208.

Siegel, B.S. 1986. *Love, Medicine and Miracles.* New York: Harper & Row.

Simon, J. 1960. The therapeutic value of humor in aging adults. *Journal of Gerontological Nursing* 14(8):8-13.

Sommer, R. and H. Osmond. 1960. Symptoms of institutional care. *Social Problems* 8:254-263.

Stenback, A. 1980. Depression and Suicidal Behavior in Old Age. In J.E. Birren and R.B. Sloane, eds., *Handbook of Mental Health and Aging.* Englewood Cliffs, NJ: Prentice-Hall.

Stotsky, B.A. and J.R. Dominick. 1969. Mental patients in nursing homes: isolation, depression and regression. *Journal of the American Geriatrics Society* 17:33-34.

Swanson, D. 1977. Minnie Remembers. In J. Grana, ed., *Images: Women in Transition.* Winona, MN: St. Mary's College Press.

Tate, J.W. 1980. The need for personal space in institutions for the elderly. *Journal of Gerontological Nursing* 6:439-449.

Tobin, S.S. and M. Lieberman. 1976. *Last Home for the Aged.* San Francisco: Jossey-Bass.

Vortherms, R.C. 1991. Clinically improving communication through touch. *Journal of Gerontological Nursing* 17(5):6-10.

Watson, W. 1975. The meaning of touch. *Journal of Communication* 25:104-112.

Weber, H.I. 1980. *Nursing Care of the Elderly.* Reston, VA: Reston Publishing.

Weiner, R.D., H.J. Rogers, et al., 1984. ECT Stimulus Parameters and Electrode Placement. In B. Lerer, R.D. Weiner and R.H. Belmaker, eds., *Basic Mechanisms.* London: John Libbey.

10

Social Work and the Suicidal Older Person

Elizabeth J. Clark, PhD

Since the early 1980s, suicide among the elderly has increased dramatically. From 1980 through 1986, 36,789 suicides of persons over age 65 were reported, with white males having the highest rate (Meehan et al. 1991). The number of reported suicides is, indeed, alarming and it should be noted that for the elderly, as with all age categories, there is a serious under-reporting of suicidal behavior. For example, Miller (1979), an expert in geriatric suicide, estimates that at least 10,000 people 60 and older commit suicide each year. These suicides may be caused by less obvious forms of life-threatening behavior.

According to Butler and Lewis (1982), suicide in the elderly may be "subintentional" or passive. It may be a long-term process of "suicidal erosion" or chronic suicide which can include refusing to eat, not taking medicines, delaying treatments, taking physical risks, or drinking too much. Passive suicide frequently is related to depression and losing the will to live. Two other categories of suicide that concern the elderly are *rational* suicides and *assisted* suicides.

RATIONAL SUICIDE

Sorenson (1991) concludes that our society considers suicide a viable option for the elderly when it is triggered by incapacitating illness, inevitably diminishing health, declining resources and feelings of being a burden to others. Pretzel (1972) also discussed types of suicide that are considered by some as rational behavior among the elderly. In addition to terminal illness, he includes circumstances that are not desperate, but situations in which the individual no longer receives pleasure from life. He also includes love-pact suicides—the double death of two people committed together as an expression of mutual love and devotion. Recent publicity and media attention about the increase in assisted suicides or "self-deliverance" for the dying (Humphry 1991) also point to the growing incidence of rational suicide.

CAUSES OF GERIATRIC SUICIDE

Geriatric suicide is a complex phenomenon. Stenback (1980) summarized a number of studies that attempt to explain why the elderly commit suicide. He found that depression was clearly a major factor. Miller emphasized that no one factor is in itself suicidogenic and detailed eight patterns of geriatric suicidal behavior (1979). These are reactions to:

1. physical illness
2. mental illness
3. retirement
4. death of a spouse
5. lack of independence or threat of institutionalization
6. pathological personal relationships
7. alcoholism and drug abuse
8. multiple losses

All of these situations are closely linked to loss which is a constant occurrence in the lives of the elderly. Clearly, the longer people live, the more personal losses they will experience. In the later years of life, these losses may accumulate suddenly, occur in rapid succession, or with frequent repetition (Goodstein 1984). Still, only a small minority of older persons who experience multiple losses commit suicide. The crucial factor that seems to determine whether a person will react by committing suicide appears to be how well developed and effective his coping abilities are (Miller 1979). However, an onslaught of traumatic events may result in a depletion phenomenon (Cath 1965) that interrupts or prevents a person's ability to adjust to crisis and disrupts the normal crisis-disorganization and recovery-reorganization process (Hill 1958).

Osgood and associates (1991) found loss to be a major factor contributing to suicide among residents in long-term care facilities. Significant and multiple losses for this group included loss of a spouse, friends, pets, money, personal possessions, control, independence, physical mobility and sensory/perceptual functions.

All losses precipitate grief responses that are either of greater or lesser intensity. For the elderly, loss of a spouse is generally considered to be the most significant loss and conjugal bereavement has been linked to increased mortality and suicide. MacMahon and Pugh (1965) found the risk of suicide in a widowed population to be particularly great during the first 4 years of bereavement and McConnell (1982) was able to link the grief reactions of aged widowers to suicide. Likewise, Bock and Webber (1977) found older widowers are at considerably greater risk of suicide than older widows. Both of these studies highlight that the elderly widower experiences greater social and emotional isolation than the elderly widow.

The typical grief response is often altered for the elderly. Most notably, the tasks of grieving are often incomplete, resulting in what is termed prolonged or chronic grief (Parkes and Weiss 1983) or complicated bereavement. Grief and its expression are bound by cultural influences and societal expectations and the elderly appear to be particularly vulnerable to these constraints. Butler and Lewis (1982) contend that older persons today do not receive the necessary cultural support for grief and mourning. Perhaps even more harmful is the fact that society views loss and grief in later life as normal and expected and little concern is given to the special problems that the elderly widow or widower may have to contend with (Clark 1990). This lack of concern and support for the bereaved elderly increases their loneliness and isolation, prolongs depression and contributes to maladaptive behavior such as alcoholism and suicide.

SOCIAL WORK INTERVENTION

In the late 1950s Batchelor stated that "We now know enough about the etiology of suicide in old age to be able to make some practical suggestions about prophylaxis, which has both social and medical aspects" (Shneidman and Farberow 1957). Suggestions included integration of the elderly into the community, allowing employment for as long as the person desires and is capable of working, fostering an understanding of their psychological and social needs and prompt treatment of depression and mental illness. Unfortunately, in the three decades since Batchelor made his well-founded suggestions, little progress in the prevention of geriatric suicide has been made. In fact, the failure of our mental health system to meet the needs of the elderly has been well documented (Osgood 1985). On a more positive note, today there is a resurgence of interest in the elderly and in the development of creative and effective intervention strategies for the problems that are particular to old age. Yet there is still much to be done. Social workers have several mandates with regard to geriatric suicide—education, intervention, research and advocacy.

Education

Social work curricula must be expanded to provide a greater emphasis on comprehensive mental health services for the elderly including the correlates of geriatric suicide. Also needed is a wider dissemination of suicide prevention fundamentals based on current clinical knowledge and research findings. Also important is the recognition of behavioral characteristics of known high-risk groups and subpopulations (the elderly widower, the newly institutionalized and the older alcoholic). A concomitant educational campaign needs to be undertaken to reduce ageism and negative stereotyping of the aged in our communities and to highlight the special needs and problems of our growing elderly population.

Intervention

There is a shortage of skilled therapists who can treat the self-destructive elderly. Social workers are well-trained in psychosocial assessment and in recognizing and evaluating the contextual sources of personal distress (Waitzkin 1991). These skills are directly applicable to intervention with the elderly person with suicidal tendencies.

Social workers and other mental health professionals need to develop uniform case-finding techniques and procedures for identifying elderly persons who are at risk for suicidal behavior. Suicide risk assessment should be incorporated into social work intake interviews at agencies and institutions to provide services for the elderly and social workers should assume the responsibility for establishing an agency or hospital protocol for assessing the suicide potential of high-risk elderly subpopulations. This may include an assessment checklist or profile that could be used for screening and better case-finding (see Osgood 1985 for an example). Even just asking emergency room staff to notify the hospital social worker when they note certain psychosocial factors in an elderly patient—recently widowed elderly men, those whose records indicate prior suicide attempts—could contribute substantially to the reduction of geriatric suicide.

Another under-served population includes the survivors of suicide—the family and friends of the person who took his life—because this group, too, has special needs; they may have intense guilt feelings and other psychological distress and their bereavement processes do not always follow a normal course (Worden 1982).

Social workers will need to explore and develop intervention strategies and techniques specific to the elderly. These may include techniques such as brief problem-centered therapy, creative arts therapy, sympathetic listening and grief counseling.

Research

A variety of research efforts are needed to fill in the gaps that presently exist regarding services tailored specifically to the elderly. While traditional research studies must be continued, other types of useful research should also be explored. One research activity lacking in most towns and cities is a community analysis of existing social and health care services that are aimed at geriatric suicide prevention. A community resource guide specific to geriatric suicide should be developed and disseminated. Another related activity is a public education campaign to provide information about the availability of mental health services for elderly persons, especially those relevant to suicidal behavior.

At the completion of the community analysis, gaps in suicide services could be addressed by a coalition of care providers. It is important to note that telephone hotlines and support groups—interventions frequently used successfully for younger persons who are suicidal—are not particularly efficacious for the elderly. Of all the calls to suicide hotlines, only 3 percent of them are made by persons over age 65 (Barrow 1989). Likewise, older persons tend to be more reluctant to join groups. This may be due to a lack of experience with the group process, or because the elderly are cautious about divulging personal information (Furukawa and Shomaker 1982). Mobility and transportation problems are other obstacles that hinder the elderly from becoming members and attending therapy or support groups on a regular basis.

The relatively new programs that do seem to have potential for suicide prevention for the elderly include telephone reassurance programs in which a caller can check on older persons daily by phone. These calls may be a meaningful part of each day for an elderly person (especially those living alone) and may provide much-needed ongoing support (Barrow 1989). Another area to be explored is peer counseling and outreach for elderly clients (Steiner 1982).

Advocacy

Last, but certainly not least, is the need for advocacy based on research and clinical intervention specific to the needs of the geriatric population. This may include actions such as obtaining community support for outreach programs and additional services, or it may take the form of lobbying for research dollars or against restrictive legislation. Advocacy also means helping the community and health care professionals recognize the interrelated factors that can lead the elderly to isolation, alienation, alcoholism, chronic grief and suicidal behavior.

With the growing number of seniors in our society, the problem of geriatric suicide will increase. Social workers as well as all those in a helping position can and should take a leadership role in addressing this serious public health issue.

REFERENCES

Barrow, G. 1989. *Aging, the Individual and Society.* St. Paul, MN: West.

Batchelor, I. 1957. Suicide in Old Age. In E.S. Shneidman and N.L. Farberow, eds., *Clues to Suicide.* New York: McGraw-Hill.

Bock, W. and I. Webber. 1972. Suicide among the elderly. *Journal of Marriage and the Family* 34:24-31.

Butler, R. and M. Lewis. 1982. *Aging and mental health.* St. Louis: C.V. Mosby.

Cath, S. 1963. Some Dynamics of the Middle and Later Years. In H. Parad, ed., *Crisis Intervention.* New York: Family Service Association of America.

Clark, E. 1990. The Interrelatedness of Loss and Pathological Grief in the Elderly Population. In E.J. Clark, J. Fritz and P. Ricker, eds., *Clinical Sociological Perspectives on Illness and Loss.* Philadelphia: The Charles Press.

Furukawa, C. and D. Shomaker. 1982. *Community Health Services for the Aged.* Rockville, MD: Aspen.

Goodstein, R. 1984. Grief reactions and the elderly. *Carrier Foundation Letter* 99 (June):1-5.

Hill, R. 1958. Generic features of families under stress. *Social Casework* 39(2).

MacMahon, B. and T. Pugh. 1965. Suicide in the widowed. *American Journal of Epidemiology* 81:23-31.

McConnell, K. 1982. The aged widower. *Social Work* 27:188-189.

Meehan, P., L. Saltzman and R. Sattin. 1991. Suicides among older United States residents. *American Journal of Public Health* 81:1198-1200.

Miller, M. 1979. *Suicide After Sixty.* New York: Springer.

Osgood, N. 1985. *Suicide in the Elderly.* Rockville, MD: Aspen.

Osgood, N., B. and A. Lipman. 1991. *Suicide Among the Elderly in Long-Term Care Facilities.* Westport, CT: Greenwood.

Parkes, C. and R. Weiss. 1983. *Recovery from Bereavement.* New York: Basic Books.

Pretzel, P. 1972. *Understanding and Counseling the Suicidal Person.* Nashville, TN: Abingdon.

Sorenson, S. 1991. Suicide among the elderly: issues facing public health. *American Journal of Public Health* 81:1109-1110.

Shneidman, E.S. and N.L. Farberow. 1957. *Clues to Suicide*. New York: McGraw-Hill.

Steinner, L. 1982. Peer counselors bridge gap in mental care for the elderly. *Milwaukee Journal*, December 9, p. 1.

Stenback, A. 1980. Depression and Suicidal Behavior in Old Age. In J. Birren and B. Sloan, eds., *Handbook of Mental Health and Aging*. Englewood Cliffs, NJ: Prentice Hall.

Waitzkin, H. 1991. *The Politics of Medical Encounters*. New Haven, CT: Yale University Press.

Worden, J. 1982. *Grief Counseling and Grief Therapy*. New York: Springer.

11

The Elderly Suicide:
Those Left Behind

Rochelle Balter, PhD

Although the amount of anecdotal and research literature about suicide has expanded greatly over the last two decades and clinical material concerning the survivors of suicide has received more and more attention (especially concerning survivors of adolescent suicide), there is still relatively little interest in suicide among one very large and high-risk group—the elderly. And if the elderly have been relatively ignored, so too have their survivors.

Statistics indicate that white males of 75 to 85 years of age have a higher rate of suicide than any other age group in the United States and that elderly males and elderly females commit suicide three to four times more often than younger adults of the same sex (Saul and Saul 1989). However, these data are not reflected in the literature concerning survivors of suicide. The majority of the studies on this topic have focused on parents who have lost a child to suicide as well as spouse survivors under the age of 45. Older adults have been excluded from suicide survivor studies because their declining health is seen by many as a contaminating factor (Lundin 1984).

As stated elsewhere in this book, older people who try suicide tend to be more successful in completing their attempts than their younger counterparts. Elderly people tend to be very serious in intent and therefore use more lethal means when they try to kill themselves such as shooting, jumping and hanging (Miller 1979). They communicate their suicidal intent less often than younger people and this is probably an indication that their suicidal intent is most likely meant to end life rather than a means of attracting attention or a call for help.

Miller (1979) points out that little priority has been given to investigating geriatric suicide or to intervening with those considered high risks, mainly because senior citizens are viewed by many as a group who are no longer wage-earning members of society and, therefore, are not a serious economic loss. Also, many purposely ignore geriatric suicide because they believe that among older people, suicide is a rational act. In other words, if an individual is advanced in years, in poor or declining health, with little possibility of improvement, the act of suicide may be seen as self-chosen, voluntary euthanasia (Miller 1979). Since much of the data concerning suicide comes from census and death records and from surviving family members, the exact reasons for the suicide often cannot be ascertained (McIntosh 1986) and this is particularly true for the elderly. Among the known factors that contribute to elderly suicide are retirement, isolation, bereavement and poor economic conditions. Geriatric suicide is also often attributed to more than one problem (Achté 1988; Miller 1979). Much more appears to be known about the elderly suicide (although much of what has been written is based on speculation) than is known about survivors. Let us consider those left behind when an older individual commits suicide.

SURVIVORS OF SUICIDE

There is a great deal of speculation about what happens to survivors of any suicide. Shneidman (1969) wrote: "the person who commits suicide puts his psychological skeleton in the survivor's emotional closet—he sentences the survivor to a complex of negative feelings, and most importantly, to obsessing about the reasons for the suicide death" (Ness and Pfeffer 1990).

Bereavement following suicide is thought to differ from other bereavements. Cain (1977) painted a rather bleak portrait of the suicide survivor as someone who may have to face the problems of denial, reality distortion, "desperate lonely neediness; disillusioned, with doubt-filled distrust of human relationships." Other problems are guilt, feelings of shame, dishonor, a sense of stigma because the death was a suicide, identification with the suicide, incomplete mourning and "depression and self-destructiveness bred of guilt, shame, rage." Hauser (1987) also describes problems of the suicide survivor that are different from those of other bereavements. Hers are not quite as bleak as those listed by Cain (1977). She states that the sudden and unexpected nature of the bereavement of suicide as well as the violence often connected with suicidal deaths can affect the bereavement process. Survivors may experience a great deal of anger that can lead to distorted communications. They may search for the meaning of the death, a process that other types of bereavement might not engender. There may also be a possible loss of social support. Researchers have begun to examine some of the facets of survivors' reactions to suicide and their findings do not support Cain's bleak description of the suicide survivor.

A number of studies have examined the stigma associated with suicide (Barraclough and Shepherd 1976; Rudestam 1977, 1990; Shepherd and Barraclough 1974; Solomon 1982-83). Barraclough and Shepherd (1976) and Shepherd and Barraclough (1974) studied 17 widowers and 27 widows after an average of 58 months following the suicides of their spouses. The subjects were interviewed by two psychiatric social workers using a questionnaire covering health issues, economic issues, the experience of the inquest and the coroner's report, and how others reacted to them, including family, friends and the public. The study found that some widows and widowers were better off than before the suicide and that others fared worse. There was a lack of consistency among responses. Some of the spouses felt relief, especially when the suicide had been preceded by a long illness or by abnormal and disruptive behavior. Barraclough and Shepherd (1974) reported that only two of the respondents felt that they had been treated correctly at the coroner's inquest or by the media, and nine respondents complained that others responded to them negatively.

Solomon (1982-83) examined the relationship between actually encountering stigmatizing events and the self-perceived stigma felt by suicide survivors. His subjects were 90 volunteers who responded to an advertisement in the Alberta media calling for volunteers who had experienced bereavement because of suicide in the last 20 years. His subject pool consisted of 69 women and 21 men. They ranged in age from 15 to 65 and the largest groups of respondents were spouses, siblings, friends and parents. All were given a structured interview that included demographics of the person being interviewed and also of the deceased, the individual's attitudes and opinions concerning suicide, and pre-death and post-death circumstances and events. Stigma was assessed both by direct questioning and by asking about potentially stigmatizing events such as lack of discussion about the suicide. Solomon divided the subjects into two groups based on responses to the question, Did they or did they not feel stigmatized by the death being a suicide? He hypothesized that those who felt stigmatized (n=28) were more likely to have encountered more potentially stigmatizing events than those who did not feel stigmatized. His results indicated that stigmatized subjects were more likely to have experienced gossip and negative reactions from public officials (and they also changed residence within a month following the suicide) than members of the nonstigmatized group. Fifteen of those in the stigmatized group said that they had experienced more stigmatizing events. However, three respondents in this group reported that they had not experienced any stigmatizing events.

Rudestam (1977) interviewed 39 suicide survivors. He found what Solomon (1982-83) called stigmatizing events were not universal. About half of those interviewed did not want to discuss the suicide and almost a third of those interviewed lied about the cause of death. In all, the research evidence does not support Cain in his contention that all suicide survivors experience shame and stigma.

A number of researchers have reviewed the literature on suicide survivors (McIntosh 1987; Van der Waal 1989). McIntosh (1987) focused on family survivors and found consistencies in parental reactions to the suicide of a child, including guilt and shame. No literature was found on reactions of siblings with the exception of one unpublished qualitative dissertation. The studies on child survivors were difficult to evaluate because of the manner in which the information was communicated. Often, the only children available to evaluate were in a disturbed population. The research indicated that widows bereaved after suicide were similar to widows bereaved after natural death except that suicide-bereaved widows appeared to experience more guilt than other widows.

Van der Waal (1989) attempted to frame his review within the concept of grief work and theoretical expectations of the suicide survivor. As with previous reviews, the study populations consisted mostly of small samples with different times of post-suicide evaluation. His review findings on family survivors essentially agree with McIntosh's. He added, however, the need to search for meaning, the relief sometimes felt by survivors, especially if presuicidal illness existed or marital difficulties and depression were present. Most studies have indicated a 15 to 20 percent finding of depression among survivors, as well as some suicidal thoughts. Van der Waal (1989) as well as McIntosh (1987) cautioned that no real conclusions could be drawn from the literature because of the difficulties of sample size and composition, the way in which subjects were obtained, the self-report measures utilized, inaccuracy of remembering (especially among subjects interviewed years after the occurrence), as well as other research flaws.

Therefore, what conclusions can be reached from this research? One can state that Cain's very pessimistic view of the problems encountered by suicide survivors has received only minimal support from other researchers. Hauser's (1987) summary of bereavement problems has received some support; however, it appears that some suicide survivors are in better condition after the suicide (Shepherd and Barraclough 1976) and that some of the stigma experienced by the suicide survivor is self-generated rather than coming from others (Solomon 1982-83). Negative and blaming attitudes of others toward the suicide survivor seem to be directed mainly toward the parents of children who commit suicide (Calhoun and Selby 1990; Rudestam 1990).

Depression among suicide survivors occurs with the same frequency as it does in most bereaved people (Farberow et al. 1987). Do survivors of elderly suicide experience the aforementioned reactions? Unfortunately, too few (if any) older subjects have been included in the previous studies to reach any conclusions. It is quite obvious that more research attention needs to be directed toward suicide survivors.

SURVIVORS OF ELDERLY SUICIDE

As stated previously, the suicides of elderly people are different from the suicides of younger people. Their means for suicide are more lethal and their intent is almost always to die (Miller 1979). They suffer from multiple difficulties including loneliness, retirement, loss of identity through work, loss of health (Achté 1988; Miller 1979) and uncertainty about socioeconomic status and the future (Lyons 1985). Their deaths are often overlooked or ignored (Miller 1979). What is known about their survivors?

The study of Farberow and associates (1987) deals specifically with survivors of elderly suicides. It investigated whether elderly survivors of spousal suicide experienced more psychological distress than matched survivors of natural deaths. All of the deceased whose survivors participated in this study were over 55 years of age and had resided in Southern California. The suicide survivor group consisted of 88 female and 20 male volunteers. Their names were obtained through a search of coroner's records and were initially contacted by letter and then by telephone. Those who agreed to participate in the study were interviewed in their homes and were given self-report data forms to fill in and return later. There was a 35 percent participation rate, which is comparable to that of other studies of this nature among the bereaved (Gallagher et al. 1983; Heyman and Gianturco 1973; Lund et al. 1985). The average age of the suicide survivor group in this study was 62.4 years old and the average educational level achieved was high school or vocational school. The suicide survivors were compared with a group of 95 men and 104 women whose spouses died from natural causes. The average age of the comparison group was 68, and they had similar levels of education. Both groups were compared to a control group consisting of 79 men and 65 women who were married at the time of the study and who had not experienced the death of a spouse or a divorce in the 5 years prior to the study. This group had an average age of 70. Although the group of bereaved subjects was contacted in the same manner as the group of suicide survivors, the control group was obtained through personal contact. All of the groups were asked to complete the Beck Depression Inventory, the severity index from the Brief Symptom Inventory, the Texas Grief Inventory (past and present) and a self-report on the status of their mental health. The nonbereaved controls were instructed to respond to the Texas Grief Inventories based on their most recent loss (Farberow et al. 1987). Although the authors state that data were to be collected at four time points between 2 and 30 months after the loss, the data reported were only for those collected at 2 months post-loss.

The groups' demographic data were compared using multiple analysis. The suicide survivor group was found to be significantly younger than the other two groups. Some of the survivors were in the 45- to 54-year age range. They also had significantly less skilled occupations.

The mental health variables were examined using multivariate analysis. Farberow's team found that both the suicide survivors and the natural death survivors experienced significantly more distress than the control group. However, the differences between the suicide survivors and the natural death survivors were not significant on any of the summary measures of mental health or grief when demographics were controlled for statistically (Farberow et al. 1987). When the Brief Symptom Inventory data were analyzed, both bereaved groups were found to have higher depression and anxiety scores than the nonbereaved group. The only scale that differentiated the naturally bereaved group and the suicide survivors group was that the anxiety scores were elevated in the suicide survivors.

Farberow's team concluded that there were no significant differences at 2 months post-loss between the survivors of suicide and the survivors of natural death in this age range. They stated that the results could well be due to the time of measurement and that changes in distress levels could very well occur at a later date. Farberow's team pointed out that clinical rather than research evidence indicated that suicide was more readily accepted when committed by an elderly person (Farberow et al. 1987).

This study suffers from some of the same unavoidable problems that plague other studies of bereavement; only a little over one-third of the potential subject pool agreed to participate and it is quite possible that those who did agree to participate were less distressed than those who refused to participate. The authors stated that their subjects were over 55 years of age, yet the suicide survivors were found to be significantly younger than the other two groups and 15 percent of them were between 45 and 54 years of age. This may have made the suicide survivor group less comparable. It is possible, given the clinical reservations stated by the authors, that in an older group of survivors, less distress may have been found. Although the differences were statistically controlled for using multivariate analysis, the survivors group consisted of four times as many women as men, whereas the sex of the two other groups was much more evenly distributed. Therefore, the survivors group was really a younger, old widows group. Sadly, much of the survivor literature is focused on widows. It might have been interesting if the authors had compared this group's data to findings in some of the younger widow survivor studies in order to determine if there were significant differences between this slightly older group and other younger groups studied.

THE BEREAVED ELDERLY

Since Farberow and his associates (1987) found no significant differences between older subjects bereaved through natural causes and those bereaved by suicide (at 2 months post-bereavement), it might be beneficial to examine the research on older bereaved persons. Again, much of this research is focused on widows; however, some researchers have also included widowers in their research (Caserta, Lund and Dimond 1985; Dimond, Lund and Caserta 1987; Gallagher, Thompson, Breckenridge and Peterson 1983; Heyman and Gianturco 1973; Lund, Caserta and Dimond 1986; and Rosik 1989).

Lund and his team (1986) examined gender differences in elderly people during the first 2 years after they lost their spouse. Lund's sample was gathered through obituary notices in a Salt Lake City newspaper. To eliminate a bias effect, a group of people who had not published obituaries was found and compared on demographic variables and was found not to differ from the group who had published obituaries. All subjects were over 50 years of age and were primarily Mormon. Although a breakdown according to sex is not provided, in another study using the same cohort (Dimond et al. 1987), the authors stated that the majority of the group was female. Eighty-eight of the 192 subjects were interviewed at home and the other 104 subjects were mailed questionnaires. Caserta and his team (1985) found that the only difference from the personal interview and the mailed questionnaires was that more questions were completed when the interviewer was present. The subjects' responses did not differ between groups due to interviewer effect. All of the subjects completed the Zung Self-Rating Depression Scale, the Life Satisfaction Index-A and a five-point Likert scale that describes 26 common reactions to bereavement. They completed these measures at 6 time intervals in the first 2 years following bereavement: 3 to 4 weeks; 2 months; 6 months; 1 year; 18 months; and 2 years. The purpose of the study was to see whether significant differences existed between bereaved men and women in order to ascertain whether they could be placed in a mixed support group. The results indicated that there were no significant differences between widows and widowers on the characteristics measured. More similarities than differences became apparent; both groups had similar bereavement reactions over time with a decrease in intensity over the 2-year period.

Lund and his colleagues (1986) found that the highest levels of depression and bereavement-related symptoms occurred in the first few months after the loss, that the symptoms lessened over time, and that the loss was often still not resolved after 2 years. The authors also found no evidence for a stage theory of bereavement.

In a study involving the same cohort, Dimond and co-workers (1987) looked at widows' and widowers' social support systems during the first 2 years of bereavement. They based their research on the belief that the elderly have fewer social resources and more losses to deal with than do other age groups. The research questions they asked were "What is the relationship of social support to your depression, coping and life satisfaction during the first 2 years of your bereavement?" and "To what extent does your social network explain variations in depression, coping, health and life satisfaction during the first 2 years of your bereavement?" The measures that were looked at included those listed in the previous study cited (Lund et al. 1986), as well as self-report Likert-type questions on stress and coping. Social network was measured in terms of size and strength of ties and how well those in the network knew each other. Family members and friends were included in the evaluation of the network.

Dimond's team (1987) found that most of the respondents had large supportive networks of both family and friends. Females reported stronger ties with their networks than males and those who were older and had been married longer reported stronger networks than did younger respondents. Network variables appeared to be related more to perceived coping and life satisfaction than to depression and other dependent variables. The authors concluded that further characteristics of the social network needed to be examined before usefulness could be ascertained. In our opinion, the researchers did not give enough weight to the subjects' Mormon affiliation and the emphasis this religion places on close family and community ties.

Heyman and Gianturco (1973) looked at the elderly's long-term adaptation to bereavement as part of their ongoing longitudinal study of aging. Their subjects were 14 males and 27 females who were part of a 256-person panel who had been followed by Duke University since 1955. Inclusion in the widowhood study were based on the following criteria: the persons had to have been married in 1955 when the study began; they had to have been living with their spouse until death; and comparable data had to be able to be collected before and after the event. The measures used were a physical examination, the Havighurst activities and attitudes scale and a psychiatric interview. The mean age of widowhood was over 70 for both males and females and their level of education was comparable. The mean time between bereavement and interview varied between 3 months and more than 36 months. It appears that physical examinations were scheduled regularly as part of the larger study. Therefore, the mean time between physical examinations was 36 months. The Havighurst scale, which was administered by a social worker during the interview, looked at activities in health, leisure, security, family, friends and religious activity (Heyman and Gianturco 1973). The social worker interviewers also used the Cavan Social Adjustment Rating Scale to evaluate the subjects' activities and attitudes. Psychiatrists conducted the psychiatric evaluations. The results of the study indicated that the subjects adapted well to their losses. Of the 20 women who had been rated as nondepressed before the loss, only four manifested signs of depression after the loss; however, the report did not clearly state at what point after the loss each of the four had been evaluated. When health and activity levels were examined, no significant differences were found between male and female subjects or between pre- and post-bereavement health status. The authors attributed their findings to what they believed was the stability and placidity of life among the elderly and that the elderly had a well-established support and activities network. They commented that older widows seemed to be better adjusted than younger widows. This is a direct contradiction of Kastenbaum's theory of bereavement overload among the elderly. Both Heyman and Gianturco's study (1973) and Dimond's (1987) study contradict the idea that older citizens are socially isolated and bereft of support (Miller 1979).

Gallagher and associates (1983) looked at the effects of bereavement on mental health indicators in both widows and widowers. They used part of the larger cohort that Farberow's team (1987) reported in their suicide survivors study. The subjects that Gallagher's team investigated were gathered from death certificates in Southern California. When subjects over the age of 55 died, the surviving spouses were contacted by mail and were asked if they would be willing to be interviewed. A comparison sample of nonbereaved people was gathered from local senior citizen centers. The bereaved sample consisted of 113 women and 98 men and the comparison group consisted of 78 women and 85 men. The mean age of the bereaved males was 70 and the bereaved females 66.7 years. The mean age of the control subjects was males 71 years and females 68.4 years of age. All of the subjects were asked to complete the Beck Depression Inventory, the severity index of the Brief Symptom Inventory, the Texas Grief Inventory (past and present) and a self-rating of perceived mental health, as in the Farberow (1987) study. Gallagher and colleagues (1983) found that the bereaved were significantly more distressed at 2 months post-bereavement than was the nonbereaved comparison group. There were no significant differences between the males who were bereaved and the females who were bereaved; however, both groups indicated more psychological distress than did the nonbereaved group. A mild depressive reaction was seen in some of the respondents, but there did not appear to be any serious pathology present. These findings agree with those of Heyman and Gianturco (1973) and raise the question as to whether there is a difference in bereavement reactions between older and younger individuals.

Gallagher and co-workers (1982) reviewed the literature on psychosocial factors in elderly bereavement. The review, however, focuses more on bereavement in younger subjects than in older subjects. When looking at coping strengths, the reviewers cite the role of the degree of religiousness as having a probable positive effect on bereavement in older individuals.

Rosik (1989) investigated the role of religion in 159 elderly widows and widowers in Southern California. He distinguished between intrinsic and extrinsic religious orientation. Intrinsic orientation is defined as religion for its own sake and extrinsic orientation is defined as the use of religion to meet an "undetermined" end. Rosik hypothesizes that the more extrinsic the bereaved's religious orientation was, the more depression and grief would be manifested, whereas intrinsic orientation would be negatively related to grief and depression. He also hypothesizes that there is a negative relationship between a proreligious stance and grief and depression and stated that the expected relationships would increase as time elapsed following the loss.

Rosik recruited his subjects from 12 self-help bereavement groups in Southern California. The widows' ages averaged 63.8 years and widowers' ages 68.3 years. Intrinsic/extrinsic religious stance was measured using the Gorsuch and Venable scale. The Geriatric Depression Scale and the Texas Grief Inventory were also administered. A self-report physical health measure was given and socioeconomic status was assessed using the Hollingshead scale. The data were analyzed using hierarchical multiple regression. The time range between bereavement and testing ranged up to 10 years. Widows and widowers indicated mild levels of depression; the widows' level of depression decreased and the widowers' mild level of depression remained constant. Extrinsic religious orientation was found to be correlated with increased levels of grief and depression, however, the opposite was not found. Intrinsic religion was not found to be negatively related to grief and depression even when the order of entry in the regression was changed. Proreligious beliefs in this study were correlated with higher rather than lower distress. No effect was found for time elapsed since death.

Rosik had difficulty explaining his results and looked to interfering or confounding beliefs for an explanation. It is well known that it is normal for people to question faith after a loss, and this too may have had an impact on his results. However, what is most interesting is that, as with other assumptions regarding the bereaved elderly, this too is not supported.

Herth (1990) explored the relationship of hope, coping skills, concurrent losses and place of death of the deceased to grief resolution in elderly widows and widowers. Herth's subjects were 75 recently bereaved spouses who were identified through the records of two hospices, two hospitals and two nursing homes in a southwestern city. The subjects ranged in age from 65 to 94 and were predominantly female (62 percent). Each subject completed a general demographics information form and the Herth Hope Scale which was designed specifically for this study. Data were also collected on the number of concurrent losses suffered by the bereaved, the length of illness of the deceased and the number of predeath visits by the bereaved's support network. Ninety percent of the sample had suffered at least one additional bereavement since the death of their spouse and 67 percent admitted to more than three concurrent losses.

Herth found that those with the best recovery from grief (or grief-related symptoms) had one or no concurrent losses, a higher degree of hope and used optimistic, self-reliant coping styles. The author also found that the place of death contributed to recovery; those whose spouses had died while in a hospice made a better recovery than those whose spouses died in a nursing home or in a hospital.

Osgood, Brant and Lipman (1988) commented on patterns of self-destructive behaviors in long-term facilities (using a questionnaire mailed to facilities) and found that overt, covert and passive or life- threatening illness behaviors existed in all. Passive means included not eating and not taking medication. This may account for some of Herth's nursing home findings in addition to the guilt of having to place a spouse in a nursing home. The other factor that made hospice deaths facilitative to recovery from bereavement might have been the supportive services offered to spouses by the facilities.

OTHER FACTORS RELATED TO ELDERLY BEREAVEMENT

A number of studies have examined mortality following the death of a spouse, such as Helsing and Szlko (1981) and Lundin (1984). These studies do not focus on older subjects even though the clinical literature indicates an increased risk of mortality for widows and widowers during the first 6 months of bereavement. Lundin (1984) reports on morbidity following unexpected bereavement. He eliminated suicides from his study because of the complexity of the reactions expected. To eliminate the expected health problems of aging, he also looked at subjects where the deceased was under 65 years of age. The study was conducted in Sweden where both death and illness days are a matter of record. Thirty-two spouses of those who died suddenly and unexpectedly were compared to a control group who suffered an expected bereavement. A definite increase in both recorded illness and psychiatric days was shown for those suffering a sudden loss.

Helsing and Szklo (1981) used census tracts in Maryland to follow 1204 male and 2828 female subjects over 18 years of age who lost a spouse between 1963 and 1974. This group was compared to an equal-numbered, nonbereaved, demographically matched group in terms of mortality. They found no significant at-risk differences for married females and widowed subjects. However, they did find a higher mortality rate for widowed males of all ages than for similarly aged married males. Helsing and Szklo (1981) found that excess mortality reached statistical signifi-cance in the age groups of 55 to 64 and 65 to 74 for widowed males. They could not, however, make a comparison with younger males at higher risk because of the small numbers of young people who were widowed. Prior health factors were not available and therefore could not be factored into this study. Although, as the research has indicated, older citizens leave behind others to grieve beside their spouses, very little has been written about these survivors.

Murrell, Himmelfarb and Phifer (1988) examine the relationship between prior health status, different types of losses and health status subsequent to loss in older adults. Their subjects were taken from a larger longitudinal study being conducted in Kentucky of people over 55 years of age who were interviewed at 6-month intervals. To qualify for inclusion in this study, the individual had to have had one or more valid interviews prior to the stated loss and had to have suffered either a loss through death of a child, spouse or parent, which the authors called an attachment loss. A nonattachment bereavement was defined as a loss through death of a sibling, grandchild or a friend; other losses were defined as the loss of a home, business, pet, divorce, friend or income. If more than one loss had occurred, the losses were prioritized. The health determinants included were a general health scale, presence of medical conditions such as high blood pressure, death during the study, the onset of a new illness and utilization of medical services. Demographics were also examined as was the impact of events. The Louisville Older Persons Event Scale was developed for this study. This instrument investigated the occurrence of events and the amount of change each event engendered. The undesirability of the event and the person's preoccupation with it were assessed. The results indicated that prior health events were the best predictor of later health events. The expected findings relating attachment loss to subsequent health changes were not supported. However, an unexpected finding was observed relating other losses than bereavement to a decrease in health, leading Murrell and his team to conclude that maybe older individuals handle bereavement better than their younger counterparts.

The studies reviewed in this section have shown that many beliefs regarding the elderly and the bereaved elderly need to be questioned further. Although all of the studies suffer from some methodologic flaws (such as heavy reliance on self-report ratings, noncontrol of time of interviews and evaluations and self-selection and volunteerism), they still are cause for concern about the accuracy of the perceptions of both health and mental health professionals regarding older citizens. Interestingly, when the researchers did not find the results they expected, they turned to anecdotal and clinical perceptions for justification, such as the placidity of the older person's lifestyle (Gallagher et al. 1983) or its stability (Heyman and Gianturco 1973), yet none were overtly willing to give up Kastenbaum's image of the older individual as suffering from bereavement overload and being isolated and depressed. It is quite obvious from the literature reviewed here that more studies should be carried out with older citizens and these need to be compared with the results of the younger bereaved.

OTHER SURVIVORS OF ELDERLY SUICIDES

There is no literature concerning other-than-spouse survivors of elderly suicides. Even though there are often adult children survivors and friend survivors, they have been virtually ignored by researchers. The only comments available are anecdotal. For example, Saul and Saul (1988) talked to nursing home residents who were interviewed regarding the suicide of a fellow resident. They stated that from the family viewpoint, the very idea of an elderly relative's suicide is threatening and pain-ful...the very act itself is often taken by the person's survivors as a reproach for their inadequacies or uncaring relationships. Regarding the death of an older parent of an adult, Myers (1986) sees the loss, no matter how age-appropriate, as a particularly difficult bereavement.

SUMMARY AND COMMENTS

Adult males over 65 years of age have the highest rates of recorded suicide in the United States. They use the most lethal acts and their intent is obvious. The reasons often given for their suicides are poor health, widowhood, loss of socioeconomic status and retirement. Sometimes older individuals have few or no survivors. However, some do leave spouses, adult children and friends.

Although a good deal of literature has begun to appear regarding younger suicide survivors, many of the studies are marred by small sample size and methodological flaws. Only one study has been published con-cerning survivors of elderly suicide (Farberow et al. 1987). When these researchers compared spouses of elderly suicides to spouses bereaved by death due to natural causes and compared both to a nonbereaved control group, the only differences found between the two bereaved groups was an increase in anxiety in the group of suicide survivors. Both bereaved groups manifested more distress than the nonbereaved group. Since the older individuals bereaved by suicide were found to be similar to other bereaved seniors, the literature on bereavement in the elderly was re-viewed with interesting results. Bereaved elderly persons appear to have a less difficult time adapting to death than their younger counterparts. Contrary to popular belief, the elderly seem to have support systems that are intact and are able to adapt to bereavement without excess physical or psychiatric problems.

Aside from the methodological difficulties already mentioned, there is another serious problem with research on the elderly: researchers have no clear-cut definition of what being "elderly" means. Some of the researchers consider 45 years to be the beginning of old age, others consider 55 years old age and still others look at 65 years and older. As life expectancy increases, it should be noted that none of these groups is really elderly. A consistent definition needs to be agreed upon for mean-ingful comparative research to be conducted on this population. There is no literature concerning younger adult survivors of elderly suicide, nor of friend survivors or grandchild survivors.

The older population in the United States, as elsewhere in the Western world, is growing rapidly and staying healthy and active longer. However, attitudes toward older citizens have not kept pace with population change and are still negative. More attention needs to be paid to the problems of older citizens, especially since they will be the primary users of the health and mental health care systems in the future. Suicide and suicide survivor services are among the issues that require special attention.

REFERENCES

Achté, L. 1988. Suicidal tendencies in the elderly. *Suicide and Life-Threatening Behavior* 18:55-65.

Barraclough, B.M. and D.M. Shepherd. 1976. Public interest, private grief. *British Journal of Psychiatry* 129:109-113.

Cain, A.C. 1977. Survivors of Suicide. In S.G. Wilcox and M. Sutton, eds., *Understanding Death and Dying*. Van Nuys, CA: Alfred Publishing.

Calhoun, S.B. and J.W. Selby. 1990. The Social Aftermath of a Suicide in the Family. In D. Lester, ed., *Current Concepts of Suicide*. Philadelphia: The Charles Press.

Caserta, M.S., et al. 1985. Assessing interviewer effects in a longitudinal study of bereaved elderly adults. *Journal of Gerontology* 40:637-640.

Deluty, R.H. 1989. Factors affecting the acceptability of suicide. *Omega* 19:315-326.

Dimond, M., D.A. Lund, et al. 1987. The role of social support in the first two years of bereavement in an elderly sample. *The Gerontologist* 27:599-603.

Faberow, N.L., D.E. Gallagher, M.J. Gilewski, et al. 1987. An examination of the early impact of bereavement on psychological distress in survivors of suicide. *The Gerontologist* 27:592-598.

Gallagher, D.E., J.N. Breckenridge, L.W. Thompson, et al. 1983. Effects of bereavement on indicators of mental health in elderly widows and widowers. *Journal of Gerontology* 38: 565-571.

Gallagher, D.E., L.W. Thompson and J.A. Peterson. 1981-82. Psychosocial factors affecting adaptation to bereavement in the elderly. *International Journal of Aging and Human Development* 14:79-96.

Hauser, M. 1987. Special Aspects of Grief After a Suicide. In E.J. Dunne, J.L. McIntosh, et al., eds., *Suicide and its Aftermath*. New York: W.W. Norton.

Herth, K. 1990. Relationship of hope, coping styles, concurrent losses and setting to grief resolution in the elderly widow. *Research in Nursing and Health* 13:109-117.

Helsing, K.T. and M. Szklo. 1981. Mortality after bereavement. *American Journal of Epidemiology* 114:39-52.

Heyman, D.K. and D.T. Gianturco. 1973. Long-term adaptation by the elderly to bereavement. *Journal of Gerontology* 28:359-362.

Jones, F.A. 1987. Therapists as Survivors of Client Suicide. In E.J. Dunne, et al., eds., *Suicide and its Aftermath*. New York: W.W. Norton.

Lund, D.A., M.S. Caserta, et al. 1986. Gender differences through two years of bereavement among the elderly. *The Gerontologist* 26:314-319.

Lundin, T. 1984. Mortality following sudden and unexpected bereavement. *British Journal of Psychiatry* 144:84-88.

Lyons, M. 1985. Observable and subjective factors associated with attempted suicide in later life. *Suicide and Life-Threatening Behavior* 15:168-182.

McIntosh, J.L. 1987. Research, Therapy and Educational Needs. In E.J. Dunne, J.L. McIntosh, et al., eds., *Suicide and its Aftermath*. New York: W.W. Norton.

McIntosh, J.L. 1987. Survivor Family Relations. In E.J. Dunne, J.L. McIntosh, et al., eds., *Suicide and its Aftermath*. New York: W.W. Norton.

McIntosh, J.L. 1985. Suicide among the elderly. *American Journal of Orthopsychiatry 55:288-293*.

McIntosh, J.L. 1985-86. Survivors of suicide. *Omega* 16:355-370.

Miller, M. 1979. *Suicide after Sixty*. New York: Springer.

Murrell, S.A., S. Himmelfarb, et al. 1988. Effects of bereavement/loss and pre-event status on subsequent health in older adults. *International Journal of Aging and Human Development* 27:89-107.

Myers, E. 1986. *When Parents Die*. New York: Viking.

Ness, D.E., and C.R. Pfeffer. 1990. Sequelae of bereavement resulting from suicide. *American Journal of Psychiatry* 147:279-285.

Osgood, N.J., B.A. Brant, et al. 1988-89. Patterns of suicidal behavior in long-term care facilities. *Omega* 19:69-75.

Rando, T. 1984. *Grief, Dying and Death*. Champaign, IL: Research Press.

Rosik, C.H. 1989. The impact of religious orientation in conjugal bereavement among older adults. *International Journal of Aging and Human Development* 28:251-260.

Rudestam, K.E. 1977. Physical and psychological responses to suicide in the family. *Journal of Consulting and Clinical Psychology* 45:162-170.

Rudestam, K.E. 1987. Public Perceptions of Suicide Survivors. In E.J. Dunne, J.L. Macintosh and K. Dunne-Maxim, eds., *Suicide and its Aftermath*. New York: W.W. Norton.

Rudestam, K.E. 1990. Survivors of Suicide. In D. Lester, ed., *Current Concepts of Suicide*. Philadelphia: The Charles Press.

Saul, S.R. and S.S. Saul. 1988-89. Old people talk about suicide. *Omega* 19:237-251.

Shepherd, D. and B.M. Barraclough. 1974. The aftermath of suicide. *British Medical Journal* 2:600-603.

Shneidman, E.S. 1976. *Deaths of Man*. Palo Alto, CA: Mayfield.

Solomon, M.I. 1982-83. The bereaved and the stigma of suicide. *Omega* 13:377-387.

Van der Waal, J. 1989-90. The aftermath of suicide. *Omega* 20:149-171.

12

Helping the Suicidal Elderly: A Hungarian Perspective

Beáta Temesváry, MD

Physicians pay a high price for suppressing diseases, dying and death. Anguish, phobias and hypochondric symptoms and sleep disorders end by leading into a very grave depression which in the case of older colleagues may become chronic (Ringel 1984).

When attempting to define suicide, it is important to realize that human beings are the only creatures who are aware of their physical existence and that they can choose the time of their death. The choice to commit suicide is rarely a simple one. Stengel (1961) in particular drew attention to the ambivalent nature of those who are suicidal. Psychoanalysts in the 1930s realized that a suicidal act sometimes involves not only a longing for death, but also a wish for survival. In other words, both life-preserving and self-destructive tendencies can be present at the same time. As far as self-destructive tendencies are concerned, even healthy, non-suicidal persons may have suicidal intentions when there are disturbances in the equilibrium of the personality (Zilboorg 1936; Menninger 1974).

THE PSYCHODYNAMICS OF SUICIDE

Some people attempt suicide as a way of drawing attention to themselves, in other words, sometimes the act is a cry for help. Another feature may be the desire to break up and step out of an unpleasant situation. The element of aggressiveness is also of importance (Linden 1969; Feuerlein

1971; Henseler 1980). If we accept the hypothesis that there is a continuity between different types of suicidal behaviors, we cannot draw a clear line of demarcation between completed suicide and attempted suicide. Some people are prejudiced toward those who have attempted suicide. So as not to support this attitude we do not approve of expressions such as "demonstrative suicide" or "theatrical suicide." (Unfortunately, in the Hungarian medical vocabulary, even the term "parasuicide" has a pejorative connotation, therefore we use the term "attempted suicide.") When a cry for help is the predominant reason for an attempted suicide (that is, death is not strongly desired), it is much better to use the term "suicidal gesture."

SUICIDE OF THE ELDERLY

Old age brings with it many physiological, psychological and sociological elements that may instigate suicidal feelings. Some of the physiological causes occur with the same probability for all ages, while others are especially characteristic of this period of life (Achté 1986; Böcker 1973; Loewenthal 1964). The following (not in any order) are elements that are age-related causes of suicide among the elderly:

- financial difficulties
- separation from or death of loved one
- feeling that life is pointless
- feelings of helplessness
- somatic illness
- terminal illness
- social isolation/loneliness

Other conditions that are especially characteristic of old age include: senile depression; atherosclerosis; and the fear of death, overt or suppressed, after a confrontation with death (Blake 1979; Cawley 1978; Feuerlein 1971; Kielholz 1986). In old age, there is also a greater probability of the incidence of serious somatic diseases that are frequently the main or accessory causes of suicide (Achté 1988; Böcker 1973; Cawley 1978). Among the psychological reasons for suicide in the elderly, some personality traits that an individual has had all his life become overemphasized. Some of the reasons for this include:

1.   a decrease in ability to accommodate change (Riegel et al. 1967)
2.   a decrease in frustration tolerance (Richardson et al. 1989)

3. a decrease in self-esteem (Achté 1986; Blazer 1989)
4. a sense of pointlessness (Osgood 1982; Summa 1982)

As a consequence of these feelings, the elderly individual often chooses less stressful solutions, those that present the least "resistance."

Peculiar psychological problems result from the fact that old people live at death's door: that life is ephemeral becomes a clear reality and the fear of death acquires a particular saliency. The proximity of death, not as an acutely appearing danger, but as an everyday imminent statistical reality, affects the elderly (Améry 1979; Blake 1979; Condrau 1984). The inability of researchers to find a connection between old age and fear of death (for example, Lester 1972) can perhaps be accounted for by the presence of psychological defense mechanisms.

No less traumatic for many elderly people is the experience of a series of losses which accentuate the imminence of death—the loss of loved ones, losses of friends and acquaintances, the loss of prestige, social isolation and, the most tragic manifestation of the latter, "social death" (Améry 1979; Lasch 1982; Powell 1958; Riemann 1981; Summa 1982; Svanborg 1979). Social isolation is rendered even more difficult to endure because of physiological and psychological losses (Améry 1979; Böcker 1973; Schabacker 1984; Sainsbury 1965).

A HOLISTIC INTERPRETATION OF SUICIDE IN THE ELDERLY

A holistic interpretation of suicidal phenomena (taking into account both its physiological and psychosocial aspects) requires that we look at the young child. This early period of life is extremely important in terms of developing a suicidal personality in later life. The formation of the concept of death is well known. Experience gained from patients who have attempted suicide during childhood indicates that adult-like motivations, precipitating factors and characteristic circumstances of the act can appear much earlier than is usually imagined. An "acceleration" has taken place in recent years; even the suicidal attempts of children now exhibit adult-like psychodynamics. In Szilárd's 1978 study, the earliest age children demonstrated a true willingness to die was between 5 and 6 years of age.

Just as the child may demand competent care, so too do old people depend on their surroundings, their death, in a social sense, often occurring earlier than their physiological death. Just as in the development of personality in childhood, in the elderly, physiological factors are so tightly bound to psychosocial factors that it frequently proves difficult to separate them from each other and to determine their order of importance.

Somatic diseases have an important influence on the psychological state of the elderly patient. They can evoke a fear of death, anguish, a decreased tolerance of frustration and interfere with social functioning. However, the reverse is also true; experience of interpersonal loss, social isolation or the loss of prestige can affect a person's physiological state to the point that it facilitates the development of disease.

SPECIAL PSYCHOLOGICAL FACTORS INFLUENCING SUICIDALITY IN THE ELDERLY

The high rate of suicide among the elderly results from complex psychological and sociopsychological factors that often make the struggle against suicidality in the elderly a losing battle. Some of these special factors are discussed below.

Societal Attitudes Toward Death

The Goths and the Celts actually expected the elderly to kill themselves. Certain Siberian peoples (such as the Chorjac and Tchouctch) killed their elders because they considered natural death shameful.

Neither the Old nor New Testament specifically prohibits suicide. In Howe's 1991 book, *The Enigma of Suicide,* he states that Christianity did not take a stand against suicide until the fifth century, when the Church "realized that Christianity contained a logical dilemma: If paradise is achieved by avoiding sin, the most sensible step following baptism is suicide. St. Augustine then tried to demonstrate that suicide was a sin greater than any it could atone for. He concluded that suicide was self-murder and self-murder is a violation of the Sixth Commandment.

Today, some people consider suicide to be a sin, but not a crime. In the United States, only Texas and Oklahoma still have laws that state that suicide is illegal. On the whole, modern civilization disapproves of suicide, viewing it as something only crazy people do. This view is actually a complete simplification of a very complex subject. Consider, for example, that while some mentally ill people do commit suicide, people who are completely well mentally also commit suicide.

Besides the ready acceptance of the natural death of the elderly, the understandability of the suicide of old people, especially if it is the result of incurable illness or loneliness, has become more common in our society (Alvarez 1974; Böcker 1973; Lasch 1982; Schadenwaldt 1977; Temesváry 1991a; Vischer 1945; Wiendick 1973). Finally, most people today would prefer to commit suicide than to endure life with a painful, terminal illness and being kept alive by a life-support machine. Living wills (a legal document stating that a person will not be unduly kept alive) are now commonplace. I would be remiss not to mention Jack Kevorkian who has developed a suicide machine for those who want to die. There is a great deal of controversy over his actions and this neatly summarizes society's attitude toward suicide—ambivalence. The elderly tend to have a less fearful attitude toward death and a greater acceptance of suicide as an acceptable method of dying than do younger age groups.

Psychological Defense Mechanisms

The psychological defense mechanisms that are present in most cases of suicide also commonly appear in elderly suicides. This may be because of their need to reduce their own guilt and the stigma attached to suicide by society. Since, in fact, the social environment frequently contributes to the truly hopeless condition of the elderly, society seems to minimize its psychological burden by viewing the death or suicide of an elderly individual as a natural or unavoidable occurrence. This acceptance of elderly suicide on the basis of social norms, common sense or psychological defense mechanisms not only works against the prevention of elderly suicide, but it also provides a pattern of suicide which may be imitated by younger people. This suicide pattern is transmitted according to a still-unclear mechanism, perhaps involving imitation and identification (Temesváry 1988).

Attitudes Toward Suicide in the Elderly

This category raises the question of which social factors catalyze self-destructive behavior. Ringel (1984) says that it is a suicidal climate, but it seems more appropriate to call it a "suicidogenous" influence. The high suicidal mortality experienced in Central European cultures (predominantly in the areas of the old Austro-Hungarian empire) presumably points to such a "suicidogenous" influence (Temesváry 1991b).

Some societies or microsocieties accept self-destructive behavior, whether it is direct behavior caused by suicide or indirect by behavior such as alcohol abuse as a form of solving conflicts. This attitude, originating in part perhaps from ambivalence toward suicide, often has two faces: nonverbal acceptance, and nonverbal acceptance that is associated with verbal rejection. Our own investigations of the attitudes of our patients, began in 1986, reveal that persons who have attempted suicide often verbally reject suicide; however, in some cases these same patients see certain suicidal motivations in exceptional cases as acceptable. An acceptable motivation might be suicide by a seriously ill or elderly person. Our research indicates that the psychological barrier formed by people who have attempted suicide, manifested in a negative or ambivalent verbal attitude toward suicide, can be broken by the influence of the suicide pattern in the family. Patients whose friends and family were suicidal had a significantly more positive attitude toward suicide than others who lacked imitation or identification models.

NARCISSISM AND SUICIDE IN THE ELDERLY

The destructive consequences of a narcissistic personality pattern are often observed in the elderly and are more serious and of course more intractable than those associated with a narcissistic crisis in adolescence.

The development of a narcissistic personality develops in early childhood. To simplify, its background involves a love-deficient emotional atmosphere (a dysfunctional mother-child relationship), inadequate educational experiences and destructive behavior, all resulting in a distortion of personality. In Kohut's concept of narcissism, adapted by Henseler (1980) to suicidology, an unreal self-image and therefore a closely connected insatiable need for love are emphasized. As a consequence of the tendency to idealize, problems in relationships between partners often develop. The partner is first put on a pedestal and then quickly devalued, a characteristic of narcissistic and pathological narcissistic (borderline) personalities.

Although the development of a narcissistic personality may in most cases allow a person to function in a seemingly problem-free way, they are often considered as a time-bomb from a suicidological point of view. (Winston Churchill is a good example of a person who seemed to function problem-free. While fulfilling his role as a politician and statesman quite well, he often struggled with feelings of emptiness and narcissistic depression.) This time-bomb is not ticking loudly or conspicuously. It may be compared to the subtle cracks in a valuable Chinese vase that may be preserved for several centuries, but which can fall into pieces at any time on receiving a knock. Because of the composite nature of the psychodynamics of suicide in the elderly, the will to die and the self-destructive character of the suicidal act may be extremely strong. The closeness to death, physiological damage and the experience of loss suffered in the psychosocial sphere may have a role in this and lead to the drastic and often "overinsured" nature of the suicide act.

Case 1

A 68-year-old retired schoolmistress, afraid of losing her husband's love, took a lethal dose of a sedative and a cardiac drug. To ensure a fatal outcome, she left for their weekend house and hid in an uninhabited building. As it was the middle of winter, and she was found only by chance, her survival was little less than miraculous. For years she had suffered from heart disease and rheumatic complaints and the fear of her disease becoming worse played a part in her attempt to commit suicide. The immediate precipitating cause of her act was jealousy of her husband, who was 3 years younger and a working biologist. They had been living together in a harmonious marriage for nearly 40 years without having been disturbed by the insignificant and practically unnoticeable age difference—until the last few years. Her retirement 3 years earlier completed her professional life. Her inferiority complex was made worse by the fact that her superannuated husband was offered further employment by his employer, and this reminded her that she was older than her husband and that she was no longer a needed person. Her three adult children are married, living in remote towns, and her grandmother role is limited to the summer holidays. Her chronic heart disease is a risk factor since both her parents killed themselves at roughly the same age (67 and 68 years old) when afflicted with incurable diseases.

This case describes an emotion-oriented, love-and-acceptance-centered personality. She was reared in an "ideal" family and her relationship with her mother was "perfect and harmonious." However, thorough exploration indicates that this "perfect" mother-child relationship was troubled by a strange event. At age 23, she was the mother of a baby several months old. At the end of the World War II, the fighting front reached Hungary and many women were being raped by the Russian soldiers. Her younger sister was still unmarried. Upon the approach of the Russians, their mother snatched away the baby from the hands of her elder daughter and put her into the hands of her younger daughter "to save her from rape." The outcome was lucky—nothing happened to either of the daughters. However, this event is vividly remembered by the elder daughter, who is still reflecting on its meaning. Smiling, she now interprets the story: "It didn't hurt me. I fully understood that my mother was more anxious about my younger sister." Recalling the event gives her food for thought and she recalls that she had the feeling starting from early childhood that her younger sister was their mother's favorite child. The development of her narcissistic personality demonstrates that simple crisis intervention would have been ineffective in her case. Her somatic disease, her age and her family's suicide pattern all increase her risk of committing suicide. To solve the serious depressive decompensation, temporary ad-ministration of antidepressants was prescribed, but the most important strategy was psychotherapy. Considering her age and her risk factors, cautious insight therapy was needed, supplemented with supportive ele-ments for 6 months. Analytically oriented eclectic psychotherapy was performed two times a week for 6 weeks, then once weekly, followed by occasional sessions. The patient has now been in complete psychological equilibrium for more than 2 years. She is carefully taking care of herself and appears much younger than her age. She recently attended a cele-bration of the 50th anniversary of the award of her diploma and the other attenders were amazed by how much younger she looked than her peers. In the meantime, two of her children encountered marital crises and she immediately lent effective support to both of them. She has succeeded in considerably stabilizing her self-evaluation, does not assume unrealisti-cally difficult tasks and is less prone to breaking down and giving up her plans as she had previously done. Since she no longer fears the loss of her husband and no longer views this latter possibility as leading to the annihilation of her self-esteem, her relationship with her husband is much better. Both partners judge their conjugal state to be balanced and happier than before. She keeps her somatic disease in control and has succeeded in changing her fatalistic views regarding death that might be caused by her disease. This 2-year period of life suggests that she has overcome her narcissistic-depressive decompensation and that, despite her advancing age, a "minimal but essential change" has occurred in her personality. The suicidal example set by her parents, which formerly represented an "attractive model," has lost its attractiveness. Her present state indicates that the danger of suicide is far less than it was before. Despite this, our connection with her remains uninterrupted; the risk of suicide may always return in the event of future problems.

The "suicide pattern" is not always displayed through psychological mechanisms. The cumulative occurrence of suicide in families often involves genetically transmitted affective disorders.

Case 2

A 69-year-old man attempted suicide while hospitalized in our clinic. There have been five suicides of hospitalized patients during the past 12 years. (All attempted-suicide patients are hospitalized on arrival and there is no separate ward for crisis intervention. Some patients receive outpa-tient psychotherapy at our Crisis Clinic. The inpatient unit handles 150 to 280 attempted suicides each year.)

This patient, who was admitted for a serious endogenous depression, attempted suicide by cutting his neck one night while lying in bed. Weeks later, as a later consequence of this act, he died from an infection. Though the diagnosis was quite clear, his treatment was very difficult. All known antidepressants were contraindicated because of his cardiac decompensation and kidney and prostate problems. His severe heart disease made even electroconvulsive therapy impractable. His wife accepted the news of the attempted suicide with resignation: "It was in their blood, doctor, there was nothing to be done against it." She was talking about her husband's seven brothers and their father, all of whom had died by suicide, all by hanging.

Case 3

An 86-year-old woman, now a resident of a home for the aged, has lived for more than 40 years as a widow. She no longer has any blood relatives. After her husband's death, his family suggested that she move into a home for the elderly. By the time she recognized that she had made a stupid mistake by giving up her valuable house in the center of the city, it was too late to change her mind. Because of Bechterew's disease, she cannot stand up straight. Even when wearing very strong spectacles, she can perceive nothing but light. During examination, she turned out to be very keen-witted and to have a good sense of humor. She can recount the various natural curative procedures she has tried over the years. As she is practically blind, she frequently listens to the radio. During clinical admission, her imagination was particularly captured by a series of philosophical lectures that she "would have been pleased to read in book form if she was only been able to read." She stated that she was religious and that she had attempted suicide out of exasperation, in spite of her faith and fear of excommunication from the church. She attributes her present recovery to a "divine decision." She has reconciled herself with her fate despite her opinion that her life has no meaning and that "such old, morbid and defenseless people should not have to struggle further."

THE DANGER OF SUICIDE AMONG ELDERLY PHYSICIANS

Investigations in the United States have drawn attention to the danger of suicide among physicians. Ross and Rosow (1973) found the highest suicide mortality in female physicians, whereas others have concluded that the group at highest risk is male doctors over 60 years old. Ringel (1984) has pointed out factors that may be presumed to play a role in precipitating depression and suicide in physicians. The decisive problem is the burden of the medical profession; it has an unfavorable impact on their work and on their private lives. The critical factors are the role of the medical professional, the personality type who chooses such a career and the stress arising from the work (Feifel 1969). A major psychological challenge is posed by the "apostolic function" of the profession, as Bálint has called it, or the demands of the helper-role noted by Schmidtbauer (1985). Narcissism is involved in the physician's feelings of omnipotence and grandiosity caused by the work of treating helpless and defenseless patients, sometimes alternating with self-depreciation ("the physician treats, Nature heals"). This explains not only the increased psychical vulnerability of physicians, but also their negative attitude toward suicidal patients. This negative countertransference reaction (Tabachnik 1967; Stolze 1976; Reimer 1981) frequently conceals the physician's own hidden suicidal tendency. This phenomenon is alarming, not only because of the suicidal risk in physicians, but even more for the possibility of influencing the fate of patients who have already tried suicide, or who have it in mind, sometimes rendering it almost impossible for the physician to make a realistic evaluation of the suicidal danger of a patient. He will rarely overestimate this risk, but may often underestimate it, thereby hindering efforts to help the patient.

It is very difficult for a physician to correctly evaluate his patient's suicidal risk if he does not know which deep psychological processes disturb his own judgment. Just as an ophthalmologist must take into consideration his own eye's refractive error in order to give an objective ophthalmoscopic description, so should the examining or healing physician know his own suicidal motivation in order to objectively assess the true suicidality of his patient (Temesváry 1991a).

If a therapist suppresses his own suicidality, he develops a blind spot that does not allow him to perceive his patient's suicidal risk. The reverse may also occur; his own perhaps yet unnoticed suicidality may cause him to overestimate the suicidal crisis in his patient.

THE HUNGARIAN PERSPECTIVE

That Hungary is the country that holds the dramatic position of having the world's highest suicide rate is well known. The opinion even exists that suicide is the new "morbus Hungaricus," a term that was formerly used for tuberculosis.

The nearly linear rise in the more than 125-year history of Hungarian suicide statistics was broken by a brief decline at the time of the general economic depression in 1929 and also during World War II, and this is consistent with observations made in other countries. This was followed in the early 1950s by a further decrease in suicide during a period that was both economically and politically difficult. After this latter decrease, a new and nearly linear rise in the suicide rate occurred. Following a peak in the suicide rate in 1987 (46 per 100,000 per year), a decline has been seen in recent years (44 in 1988 and 44 in 1989). This overall trend is true for men, but not for women; their suicide rate is still extremely high.

The term "morbus Hungaricus" may seem overdramatic, but it should be evident that this analogy is to some extent reasonable. Suicide as a conflict-solving behavior has an "infectious effect." However, even in a relatively small country such as Hungary, there are considerable intra-regional differences in suicide rates. In the south of Hungary, for example, the suicide rate is well above the national average.

Historical and Social Background

In the analysis of Hungarian aspects of suicide and especially the suicide of the elderly, there are certain factors relevant to understanding the relationship of Hungarians toward death and dying which may (at least partially) give an explanation to the origin of the exceedingly high Hungarian suicide rate.

1. Hungary occupies a peculiar (almost awkward) geographical position, situated for centuries at the frontier of immense empires and characterized by an almost permanent struggle for survival. From 1526 to 1686, the major part of the country was occupied by the Turks, and Hungary always has felt that her European culture was menaced. Some decades ago Hungary was at the peak of her power and at that time the number of inhabitants surpassed those of Great Britain and France. King Matthew had been one of the most significant Renaissance rulers at the end of the 14th century. After losing an important battle, the country was divided into three parts: the territory under Turkish rule, the independent Transylvania (now part of Romania), and the area close to Austria (the Hapsburg Empire). The peculiar intra-regional distribution of Hungarian suicide rates, those in the western part of the country being almost half those in the southeastern part, is attributed by investigators to the different histories of the regions. After the 150 years of Turkish rule was over, Hungary increased its effort to achieve independence from Hapsburg rule. At the end of World War I the Treaty of Versailles caused the country to lose two-thirds of its land and one-third of its citizens. These territories were annexed to Hungary's victorious neighbors who did not anticipate the separatist tendencies that are now endangering European peace. World

War II again resulted in loss, Hungary having turned against the Germans too late. Until the recent changes in international politics, Hungary was again on the borderline, separated from the western countries by the Iron Curtain and belonging to the Eastern Bloc.

2. The "role of the defeated." Hungary is a land of "won battles and lost wars." Though it is not the only country in the world for whom this is true, the conscious acceptance of this is a peculiarity of Hungary's self-image. The crisis of World War II may be explained in part by the punitive peace treaty following World War I which plunged Hungary into humiliating poverty. The Latin proverb, wars begin with treaties, seems especially suitable here.

3. Besides the almost perpetual defense against external enemies, the effects of conflicting intra-regional interests have created a great deal of unrest and dissatisfaction that has persisted for centuries, only momentarily interrupted by the unity of her forces at the times of certain major events.

4. A considerable number of the Hungarian population are foreign and ethnic groups. In some respects, Hungary, like the United States and to some extent Switzerland, is a melting-pot and it has similar resulting conflicts. Any positive aspects of the varied population in our country have now been modified by tension following the recent radical changes and by the fact that there is a hatred of foreigners and a constant search for scapegoats.

5. Because of the situation stemming from the above-mentioned historical events and the physical position of the country, the evolution of Hungary's self-destructive image was increased by the fact that mourning was impossible, not only individually, but also on a social level. Certain major events that have caused trauma to Hungary's history during the last 150 years include: the lost war of independence (1848-49); participation on the losing side in both World Wars; creation of the Hungarian Soviet Republic at the end of World War I and the ensuing repression; the death of 200,000 soldiers in a single battle beside the Don during World War II; the deportation of nearly 600,000 Hungarian Jews to German-occupied territory (only a few of whom returned); the deportation of approximately 200,000 Hungarian civilians to the Soviet Union as retribution for World War II; resettlement of 100,000 people in Hungary as a consequence of the Stalinist politics in the 1950s; and finally the Revolution in 1956 and the subsequent repression. The often conflicting interests and the modification of concepts in accordance with the current politics rendered it impossible to mourn for

the defeated participants in the various events. The perpetual struggle against external and internal oppression during recent centuries also ruled out the healthy canalization of aggression in the society. In a society where for long periods of time the determining conditions of survival were either fighting (aggression) or survival (suppressed aggression), tolerance became an ever less desirable feature. Indeed, tolerance was ranked last by the Hungarian population in a survey of desirable educational goals in several European nations in 1991.

The most radical changes in Hungary during this century occurred during the post-war years and these changes were by no means favorable. This period witnessed a loss of ethical norms; the spontaneous or forced denial of traditional norms and moral principles; the declaration of atheism as an established "state religion"; the introduction of a one-party system instead of a multi-party one; the nationalization of large, medium and even small-scale plants and factories and the sometimes forced collectivization of farms. This decreased people's sense of stability, giving them the impression that they had lost their roots, and this could very possibly have suicidogenic influences.

Though few people in Europe today speak of national character traits, it must be accepted that in some regions or countries certain types of behavior occur more often than in others as a result of historical, economic and cultural forces. The accepting attitude of a community can promote the emergence of a certain behavior pattern. "Suicidogenous influence," an expression given to the interactions of those social background factors in the Eastern European (and, above all, in the Hungarian) culture, society and psychological milieu (Temesváry 1991b), may stimulate and promote the development of self-destructive behavior patterns.

All of this information can be summarized as follows: the evolution of Hungary's historical self-consciousness has been affected by her peculiar history, her position at the margin of colliding parts of history and her centuries-long search for an identity. Though it seems certain that the Finns constitute the bridge to the ancestors of Hungarians in Europe, even today it is unclear whether the common origin extends only to folk-groups living near the Urals in southern Russia or to an earlier Chinese/East Asian relationship. These factors have been compounded by the formation of an unstable "self-image" by Hungarians. One characteristic trait of this instability is the inability to handle and canalize aggression. An equally important role has been played by the many instances of loss that have reoccurred for centuries and by the development of a collective-guilt feeling induced both from outside and as a result of the internal conflicts in Hungarian history. The losses suffered have been viewed as a national tragedy and the mourning reaction at a social level has been suppressed in favor of survival and endurance. These factors not only hampered the development of a stable identity, but also significantly altered the collective and individual relationships toward death and dying.

It has been known since Freud and it was sensed before him, that the relationship of mankind toward death, though modified by religion, is inconsistent and conceals tension. In the Hungarian folk culture, there were peculiar beliefs about death and dying. The mainly Roman Catholic Hungarian population, with a tradition of more than 1000 years, is woven through and through by pagan elements dating back to Hungary's Asian past. More recently, a secularizing tendency has been evident.

POSSIBILITIES FOR PREVENTION AND THERAPY
FOR SUICIDAL ELDERLY

The antecedents of suicide among the elderly, with rare exceptions, occurred earlier in their lives. Therefore, curtailment of the suicidal risk in the elderly should necessarily begin with early years. This is the period of life that engenders both the tendency to a later self-destructive course of life or self-destructive behavior and the possibilities for change and prevention. At the same time, effective prevention is hindered by several factors:

1. An unfavorable effect results from philosophical views that regard suicide as a natural, dignified and humane way to die. These harmful views influence people. The suicide of Jean Améry probably attracted increased attention to this issue because of his lifelong work in suicidology. The suicides of other famous people (including writers and philosophers) also pose the question of the limits and conditions within which a self-caused "humane" death should be respected. Arthur Koestler, a writer-philosopher of Hungarian origin, ended his life by suicide in England, his suicide note illustrating a philosophical approach to suicide. A deeper analysis, however, reveals that his suicide in his declining years could be traced back to his personal and family history and to his first suicide attempt in childhood. The suicidal motivation mentioned by the patient does not necessarily coincide with the psychodynamic analysis of the act.

2. As suicides among the elderly demonstrate, there are close connections between physiological events and the psychosocial sphere and

the obstacles to prevention are complex. Bálint called attention to the need of physicians to share their responsibility with others. This is especially true in cases of suicide among the elderly, where almost all the areas (the somatic state, psychological functioning and the social situation) are equally involved. The solution is probably complex and the problem is not the responsibility of one person or one discipline. Unless suicide in the elderly is handled with as much understanding as it is in younger people (and it is doubtful how good even that understanding is), the rate will increase, spurred by the changing systems of norms, devaluation of the "socially useless" elderly and the increasingly common phenomenon of "social death" occurring long before clinical death.

REFERENCES

Achté, K. 1986. Suicidalität in Höheren Lebensalter. In P. Kielholz and C. Adams, eds., *Der alte Mensch als Patient*. Koln, Germany: Deutscher Arzte-Verlag.

Achté, K. 1988. Suicidal tendencies in the elderly. *Suicide and Life-Threatening Behavior* 18:55-66.

Alvarez, A. 1974. *Der Grausame Gott*. Hamburg, Germany: Hoffman und Campi.

Améry, J. 1979. *Uber das Altern*. Stuttgart, Germany: Klett-Cotta.

Blake, R.R. 1979. Attitudes Toward Death as a Function of Developmental Stages. Dissertation Abstracts International 30B: 3380.

Blazer, D. 1989. Depression in the elderly. *New England Journal of Medicine* 320:164-166.

Böcker, F. 1973. Suizidhandlungen alter Menschen. *Münchener Medizinische Wochenschrift* 117:201-204.

Cawley, D.H., F. Post and A. Whitehead. 1978. Barbiturate tolerance and psychological functioning in elderly depressed patients. *Psychological Medicine* 3:39-59.

Condrau, G. 1984. *Der Mensch und sein Tod*. Zürich, Switzerland: Benziger Verlag.

Feifel, H. 1969. Perception of death. *Annals of the New York Academy of Science* 164:669-677.

Feuerlein, W. 1971. Selbstmordversuch oder parasuizidale Handlung? *Nervenarzt* 42:127-130.

Henseler, H. 1980. *Narzisstische Krisen*. Reibek bei Hamburg, Germany: Rowohlt.

Kielholz, P. 1986. Prophylaxe der Altersdepression. In P. Kielholz and C. Adams, eds., *Der alte Mensch als Patient*. Koln, Germany: Deutscher Arzte-Verlag.

Lasch, C. 1982. *Das Zeitalter des Narzissmus.* München, Germany: Steinhausen.

Lester, D. 1972. Studies in death attitudes. *Psychological Reports* 30:440.

Linden, K.J. 1969. *Der Suizidversuch.* Stuttgart, Germany: Enke.

Loewenthal, M.F. 1964. Social Isolation and Mental Illness in Old Age. In P.F. Hansen, ed., *Age with a Future.* Copenhagen, Denmark: Munksgaard.

Menninger, K. 1974. *Selbstzerstörung.* Frankfurt, Germany: Psychoanalyse des Selbstmordes Suhrkamp.

Osgood, N.J. 1982. Suicide in the elderly. *Postgraduate Medicine* 72:123-130.

Powell, E.B. 1958. Occupation, status and suicide. *American Sociological Review* 23:131-139.

Reimer, C. 1981. Zur Problematik des Helfer-Suizidant Beziehung: Empirische Befunde und ihre Deutung unter Ubertragungs und Gegenübertragungsaspekten. In H. Henseler and C. Reimer, eds., *Selbstmord-Gefährdung.* Stuttgart, Germany: Frommann-Holzboog.

Richardson, R., S. Lowenstein and M. Weissberg. 1989. Coping with the suicidal elderly. *Geriatrics* 44(9):43-51.

Riegel, K.F., R.M. Riegel and G. Meyer. 1967. A study of the dropout rates in longitudinal research on aging and the prediction of death. *Journal of Personality and Social Psychology* 5:342-348.

Riemann, F. 1981. *Die Kunst des Alterns.* Stuttgart, Germany: Kreutz-Verlag.

Ringel, E. 1984. Der Arzt und seine Depressionen. In A. Soritsh, ed., *Literas, Facultas, Osterreichische Universitätstexte.*

Ross, M. and I. Rosow. 1973. Physicians who kill themselves. *Archives of General Psychiatry* 29:800-805.

Sainsbury, P. 1965. Der Altersselbstmord. In C. Zwingmann, ed., *Selbstvernichtung.* Frankfurt, Germany: Akademische Verlagsgesellschaft.

Schabacker, P. 1984. Der Suizid im Höheren Lebensalter unter Einbeziehung kommunikationstheoretischer Uberlegungen. In V. Faust and M. Wolfersdorf, eds., *Suizidgefahr.* Stuttgart, Germany: Hippokrates Verlag.

Schadenwaldt, H. 1977. Historische Betrachtungen zum Alterssuizid. *Aktuelle Gerontologie* 7:59-66.

Schmidtbauer, W. 1985. *Die Hilflosen Helfer.* Hamburg, Germany: Rowolt, Reinbek.

Stolze, H. 1976. Sicherheit und Angst des Arztes in der Begegnung mit dem suizidalen Patienten. *Münchener Medizinische Wochenschrift* 117:183-188.

Summa, D., J. Platt, D. Maywald, et al. 1982. Suizid und alter. *Medizinische Welt* 33:566-569.

Svanborg, A. 1979. Variables related to affective disorders in the elderly. *Aktuelle Gerontologie* 9:461-463.

Szilárd, J., T. Farkasinszky and B. Temesváry. 1978. Adultlike Psychic Mechanism in the Suicide of Children. Paper presented at the World Congress of Mental Hygiene and Family Therapy. Salzburg, Austria.

Tabachnik, N. 1967. Countertransference crisis in suicidal attempters. *Archives of General Psychiatry* 4:572-579.

Temesváry, B. 1988. Individual and Social Factors in the Psychodynamics of Suicide. In H.J. Moller, A. Schmidtke and R. Welz, eds., *Current Issues of Suicidology*. Berlin, Germany: Springer Verlag.

Temesváry, B. 1991a. Suicide in the Elderly in Hungary. Paper presented at the 26th Congress of the International Association for Suicide Prevention, Hamburg, Germany.

Temesváry. B. 1991b. Suicidogenenous Climate in Hungary. Paper presented at the Meeting of the Royal College of Psychiatrists, London.

Vischer, A.L. 1945. *Das Alter als Schicksal und Erfüllung*. Basel, Switzerland: Schwalbe.

Wiendieck, G. 1973. Zur psycho-sozialen Bedingtheit des Alterssuizid. *Aktuelle Gerontologie* 3:271-274.

Zilboorg, G. 1936. Differential diagnostic types of suicide. *Archives of Neurology and Psychiatry* 35:270-291.

13

Alternatives to Suicide

Robert Kastenbaum, PhD

PLAYING THE LAST CARD

To some people, self-destruction is seen as the final move to make when all other alternatives seem to be exhausted—the last card to be played. This view has been expressed by those who have attempted suicide themselves as well as those who study suicide. A 67-year-old woman, hospitalized after a near-fatal drug overdose was one of the first to share this perception with me. In a slow, deliberate, school-teacherish manner, she said the following:

> I am a used-up person. I realize that. I am a used-up person at the end of the road. But, you see, the end of the road is too far away. I don't want to walk that far alone. And I don't know how else to turn off the road. You can't go back either, and I wouldn't want to. I was always a waiting person, but now, what for? I wanted out and I could not think of a better way. [How do you feel about this now, she was asked.] I—I don't know how I should feel. This is all new to me. How would you feel?

Certain suicidologists firmly believe that suicide often proceeds from a rigid or inflexible mindset. This concept has been with us for a long time and was first associated with the observations and insights made by pioneers such as Westcott (1885), Cavan (1928), Dublin and Bunzel (1933) and Menninger (1938). Empirical studies conducted later by Neuringer and his colleagues (Neuringer 1961, 1964, 1967; Neuringer and Lettieri 1971) also provided verification for the proposition that suicidal individuals tend to engage in dichotomous thinking. In other words, certain types of people cannot find alternative methods to solving a problem other than committing suicide. For example, a man in his late fifties has been discharged from his long-term employment because his employer is having financial problems. When coupled with his pre-existing way of thinking, the stress generated by the layoff might cause him to lapse into *either-or* thinking: "*Either* I get a new job right away or I'm a total failure," or "I really screwed up my whole career, so I must be the worthless bum that Father always said I'd turn out to be," or "Those bastards at the plant had it in for me all along and just used the recession as an excuse to lay me off." An objective observer might not only disagree with both of these dichotomous and extremist propositions, but may also be able to see the job layoff in a positive way: "Listen, Buddy, maybe by being laid off you've actually been done a favor. You can use the free time to take a well-needed break. Get to know yourself again and do some of the things you've always wanted to do but didn't have the time for. Maybe you can start a new career doing something better than what you did in your old job." The laid-off man's rigid either-or perception of the situation prevents him from seeing the full spectrum of alternatives that are actually open to him, causing him to come to the premature conclusion that he only has few ways of dealing with his dilemma—one of which may be suicide. This is a typical way of thinking for those with a rigid mindset.

Sometimes discussing with the suicidal person what he is thinking and why he feels the way he does carries with it the risk that you are seeming to question his mental competence and sanity. Society is often all too ready to write off suicidal people as "crazy," as though mental illness would constitute a solid explanation for suicidal behavior even if a person was mentally unsound. Reviewing the literature on this topic, Neuringer (1987-88) reports that approximately 90 percent of the people who take their own lives are not, in fact, psychotic, not "crazy." He further notes that drawing the conclusion that suicidal people are (or were) not in their "right mind" mostly serves to reduce the anxiety that the survivors feel because of the suicide, as well as providing a convenient excuse for survivors not to consider the full implications of and reasons for the suicide.

In the following discussion, we do not equate certain cognitive features in the decision to commit suicide with "psychosis" or "incompetence." The sentient observer may feel that suicide is a bad choice, but people make bad choices all the time and are not necessarily considered crazy or incompetent for their blunders. How many of your own decisions have been a little short on logic? Have your bad decisions been made because you are "crazy"? In other words, the fact that suicide is a momentous act does not mean that the person who makes this decision based on less-than-sagacious reasoning was mentally ill at the time. In fact, particularly in old age, we often find some rigidity of thought processes combined with a basically practical and realistic view of a hard-times world.

WORKING HYPOTHESES

The above-mentioned considerations help formulate the following working hypotheses concerning suicide. (Note that a good supply of clinical reports, expert opinions and a scattering of empirical findings in no way means that these points have been proved in a precise and definitive manner.)

1. A salient feature of the suicidal person's thought processes is the perception that, when faced with overwhelming stress or sorrow, he has very few alternative ways of solving his dilemma.
2. This perception has a variable relationship to the actual situation; in other words, there may actually be a number of possible alternatives that he cannot see. On the other hand, he really may only have a few ways to deal with the situation, one of which is the wild card—suicide.
3. The most effective approaches to suicide prevention are to encourage a more flexible type of thinking on the part of the suicidal individual. Second, one should make clear that there are indeed other alternatives to suicide.
4. In turn, the development and implementation of effective approaches depend on the attitudes of the "gatekeepers" and caregivers, as well as society at large. This hinges on our own answers to the following questions: Do we really think this person should go on living? Do we really think this person should not self-destruct? And finally, What would I do if I found myself in this person's predicament?

The first two assumptions come from observations made by various suicidologists and by people like the woman whose quote opens this chapter. The third assumption is an obvious inference. The fourth assumption, however, could use a little amplification. As individuals and as a society we do not show equal concern for protecting or enhancing the lives of different types of citizens. The plethora of discriminatory "isms" rampant in today's society are all too well known. For example, some people are quite unsympathetic and even hostile toward persons with AIDS and others may feel that too much money is going to "welfare mothers," or that tax dollars should not be spent on rehabilitating those in prison.

Even apart from the most rabidly prejudiced segments of the population, most people have clear attitudes regarding who they feel deserve top priority when it comes to life-rescuing efforts. For example, physicians and nurses often feel frustration and anger when called upon to care for people who are contributing mightily to their own ailment; for example, the patient they are trying to keep alive despite severe loss of respiratory function who will light up another cigarette at the first opportunity. Although professionalism will hopefully ensure that caregivers will provide the same quality of treatment to all people regardless of who they are, why they are sick and what they are sick with, there are many whose attitudes toward, for example, a homosexual drug addict with AIDS will not compare favorably with their attitude toward caring for a hit-and-run victim.

Age is one of the major issues around which today's caregivers' attitudes and priorities vary. Studies of ageism (Palmore 1990, for example) consistently indicate that in the United States, young people and those in their "prime" are valued more highly than the elderly. Intense debate on the generational equity issue (Wisensale 1993) is anchored in the question of the societal value of older persons and how much financial (and other) resources should be "invested" in a group that is perceived by some as consuming more than they contribute. Both the lives and the deaths of older people are generally believed to be of less consequence than the lives and deaths of younger age groups (Markson and Hand 1970; Kastenbaum 1985).

There is a key distinction to be made between the following two questions: Do we really think this person should go on living, and do we really think this person should not self-destruct? Decision-makers do not necessarily hold identical views on both questions. Callahan (1987), for example, strongly advocates the restriction of health care services to elderly persons because of what he believes is a "natural" lifespan that is violated by "overliving." Of course, he does not believe in life prolongation for the elderly. However, he is also dead set against suicide. Callahan sees suicide as a sort of privilege or concession that should not be legal for aged people. If suicide is "allowed" for the elderly, then anyone else who wants to commit suicide will do so without hesitation. Within this framework, older persons are denied both the claim to continued survival and to exercising control over the timing, manner and context of their own death. Many people see no difficulty with this logic: old people are not worth keeping alive, but they should not be allowed to choose death on their own terms. I doubt that this position would provide an effective foundation for authentic efforts in suicide prevention.

Finally, the question must be raised of one's own vicarious relationship to the issue of suicide. As a clinician and then administrator in a large geriatric facility, I often heard visitors remark that they would rather die before they become "like that," referring to elderly patients. Health care professionals were apt to respond similarly. Today, with a gerontologically attuned ear open to students and colleagues, I still hear people vowing that they would rather "do themselves in" before having to face the losses and humiliations experienced by the aged. It is not for me to tell others how they should feel; however, one cannot ignore the fact that potential caregivers and decision-makers who themselves would contemplate suicide before accepting life as a sick and depressed aged person may be seriously compromising their effectiveness in suicide prevention.

CONTEXTS AND ALTERNATIVES

The following approach is only one of many that could be proposed. In the interests of simplicity without oversimplification, several basic sets of distinctions must first be introduced. Obviously there is an overall distinction between the contexts within which suicidal ideation and actions are likely to arise in old age, and the possible alternatives to self-destruction. I use the word "context" as opposed to "cause" because it is a less mechanistic and more heuristic way of framing the situation. Every context can be characterized along three theoretically independent dimensions of stress or threat: saliency (intensity), immediacy and concrete versus symbolic threat. A context is *salient* in its suicidal potential when it occupies the center of an individual's thoughts and feelings. The *immediacy* dimension refers to an individual's expectation as to just when he will actually have to face the threat or stress head-on. "One of these days the children will try to put me away in the nursing home, just as they did with my sister. But this won't happen to me, at least not for a while." In this instance, nursing home placement might represent a salient concern to this person, but she does not perceive it as an immediate threat and so her situation is less likely to require a decisive response. The dimension here labeled *concrete versus symbolic* refers to the reality level of the primary threat or stress. A newly retired librarian underwent what she considered to be a routine physical examination prior to traveling abroad. As a complete surprise, she was diagnosed with untreatable, terminal cancer. This turn of events clearly constituted a concrete threat not only to her immediate plans, but also her life values. As another example, the aging founder of a small but very successful corporation was on vacation when his partners decided to force him out of the company. He was financially well off and in good health, but the symbolic and psychological implications of this event caused him to become both suicidal and homicidal.

This general model can be applied to the suicidogenic contexts that may be experienced by anyone, although our focus here is on older adults. There is nothing magic about this model, but it can be useful in guiding our examination of the varied situations that cause aged men and women to reach the "point of no return."

What are the alternatives to suicide within the different contexts we have defined? First it is useful to distinguish between two broad classes of response that can be denoted by the familiar, if evasive, terms *objective* and *subjective.* It would be unsound and artificial to make a rigid distinction between objective and subjective alternatives to suicide in old age. The two realms are closely and dynamically intertwined and even these categorizations depend much on the observer's frame of reference. Nevertheless, the objective/subjective distinction can be a useful guide as long as its inherent limitations are kept in mind. Consider again the retired librarian. She might decide to take the next flight to Mexico with the hope of finding a cancer cure that is not available or legal in the United States. This would be an objective alternative; the action she is taking has to do with the world outside of herself. In marked contrast, she might instead decide to renew her religious faith or repair a long-term relationship that she has neglected. This latter action would be a subjective alternative in its aims, and to engage in it involves working with her own thoughts, feelings and values. The above alternatives involve both objective and subjective components, but the key point is whether or not the individual is trying to cope with a potentially suicidogenic situation through actions outside of herself or through creating a more acceptable state of mind and spirit within.

The final point to be made here is a distinction that many suicidologists have recognized in the course of their clinical or research observations—intentionality, a puzzler of a concept that we do not seem to be able to solve or leave alone. The distinction of intentionality is a fairly subtle one: did this person intend to kill himself, to actually die and end it all, or was his real intention to escape from an unbearable situation or state of mind? The outcome might be the same regardless of what a person's intentions are (or were). However, if we know that a person is suicidal and if we can help him *before* he attempts a potentially fatal suicide act, it can be useful to know whether he really wants to die or whether he is attempting suicide to accomplish a different objective. From the standpoint of counseling or other interventions, we might find that differential courses of action are advisable for the person working with someone who is honestly seeking death as opposed to those who are seeking something else and using self-destruction only as a means to that end. (We will look at a few "something else" examples below.)

We are now ready to examine the relationship between individual and context. A person might select either a (primarily) objective or subjective alternative when experiencing the stress and threat of a suicidogenic context. If it is indeed suicide rather than an alternative that is selected, the underlying intention may be to die or to exchange one's present intolerable situation for a condition that is believed to be more acceptable.

ILLUSTRATIVE SUICIDAL CONTEXTS AND ALTERNATIVES IN LATER ADULTHOOD

The following examples are not intended to represent all possible contexts and alternatives for all elderly adults. Indeed, comprehensiveness would be a chimerical pursuit because of the fact that contexts are so numerous and dynamic and, as they say, "new people are getting old all the time." I have merely chosen some examples that have I have personally encountered and therefore can share with a reasonable degree of confidence.

Context I: Health and Body Integrity

Health-related issues invariably rank at or near the top of the concerns typically expressed by the elderly. Of course, this concern has an indisputable basis in fact. Older people experience a disproportionately large number of illnesses and disabilities and rely on more medications and assistance devices compared to younger age groups. To note just one example: it has been estimated that the annual incidence of falls by elderly people is as high as 625 per 1000 persons; even the most conservative figures indicate that more than one in ten elderly have suffered a fall (Tideiksaar 1989). The risk of this occurring and its life-threatening consequences will continue to increase as people age.

The risk to health, body integrity and life itself is concrete and palpable in old age. It would be an ignorant mistake to stereotype the aging person's concerns as "hypochondriacal"; everyone knows that as the body ages, it does not work the way it used to. This means that one of the major reasons that contribute to elderly suicide is a significant feature of daily life for most older men and women. The question of why some older people turn to suicide when they can no longer bear their health-related problems and why others seem to be able to live with them is related to what the other alternatives are and whether people are able to find them. These related questions will be addressed in the following brief case examples and in the equally brief analyses conducted within the framework of the model presented above.

Eleanor: Loss of Mobility and Independence

After Eleanor's second fall she had to spend a convalescence period in a skilled care facility, an experience that disturbed her even more than the injury. Her return home was also fraught with tension. "Ed's in the tottering stage," she complained. Eleanor wasn't sure about resuming her role of looking after almost all of her husband's needs and she was sure that she did not want to end up in a nursing home because of overworking herself so that Ed could stay at home instead of being moved to a care facility. Furthermore, she was now dependent on a walker to get around, could no longer drive and did not want to struggle with the increasingly difficult physical demands required to maintain the household.

Ed was not totally sympathetic. "Drop dead and get it over with" was one of his more blunt responses to her complaints. Eleanor actually played with the idea of doing just that. She collected a few pills and information about which drugs do what. At this point, Eleanor's situation could be (perhaps overly simply) summarized as follows:

1. She has had a foretaste of the immobility and dependency that could be her fate from now until the end of her life.
2. The stress/threat factor caused by her current situation has become salient and the threat itself is primarily concrete (actual loss of function and home living). The immediacy dimension is more complex; she recognizes that the "moment of truth" has not yet arrived, but she has just recently experienced a sample of what the unacceptable outcome might be.
3. The overdose suicide she is considering would instantly eliminate all of her problems; she was not so much considering the effect of her suicide on others, nor was she longing for death as such.

Eleanor did not pursue the self-destruct option (although she did not entirely abandon the idea either). Instead, through peer counseling (provided through a retired social worker), she has been able to feel justified and not guilty about resigning from her role of nursemaid and keeper to her husband. Instead, they have managed to persuade Ed to enter a local nursing facility. Fortunately, this has helped their deteriorating relationship to improve; they no longer have to hassle each other about daily care issues and each has more space in which to live. A widowed friend has moved in with Eleanor and provides her with companionship; she also helps her with light housekeeping and drives her wherever she needs to go. The prospect of increased immobility, dependency and eventual admission to a nursing care facility has not and cannot be erased from Eleanor's mind, but it has certainly decreased in saliency.

Eleanor's overall alternative to suicide had two major components: load-shedding (Take a hike, Ed!) and positive restructuring (Come right in, Gertrude!). Sometimes an effective alternative may only require eliminating the negative or accentuating the positive, or often both moves are necessary, as they were in this case.

What follows are several other people's confrontations with suicide that revolved around the general health and body integrity context.

Roger: Fear of Pain

A widower living alone in an adult community, Roger knew that his life expectancy would last, at most, for only a few seasons. He found little pleasure in the life that he was now leading. Overshadowing everything was his fear that the time would come when his cancer-related pain would get out of control. Death itself was not especially frightening or salient to him. It would just mean no more "creeping around like a ghost" and, more importantly, no more pain and fear of pain. Roger deliberately made plans for the time when the pain that he knew was on its way would begin—he would terminate his life. He made two determined efforts to kill himself. Both attempts could have been fatal, but somehow the gun he had discharged into his mouth hadn't done the job ("The bullet was too damn old, just like me!") and all that happened when he placed his head inside the oven was that he developed a terrible headache.

Roger did not try a third time. He was not an angry person with the need to make an explosive commentary, nor was he a self-punishing person who needed to destroy the evidence of his failed attempts. Essentially, he did not want to be alone with his pain and he did not want to keep worrying about when it might become too much for him. A counselor associated with the hospital took the initiative to serve as intermediary with Roger's physician. The doctor made it clear to Roger that he understood Roger's fear of the pain he would inevitably be encountering and promised Roger that he would provide him with effective and complete pain control. In other words, the physician promised Roger that his nightmare of physical agony would not take place. Roger was now convinced that his physician cared about and would not abandon him. Liberated from his terror of unrelieved pain, Roger continued to live independently in the community, living each day for its little pleasures until he fell asleep in his own bed one night and did not awaken. For

Roger, all that was needed as an alternative to suicide was the relief of his apprehensions of a life haunted by pain. The prospect of death remained salient, but it was no longer a prospect that frightened him.

Karl: Deprived for His Own Good

One of the vanishing generation of traditional New England farmers, Karl was a thin, wiry man with a leathery skin. Not much was known about his social history and Karl himself did not offer any information. At some point in his mid-sixties, he became confused and withdrawn. He was in and out of mental institutions for a while and then was finally admitted to a state-operated geriatric facility that was a combination of a general hospital, nursing home and residential community. Karl was no trouble to anybody, pretty much kept to himself and stayed on the fringe of social interactions and activities in the facility. He had a variety of medical problems that were managed primarily by minimal medications and good nursing care.

My first meeting with Karl was when I learned that he was going to be one of the participants I would be interviewing and testing as part of a pilot study on drug effects in geriatric patients. I remember Karl well because he was the first patient to participate in my first post-doctoral study and also because he had surprised me by opening up after only a few minutes of conversation after initially seeming so withdrawn and unapproachable.

I had my second interaction with Karl after he had made an unexpected and near-fatal suicide attempt by trying to hang himself with a belt. Looking as remote and affectless as ever, Karl did not mind explaining to me his reasons for attempting suicide: "They won't let me eat." When I looked into this, I discovered that Karl had been put on a restricted diet in order to establish a baseline for a new evaluation of his complex medical status and thereby perhaps work out a better balance of medications, dosage levels and other treatment regimens. But from Karl's point of view the hospital had taken away one of his last remaining pleasures. (Karl could and did eat rather prodigiously.) His connection to life had been tenuous for a long time and now, with this last deprivation, he did not see any point to continue living. The idea of hanging himself just came into his mind one day and he got up and did it the first chance he had.

Karl's solitary lifestyle, the conditions of institutional life and his precarious medical situation were so closely intertwined that one cannot speak of one issue without discussing the others. Nevertheless, it seems evident that his health problems contributed in two ways to his attempt to commit suicide: it prompted his doctors to put him on a deprivation diet and it also shaped a state of mind in which physical distress, drug effects and change in nutritional status contributed powerfully to his decision-making. The diet (even though it may have been only temporary) was a concrete experience to him, but its symbolic implications were far more important, for it took away his only remaining pleasure.

The farmer needed help. He needed to be offered pleasures that fell within his limited range of acceptance and tolerance. Hospital staff members, representing all the clinical specialties, were highly sympathetic to Karl and carried out interdisciplinary discussions to arrive at a new plan to lure him back to wanting to live. Unfortunately, Karl never fully recovered from his suicide attempt and died before the staff could try out a plan.

Theoretically, the alternative to suicide had been to heap unlimited food on the farmer's plate, but to somehow change Karl's perception that the world could still provide him with some sort of pleasure, a kind of "custard-pudding love" that he wanted and needed. As this case demonstrates, all too often "theoretically" is not good enough.

Context II: Isolation and Loneliness

Isolation can be taken as an exterior aspect and loneliness an interior aspect of the alienation dimension. For example, an elderly widow, outnumbered by a younger and coupled crowd at a social event, feels isolated and this causes her to feel lonely. Involuntary isolation and loneliness must be distinguished from being alone by choice and preference. When isolation is imposed on a person, tension, despair and loneliness develop.

The literature on adult development and aging includes some surprises regarding the social interaction and support systems of elderly persons. Many older adults have satisfying friendships and social contacts (see Matthews 1986). Not all elderly people are lonely. Nevertheless, health problems, limited mobility, loss of significant others through relocation or death and age-discriminatory attitudes of others (Palmore 1990) all contribute to the possibility of isolation and loneliness in old age.

The increased risk of suicide in old age, especially among white males, is not independent of isolating circumstances. It has been noted (Kastenbaum 1993) that high-risk elderly persons tend to have characteristics that reduce the likelihood of open and substantive communication. These people tend to be males who live alone, reside in low-income, transient urban areas, and suffer from depression. Males have an increased risk because they have a lower probability of seeking help, as Stroebe and Stroebe (1989) and others have shown.

Below is a sampling of alternatives selected by individuals who fall into the isolation/loneliness context.

Max: The Bottom Just Fell Out

Sadie and Max had often teased each other with the joke: "When one of us dies first, I'm taking the next plane to Florida." Max was convinced that Sadie would end up an affluent widow because "I'm in such lousy shape, and men, you know, we always seem to crap out early." When Sadie died before he did, Max was devastated and felt that the bottom had dropped out of his world. "I didn't realize how much I counted on her."

Max differs from individuals we have already discussed in that he was able to come up with a number of alternative responses to his situation. He tried "getting religious again" but this venture did not work. However, as a consequence of that action, he did reestablish a welcome relationship with a former friend as well as with his supportive family. Max then turned to drinking. "The most ridiculous thing I ever did! I couldn't even get drunk! It made me feel disgusted with myself!" His third try was to move out of the apartment that he and Sadie had lived in and out of the neighborhood that reminded him too much of Sadie and the life they had once shared. "I couldn't bring myself to go to Florida. That would have been a sick joke." He did relocate to a sunbelt state, but he hated it. Surrounded by strangers and an alien environment, he felt more isolated and lonely than ever. He finally went out and bought a handgun and spent an evening staring at it.

"I sat there stunned. Is this me?' I kept asking myself. Am I a killer?' I felt like a murderer. No, that was not me."

Max returned to his old neighborhood, though he had no clear plan in mind. He drifted over to the library he had used many years before as a schoolboy. The familiar feeling of the library was somehow comforting and books once again felt like his friends, as they had been when he was (in his mind) a clumsy and unpopular child. From becoming a regular at the library, Max found ways to make himself helpful to the short-handed staff. Before long, he was an unpaid library assistant who took a fatherly interest in the younger staff members and "the kids who come there looking for something that they couldn't find in a book, but maybe I could!"

Max found his own way back to a peaceful existence, at least partially, by returning to and bonding with his former community and finding a renewed source of friendship and familiarity in books. He realized that he could not manage without familiar supports (for example, the neighborhood) and could not turn himself into a new person (deeply religious, suntanned golfer, self-murderer). In his own distinctive manner, Max had found enough connections to maintain a continuity with who he had been before Sadie's death and who he was afterward, even though "I still think about Sadie all the time, all the time." A life-preserving alternative to suicide does not necessarily provide an escape or relief from sorrow.

Thelma: Going to a Better Place

Thelma had been an attentive but quiet and nearly invisible presence during her husband's last days of life. Nominally, Thelma was the principal family caregiver, but hospice staff and volunteers soon discovered that her unmarried sister was more on the ball in terms of learning and carrying out procedures designed to keep Ralph as comfortable as possible. Thelma seemed to understand and approve of the hospice caregiving program. She was also strongly attached to her husband, yet seemed to be somewhat detached from all that was occurring around her.

After Ralph died, Thelma decided to take her own life by poisoning herself with carbon monoxide in the family car—a move that caught everyone off guard. Later, an undated note in her handwriting was found tucked like a marker between two pages of the Bible. Unfortunately, no one thought of looking to see if Thelma had chosen a particular place in the Bible for her note. It read: "I will be with Thee again."

Is it justifiable to interpret this cryptic note as the expression of intention for reunion in the next life? Her family thought so. The sister was certain that Thelma had considered Ralph dead from the time his cancer was diagnosed and had just been waiting for the drama to play itself out. But she also thought that Thelma was more interested in oneness with God than in continuing her relationship with Ralph in life after death. An only surviving child, an adult daughter, Thelma used to say that her mother was more interested in the next life than the present one, but she did not claim to understand how her mother's mind worked. Ralph's sister-in-law wickedly volunteered: "It was a marriage made in Heaven—and it should have stayed there!"

Bereavement and loss would not have deprived Thelma of her social support system, which was fairly substantial and close at hand. From what could be learned about her preexisting personality and family interaction patterns, she had not been overwhelmed by the fear of isolation and loneliness with Ralph's impending absence. It seemed more in keeping with her outlook on life to suggest that Ralph's departure provided her with a cue to depart this world for a better place. Unlike the other individuals we have considered here (but similar to many we have not),

Thelma *wanted* death. For her, death was the passport to union or reunion with the real or symbolic figures at the center of her inner life.

OTHER CONTEXTS, OTHER ALTERNATIVES

Following is a brief survey of some additional suicidogenic circumstances in old age. Again, the coverage is far from comprehensive and each of the examples presented would require systematic attention if we were discussing the challenge of determining effective prevention or intervention services.

Other Suicidogenic Contexts in Later Life

Loss of Control

Actual, suspected or anticipated loss of control is a frame of mind within which suicidal intentions can often develop and mature. Among elderly adults, memory deficits and other difficulties in the perceptual/cognitive sphere are often particularly salient threats. Specifically, I am referring to the threat to one's sense of efficacy and independence as indicated by the ability to detect, organize and make sense of information. Aging is sometimes accompanied by the fear of becoming senile. Although gerontological studies indicate that most elderly people do retain mental competence and good judgment, the public's recent heightened awareness of Alzheimer's disease and related dementias has unfortunately heightened people's fear of becoming senile. Some aging individuals might consider suicide even if dementia is not on the horizon; a person can become anxious and depressed just by the thought that he will at some point no longer be able to function intellectually on the level to which he has become accustomed (somewhat like a faded athlete who is still adept in the physical activities of daily life, but who is despondent about the loss of the exceptional abilities that were once his personal strength). The interactive nature of this context often becomes evident as the troubled individual interprets or overinterprets social and environmental cues regarding the suspected unraveling of memory and other cognitive functions.

Flunking Life's Exams

An adult child's stormy divorce or bankruptcy are examples of events that can trigger the elderly adult's sense of having failed to meet his obligations. One salient, negative outcome has the tendency to recruit other incidents that have occurred throughout life that the elderly person now interprets as a general indictment. As negative events and outcomes unfold, the inclination to attribute them to one's own failings is often intensified by the depressive overtones that are not uncommon in later life and the lack of positive-minded intimate companions who can offer a credible line of defense against these feelings. Under these circumstances, suicide can be envisioned as a way of paying off debts and punishing oneself for having flunked the exams of life.

Lifting the Burden from Others

The first individual we discussed in this chapter considered herself to be a "used-up person." She is just one of many elderly adults who have come to this conclusion. Furthermore, the reason that older men and women are likely to feel that they are burdens to others is no mystery: Callahan's (1987) book might influence many people and so, too, do the many societal exclusions and condescensions that target the aged today.

I have known many aged people while they were in their last months prior to death. Few were suicides. Most, however, had interpreted interpersonal and societal messages as an indication that they were useless and used-up souls who should take the hint and depart this life as soon as possible. Although poorly understood, having a "will to live" is a significantly positive force in old age and is, perhaps, even more consequential when a person is so frail and vulnerable that all he has to do is open the door to give death entry.

Whether a particular death is classifiable as suicide or as a suicide equivalent may be less important than recognizing that it was potentiated by an individual's conclusion that his life had become a burden to everybody.

Some Other Alternatives in Later Life

Symbolic-Substitute Actions

This type of alternative takes the place of a direct or covert suicide attempt. When effective, it borrows its power from the original or latent intention of manifest self-destruction. A turning point in one man's therapy came when, as an embittered, self-despising person approaching retirement, he developed the ability to differentiate between himself and his "albatross" (we had read Coleridge's "The Ancient Mariner" together). He found that he could symbolically destroy his personal albatross—feelings of misdeeds and a lack of self-worth—rather than killing himself as a means of removing the dead weight from around his neck. Symbolic and substitute actions can often be helped by the use of rituals and participation from meaningful people in a person's life. It is a fairly dramatic and sometimes highly effective approach, but applicable only among a limited range of individuals and situations.

Externalizing the Evil

This is a much more widespread and spontaneous tactic, although it does have something in common with symbolic suicide and murder—the detachment and distancing of the stress/threat. I have suggested elsewhere that racism and other forms of bigotry among some elderly people represent an effort on their part toward obtaining coherence and control in a world that is not behaving as they had expected it would (Kastenbaum 1992b). This "fortress mentality" also provides a bulwark against suicidal impulses. In other words, one is not one's own worst enemy, nor has one failed a test or lost abilities and competencies; others are to blame. Bigotry, close-mindedness and paranoia are not universally admired characteristics, but for some people, these attitudes can be an effective line of defense against being overwhelmed by inner doubts and conflicts.

Rest and Recentering

Suicidal older people often become terribly tired and frustrated after enduring repetitive rounds of hassles, disappointments and failed efforts to improve their situation. Often all that is needed is a few nights of good, sound sleep, a change of scene and companionship which can provide the opportunity to see oneself in a different light. Timing and finesse are important considerations here; the recentering alternative should depend on the individual's life and circumstances. If effective, it is possible for the "tripper" to return to the original problem situation with a different perspective. Therapists can also enhance this approach by introducing, when feasible, constructive modifications to the problematic situation.

Separating Fact from Fancy

There is much outdated, incomplete and downright inaccurate information in circulation about issues that are of great importance to elderly adults. I have already mentioned an example in which a physician was able to completely assuage a terminally ill man's fears by promising to keep his pain under control. Elderly patients should be given the same type of patient education that patients of any other age receive. Physicians and nurses should not assume that elderly patients will not want to know what is wrong with them and that they will not want to know how they can or cannot be helped. When honesty and up-to-date, relevant and useful information is provided instead of hearsay, it can, in some situations, assuage a patient's fears—fears that otherwise might generate suicidal intention.

Financial information is perhaps second in importance only to health for most patients. It is advisable to make sure that the elderly patient has not made any erroneous assumptions or does not have any unreliable information that might cause unnecessary worry.

Articulating and Fulfilling Underlying Values

Although this may seem to be an unlikely concept, there is reason to believe that some elderly people contemplate suicide as a way to survive (Kastenbaum 1992b); in other words, a person is willing to surrender his life in order to preserve something that he believes is more precious than his own existence. He may have difficulty articulating this belief, even to himself. Not infrequently, when a person thinks this way, it proves to be a core aspect of his self-concept. A man may be ready to commit suicide to salvage his sense of honor or pride, or a woman may want to end her life prematurely to keep a secret or to maintain an illusion that she believes she has been working effectively on her children. Whatever the particular value is, we can reduce the likelihood of suicide by helping the individual to articulate and consider the value clearly and then to find an alternative way of preserving it. Usually, pointing out that by being alive they will be able to appreciate the success of their efforts will seem more appealing than having to give up everything else to save this precious symbol.

These examples of contexts and alternatives are intended only as a starting point for those who believe that life is as precious in age as it is in youth, and for those who appreciate the difference between the acceptance of mortality and the retreat from pain and sorrow. The last card we turn over need not be the joker.

REFERENCES

Callahan, D. 1987. *Setting Limits*. New York: Simon & Schuster.
Cavan, R. 1938. *Suicide*. Chicago: University of Chicago Press.
Dublin, L.I. and B. Bunzel. 1933. *To Be or Not To Be*. New York: Smith & Hass.

Kastenbaum, R. 1976. Suicide as the preferred way of death. In E.S. Shneidman, ed., *Suicidology: Contemporary Developments*. New York: Basic Books.

Kastenbaum, R. 1985. Dying and Death. In J.E. Birren and K.W. Schaie, eds., *Handbook of the Psychology of Aging*. New York: Van Nostrand Reinhold.

Kastenbaum, R. 1987. When a long life ends. *Generations* Spring, pp. 9-14.

Kastenbaum, R. 1991. Racism and the older voter. *International Journal of Aging and Human Development* 32:199-209.

Kastenbaum, R. 1992a. Death, suicide and the older adult. *Suicide and Life-Threatening Behavior* 22:1-14.

Kastenbaum, R. 1992b. Suicide Among Elderly Americans. In H. Radebold and R. Schmitz-Scherzer, eds., *Suicide in Old Age*. Darmstadt: Steinkopf.

Kastenbaum, R. 1993. Encrusted Elders: Arizona and the Political Spirit of Postmodern Aging. In T. Cole, A. Achenbaum and R. Kastenbaum, eds., *Voices and Contexts*. New York: Springer.

Markson, E.W. and J. Hand. 1970. Referral for death. *International Journal of Aging and Human Development* 1:261-272.

Matthews, S. 1986. *Friendships Through the Life Course*. Beverly Hills, CA: Sage.

Menninger, K. 1986. *Man Against Himself*. New York: Harcourt, Brace & World.

Neuringer, C. 1961. Dichotomous evaluations in suicidal individuals. *Journal of Consulting Psychology* 25:445-449.

Neuringer, C. 1964. Rigid thinking in suicidal individuals. *Journal of Consulting Psychology* 28:54-58.

Neuringer, C. 1976. The cognitive organization of meaning in suicidal individuals. *Journal of General Psychology* 76:91-100.

Neuringer, C. 1987-1988. The meaning behind popular myths about suicide. *Omega* 18:155-162.

Neuringer, E. and D. Lettieri. 1971. Affect, attitude and cognition in suicidal persons. *Life-Threatening Behavior* 1:106-124.

Palmore, E.B. 1990. *Ageism*. New York: Springer.

Stroebe, M.S. and W. Stroebe. 1989. Who participates in bereavement research? *Omega* 20:1-30.

Tideiksaar, R. 1989. *Falling in Old Age*. New York: Springer.

Westcott, W.W. 1885. *Suicide*. London: Unwin.

Wisensale, S.K. 1993. Generational Equity. In R. Kastenbaum, ed., *The Encyclopedia of Adult Development*. Phoenix: The Oryx Press.

14

Sara Teasdale: Case Study
of a Completed Suicide

David Lester, PhD

It is useful to examine individual cases of suicide in detail in order to determine whether the abstract generalizations that are often made about suicidal behavior have relevance for individuals. It is difficult to choose just one case for several reasons. First, of course, no suicide can be typical of all suicides or illustrate all of the possible psychodynamics of suicide. Second, there is an insufficiency of data on the majority of suicides. Fortuitously, I have recently been engaged in a project examining the lives of famous suicides about whom biographies have been written. I find that biographies provide a wealth of detail not available for the ordinary suicide. Third, the most significant feature of the majority of all suicides is that the victims are psychiatrically disturbed. Virginia Woolf most probably had a bipolar affective disorder. Ernest Hemingway was treated for depression and had symptoms of alcoholism and paranoia as well. The psychiatric disorder, though critical in determining the suicidal outcome, usually dominates any discussion of the case and obscures everything else. And finally, a case of suicide is almost always an example of treatment failure. Ernest Hemingway killed himself despite his treatment at the Mayo Clinic. Anne Sexton committed suicide despite (or perhaps because of) her psychotherapy.

In light of these considerations, I have chosen to present the case of Sara Teasdale, the American poet. A good biography was written about her (Drake 1979) and she did not appear to have a major psychiatric disorder. Sara was never in psychiatric treatment, and it will be useful to consider how she might have fared today when treatment resources are more available. Would she have sought those resources and might they have helped her?

SARA'S LIFE

Sara Teasdale was born on August 8, 1884 in St. Louis, Missouri. She was the fourth child, had a brother George aged 20, a sister Mary (Mamie) 17 and a brother John, who was 14. She was christened Sarah Trevor, but later dropped the final "h." At home she was known as Sadie.

Sara's father had intended to study law but instead went into business at the age of 17 after his father died suddenly. He became a successful wholesaler of dried fruits, beans and nuts. He met his wife at the Third Baptist Church, where they were married in 1863. They were devoutly religious. When Sara was born, her mother was 40 and her father was 45. Sara was almost like a grandchild in the family, only 5 years older than the first grandchild.

Her mother was by far the dominant parent. Like her daughter, she, too, had a sickly childhood, but she became physically transformed when she got married. She became an energetic and domineering mother. Sara's biographer speculates that to have had a daughter at the age of 40 was unheard of in Victorian times, especially because it advertised the fact that she and her husband still engaged in sexual intercourse. Her determination to bring her daughter up as the model of gentility was possibly an attempt to compensate for this shadow on her virtue.

Sara was watched over anxiously from birth and had an early tendency to frailness. She was never strong, got colds frequently and was easily exhausted. When she caught a common cold, she was treated as if she had pneumonia and immediately put to bed. For much of Sara's life her family employed a nurse to be with her to ease the burden of daily tasks and to see that she did not tax her strength. Drake suggests that this concern led to Sara's life-long anxiety about her health. Her mother crippled Sara by her smothering kindness and lavish attention. Sara's sickliness was not a cause of her lack of energy; rather it was a result of Sara's attempts to suppress her energy.

Sara was not exceptionally pretty and she always regretted this. She was indulged, surrounded by luxuries, given whatever she needed and excused from household responsibilities. Sara never cooked, mended or cleaned the house. She was a placid, sweet-tempered and obedient child who learned to inhibit her hostile impulses. Drake reprints a photograph of Sara at age 5, looking cute for the photographer, but clenching her right fist by her side, perhaps to help her suppress her inner feelings.

Sara was educated at home until she was 9. Thereafter, she attended private schools. Her parents discouraged her from playing with other children because of her frailty and she became rather shy. At school, Sara did not go to parties, engage in athletics or have typical teenage fun. She was asked to be on the commencement program, but she declined the honor.

Although her parents were not especially interested in literature, Sara soon developed a passion for it and her older brothers and sisters encouraged her to pursue her poetic gift. The schools she attended gave her an excellent education in literature and the arts, so even without a college education, Sara became well-read and informed in the arts.

The Young Adult

At school, Sara made several close friends and after graduation, they formed the nucleus of a group of women interested in the arts. They called themselves the Potters and they decided to produce an artistic monthly magazine containing their literary and artistic efforts. Each month they produced an issue of *The Potter's Wheel*, from November 1904 until October 1907, 36 issues in all. The group also wanted to improve its skills and so criticism from readers was encouraged. Sara's poems first appeared in print in this magazine and her first published book of verse contained many of these poems. From the beginning, Sara was very conscientious about her writing and was distressed by any flaws in her poems. She worked hard to improve them and relied on her associates for constructive criticism.

Sara's friendship with women continued to play a major role for the rest of her life. Williamina Parrish, one of the Potters, played a prominent role in Sara's life, helping her to organize the poems for her first collection. Women played a nurturing and guiding role for Sara throughout her life, taking the place of her mother in supporting her. Sara always seemed to need a friend to help her complete a book of poems. (After Williamina Parrish came Marion Stanley, Jessie Rittenhouse, Marguerite Wilkinson and Margaret Conklin.) Later, however, she became less dependent upon them and her final friend, Margaret Conklin, was more like a servant and a daughter to Sara. In her early years, Sara's heroes were women—Sappho, Guinevere and the actress Eleonora Duse. However, she also needed fantasy male figures for her love poems. Until she was 28, though, the lovers about whom she wrote her poems were almost entirely imaginary.

In 1905, Sara and her mother took a trip abroad for 3 months. By the time the boat reached Greece, a place that had for a long time fascinated

Sara, she was ill with a fever, but she managed a little sight-seeing and then recovered enough to visit the Holy Lands, Egypt, Italy, Paris and London. Sara enjoyed the trip immensely and took many more trips abroad throughout her life.

The fame of *The Potter's Wheel* spread through the literary circles of St. Louis, eventually reaching the attention of William Reedy, who ran the *St. Louis Mirror*. In May 1906, he included a poem written by Sara. Soon the poems published in the *Mirror* established her reputation as a lyric poet.

In 1907, *Poet Lore* accepted one of her sonnets and later that year published a book of poems (which her family had to subsidize). Reviews of the book were favorable, such as the one written in *The Saturday Review* of London. In 1908, *Atlantic Monthly* accepted one of her poems and Putnam brought out a full book of her verse in 1911. Reviews in *The New York Times* and *Current Literature* praised it and she soon became a member of the recently founded Poetry Society of America. From the beginning, Sara had the tenacity to submit her work again and again to periodicals until it was accepted. She shrewdly sent copies of her books to supportive reviewers and she made a vigorous effort to cultivate friends in the literary field.

Sara continued to live at home, in a suite of rooms on the second floor, with a door that separated her from the rest of the house. Friends did not drop in on her casually. Instead, even close friends had to adhere to fixed, scheduled meetings and their visits were kept brief so as not to overtax Sara's health. There were two main sides to Sara—the distraught, sickly person who withdrew into isolation and the witty, intelligent and candid companion. This social side appeared, however, only with those whom she knew well. She preferred to develop new relationships by exchanging letters.

There is no sound evidence that Sara was truly sickly. She had illnesses and fevers to be sure, but no more than the average person. Sara would get involved in social activities and these seemed to arouse desires in her that she could not cope with. At that point, she would retreat into exhaustion and sickness and withdraw to a clinic or a hotel away from everyone so that she could "reorganize herself." Sara once pondered whether, had she been born into a poor family, she would have had better health. More likely, if she had not been so suppressed as a child and so repressed as an adult, she would have had no need for retreating into sickness.

In 1908 and 1909, because Sara's health continued to be a problem, she spent some time in San Antonio and also at a hospital in Connecticut where she hoped to recover. Thereafter, whenever life became too much for her to handle, she escaped to a hospital under the guise of being sick. In San Antonio, she made the acquaintance of Marion Stanley, another poet with whom she developed a close friendship. Marion tried to get Sara to see herself honestly and to help her to get free of the cycle of chronic sickliness. But even though every visit she made to see her parents in St. Louis brought on depression (and a desire for death), causing a retreat into the patient role, Sara did not appear to have the strength to leave home and try to build a healthy life for herself. She was overwhelmed by the aggressive vitality of her mother and it was only through the patient role that she and her mother knew how to relate to each other in a semblance of a loving relationship.

In 1909, though, Sara decided that she did not want to live at home with her parents forever, especially because her mother was so domineering and suffocating, but neither did she want to be independent, which meant supporting herself. (If she ever had to do that, she said, she would kill herself.) She decided that she needed a husband to support her, so she began to look around.

In 1908, Sara began a correspondence with the writer John O'Hara, then living in New York, which developed into a life-long friendship. Sara developed an infatuation with O'Hara, fueled by her fantasies about him, made possible by the fact that she had never met him face-to-face. Indeed, she was scared by the prospect of real love and avoided meeting O'Hara on several occasions. She eventually met him in January 1911; this meeting promptly put an end to her romantic feelings for him.

In 1911, Sara persuaded her parents to let her go to New York (at age 28 she still needed their permission), and she began to go to the city for meetings of the Poetry Society, building up close relationships with the other writers who attended. When away from New York, she kept in touch with her friends by letter. Interestingly, when she was in New York, Sara showed little of the exhaustion and illness that plagued her in St. Louis.

In the summer of 1912, Sara and her friend Jessie Rittenhouse took a trip to Europe and on the boat back Sara met Stafford Hatfield, an Englishman with whom she became infatuated. It is not clear whether he wanted Sara to become his lover or whether he wanted her to return with him to England as a friend. Sara could not cope with the anxiety she felt about the relationship and, as a result, fled back to St. Louis. From afar, Hatfield was no longer as interested in Sara as he had once seemed, eventually ending the relationship completely. This episode persuaded Sara that she had to plan more purposefully to get married or else she would remain a spinster forever. Since erotic emotions scared her, she thought that perhaps rationality could find her a husband.

The next romantic figure to enter Sara's life was the poet John

Wheelock. Although Sara fell in love with him and gave him every opportunity to declare his love for her, he never did. In 1913, Sara began a
correspondence with the poet Vachel Lindsay, and they finally met in St.
Louis in 1914. After this meeting, their correspondence grew and eventually
Lindsay fell in love with her. However, at the same time Sara was introduced
to Ernst Filsinger, who owned a shoe business in St. Louis. He was also
attracted to Sara and she soon was faced with deciding who she wanted to
marry. John Wheelock was still the man she thought she loved, but he did
not want her. So she had to choose from two men—Lindsay and Filsinger—
neither of whom she loved, but who both seemed to love her.

During this period, Sara's father suffered a stroke and her mother's
health also became poor. These events happened at a critical time for
Sara. The poor health of her parents made the question of what would
happen to her once they died more urgent. Lindsay was poor and too
egocentric to be a caring husband to Sara. Ernst Filsinger appeared to fit
the role of husband much better. His and Sara's interests and natures
seemed harmonious and he appeared to worship her. He would make a
good husband and father for her children. Despite the misgivings that
Sara felt—a point she did not tell anyone till many years later—they were
married in St. Louis in December 1914. Sara was 30 years old.

Their marriage was a disaster from the beginning. Sara could not bear
to sleep with Ernst, so they always had separate bedrooms—at home, in
hotels and even when they were on a boat they took separate cabins. Sex,
apparently, was also a disaster. Soon after the wedding, Sara developed a
bladder problem that caused her excruciating pain and lasted for 2 years.
This probably detracted greatly from their already-limited sexual relationship. Sara would probably have had difficulty having a sexual relationship
even with a man she loved passionately. And she was certainly not passionately in love with Ernst. Once again Sara turned to illness to resolve
interpersonal problems.

Life must have been difficult for Sara at this point. She had chosen the
conventional life of marriage partly to get away from her parents, partly
for security and partly because she was a conventional person who
expected to live conventionally. But since love was absent from her
marriage, which was held together mainly by mutual respect, Sara felt she
had failed. She was faced with a difficult interpersonal relationship, an
absence of love and an uncertain future. As Sara saw it, she had one
solution open to her—illness.

Sara and Ernst had made their home first in St. Louis and then in New
York City. They chose to live in hotel apartments to spare Sara the strain
of running a house and staff. Ernst was proud of Sara's poetic talent and
encouraged her in every way he could. Her third book of poems came

out in 1915, again receiving excellent reviews. Her next book, published in 1918, received an award that was the forerunner of the Pulitzer Prize.

Married life soon developed a clear pattern. Sara continued to write poems and edit other poets' collections. Ernst became involved in international trade and frequently had to travel all over the world. But because he had to move at a pace that would strain Sara too much, she stayed in New York or took trips to secluded spots around the country. Sara's health was so frail that even socializing was restricted. Instead, she would send Ernst in her place—to important meetings, occasionally to read her poems and even to social events, where she would have her friends accompany him. Ernst took care of her mail and correspondence when she was away and occasionally handled her business affairs. Sara even turned down honors because to receive them would mean attending evening dinners or traveling too far.

Before long a conflict developed in their relationship. After his shoe business had gone bankrupt, Ernst had entered international trade. He soon became an expert, giving talks all over America and traveling throughout the world. Sara encouraged him; she wanted Ernst to be successful and she also wanted financial security. But she resented the fact that he threw himself so energetically into his work. She repeatedly told him to take it easy. (Ernst probably threw himself into his work because of the frustrations arising out of his marriage.)

Despite her resentment, Sara missed her husband greatly when he began his trips, but after he came back she was unable to cope with him. She would become depressed, fall ill and leave for the hospital in Connecticut or go to a favorite vacation spot. In fact she seemed most content when she was by herself in the hospital or at a resort hotel—as long as Ernst stayed in New York City. However, much as she found life with Ernst difficult, his presence at least kept her depression at bay and took her mind off self-destructive thoughts. It was during Ernst's absences that Sara felt closest to him.

Surprisingly, in 1917 Sara became pregnant. Although she thought she wanted to be a mother, when the pregnancy became a reality, she realized that it threatened to interfere with her career. (More importantly, it threatened her role as patient.) How could Sara cope with taking care of someone else? She couldn't, and instead chose to have an abortion.

For much of their life together, Sara and Ernst's financial position was not secure. Though they could afford a comfortable life style, especially because of the supplemental money from Sara's writings, they had to borrow from Ernst's family to get by in the early years. Sara occasionally considered ways of increasing her contribution to their income, but she never did much about it.

The absences due to Ernst's traveling increased. In 1920 and 1921 they were together for only 6 weeks. They became sarcastic toward each other, brought up old annoyances and both of them felt pain over new trifles. Ernst grew more defensive, moody and irritable and his explosive temper showed itself.

The Divorce and Final Years

Sara's decision to divorce Ernst in 1929 came as a surprise to her friends. Sara feared abandonment and her fear had only increased because of his repeated absences. (In a letter Sara wrote to Ernst just before he left on the trip during which she would divorce him, she listed his previous trips in 1919, 1920, 1923, 1925 and 1928.) Eventually she began to fear that he would be attracted to another woman. (This was likely, of course, since she would not be his lover and since he was away so much. However, there is no evidence that Ernst ever behaved in a way to reinforce her fears.)

She had discussed divorce with Ernst before, but he had always protested. She therefore planned to get divorced in Nevada while he was away. She divorced him for mental cruelty and begged him not to contest it. Although she expressed euphoria at being free when she was back in New York, she soon sank into depression. After the divorce, Sara lived in hotel apartments by herself, just as she had done while she was married. Her life changed little, except that Ernst no longer made occasional visits.

Sara then met a young student, Margaret Conklin, who became her close friend. Margaret would visit Sara daily and they once went to Europe together. Interestingly, though, Sara showed little concern for Margaret. She would eat her meals (sent up from the hotel kitchen) in front of Margaret without ever worrying whether her friend had eaten. Typically, Sara had little concern for others. Because she had been in the patient role all her life, with others taking care of her, Sara never learned that sometimes people should take care of others. If Margaret upset Sara in some trivial way, she would banish her from visiting for days at a time.

Sara grew more and more inflexible. She still gave friends specific appointment times for their visits, but she started to keep them waiting if they arrived a few minutes early. These latter years illustrated quite clearly her egocentricity, her lack of caring for others and her basic selfishness.

In the final years of her marriage, Sara had experienced periods during which she could not write. These barren spells became longer and longer—several months in 1920, 5 months in 1925 and longer during the period leading up to her divorce. However, even after the divorce, writing was not easy.

Sara had experienced periods of depression throughout her life. In later years she lost weight, suffered from insomnia (though in creative periods she would work on her poems during the night) and she also had trouble getting up in the mornings, all of which are typical symptoms of depression. She took Veronal to help her sleep. Her moods varied with the seasons. Her depressions were worse in winter and she hated the cold weather since it also brought on respiratory illnesses. As she grew older, external events led to an intensification of her depression (events such as the marital problems of her friend Louis Untermeyer and the suicide of his son).

Sara's father died in 1921 at the age of 82 and this was a severe loss for Sara. Her mother died in 1924, as did her older brother George. In 1928, her friend Marguerite Wilkinson drowned. Later that year, Sara was injured in a taxi cab accident. In September of that year, Ernst's father died.

Sara grew more and more concerned over her finances. After her parents' death, she found that her inheritance was not as great as she had expected. The stock market crash in 1929 increased her anxiety. Although she had asked for no alimony, Sara tried to get Ernst to set up a trust fund for her. She worried whether she could afford to renew the lease at her hotel and she decided to move to a cheaper apartment. Her concerns became an almost nightmarish obsession. (Sara left an estate of almost $84,000.)

Many of Sara's friends had moved away from New York City and she was often lonely. However, despite the fact that she craved company, she often rejected offers from friends to visit her, usually feigning illness. In 1931, Vachel Lindsay killed himself by drinking a bottle of Lysol disinfectant and this caused Sara much distress. For many months after Lindsay's suicide, Sara feared that she was about to have a complete physical breakdown or die in an accident.

Sara was no longer able to write productively, but her friend, John Wheelock, suggested that she write a biography of Christina Rossetti. Macmillan gave her an advance on the project and she had written about 100 pages at the time of her death.

In August 1932, Sara went to England to gather material for the biography, but she developed pneumonia. She came back to America in September 1932 and her recovery was slow. She had failed to build a fruitful life after the divorce and now the only thing that seemed to lay ahead for her was ill health. She worried that her heart had weakened and that her blood pressure was fluctuating too much. Her friends were very concerned over her despondency. She was taking sleeping pills regularly and seemed severely depressed.

During the fall of 1932, Sara's despondency deepened as more of her friends died and in December she began to collect a supply of sleeping pills. She now feared having a stroke like her father and brother. (The latter lived for 20 years after having a paralytic stroke. He died in 1917 at the age of 47.)

In December, Sara went to Florida to stay with Jessie Rittenhouse, but lay in bed all day with the drapes closed. Jessie discussed the situation with Sara's doctor and nurse and they felt she should return to New York to seek psychiatric help. She developed an obsessive, but unfounded, fear that her blood vessels were beginning to rupture, increasing her fear of a stroke. On January 27, 1933, a blood vessel did break in her hand, making her frantic with the idea that her long-awaited stroke was at hand.

On the evening of January 29, 1933, Margaret Conklin came to visit her. They read and listened to Beethoven's Fifth Symphony. Sara was found at 9 o'clock by her nurse, dead in her bath after taking an overdose of sedatives. The water was still warm. Perhaps the nurse could have saved her had she checked earlier.

DISCUSSION

Drake (1979) points out that four major women poets of the nineteenth century (Emily Brontë, Christina Rossetti, Emily Dickinson and Elizabeth Barrett Browning) were all recluses like Sara. All four belonged to very close family units that fulfilled their desires for affection and intellectual stimulation. Sara ventured out more than her predecessors, but continually retreated into seclusion because of her "illnesses," becoming almost a total recluse by the end of her life.

The Victorian era encouraged women in the creative arts but at the same time undermined their self-confidence; they were allowed to dabble, but they were not supposed to achieve. When they did write poetry, they mostly wrote about protective love and the desire to submit to the ideal lover. However, it was not always easy for them to find romance in their own lives. They often ended up renouncing love for men and substituting an attraction to death. They frequently had mysterious physical weaknesses and chronic ill health, a neurotic way of resolving the conflict between their personal desires and the conventions imposed upon them by society.

Sara was a chronically depressed woman whose depression worsened as she grew older. In middle age, concerns that were mild as a young adult grew to be irrational obsessions. She feared poverty and an imminent death, though neither was very likely. It is unfortunate that Sara contracted a real illness (pneumonia) at this time and that a blood vessel did break in her hand. Her irrational concerns no longer seemed so irrational to her.

Sara had struggled to lead a conventional life, but she never learned to form and maintain healthy interpersonal relationships. The patient role she learned as a child was of no use to her in marriage. Simply put, she failed to mature. She remained a child, as evidenced by her failed marriage and the self-centeredness she displayed in her friendships.

Her childhood led her to repress her basic emotions. Her anger, curiosity and sexuality were all suppressed by her aged parents, and in particular by her mother. She married at age 30 with no realistic idea about the responsibilities of a person involved in adult relationships.

The prospect of having a child frightened her so much that she had an abortion. One event that could have turned her life around was motherhood. The easiest change for a person to make in life is to switch to a role that is complementary to what one already knows. Perhaps Sara could have become the nurse (mother) taking care of the patient (her baby) after her years of experience as the patient. But as it happened, she panicked and avoided the experience.

By the end of her life, Sara was finding it hard to write creatively, she was lonely and isolated and her irrational fears and depression were getting worse. She had often contemplated death and finally she planned it. She had long used sleeping pills and knew the peace they brought her. So she sought the ultimate peace, not in bed, but in a warm bath, as if seeking the womb from which she may have wished she had never emerged.

TREATMENT POSSIBILITIES

Sara did not have a traumatic childhood and she did not show any significant psychological distress as an adolescent. Thus there would have been no reason for the family to seek counseling for Sara or for the family. Although Sara's motivations in her marriage were not necessarily those that would improve the chances of a successful relationship, again counseling would not have been indicated. The first opportunity for counseling occurred soon after her marriage as a result of the sexual difficulties experienced by Sara and her problem of sharing an intimate life with her husband. In the early 1900s, marriage counseling was not an option and it is unlikely that such a couple would seek such counseling today, especially since Sara did not have exposure to psychology courses and a college counseling center that might have made her receptive to seeking help. Marriage counseling at this juncture might have enabled Sara and Ernst to build a mutually satisfying marriage, preventing the alienation and subsequent divorce that left Sara alone, depressed and acutely anxious.

Sara was subject to depression and exhaustion, and during her stays at clinics she would clearly have benefitted from appropriately focused psychotherapy, perhaps supplemented by antidepressant medication, to help her understand and relieve her depression and to realize that she chose to be sick instead of confronting and coping with life's problems.

In her final years, Sara had many friends who could see that her psychological state was worsening and who, had treatment been readily available, could have tried to get her to see a psychotherapist or psychiatrist. Sara's anxieties over health and finances were clearly irrational and cognitive therapy could perhaps have helped her change her dysfunctional thinking patterns.

Sara committed suicide in 1933 at the age of 48 at the brink of her senior years. Today, antidepressants for her depression and mild tranquilizers for her anxiety might enable Sara to face a continued existence. However, her immaturity would ensure the continuation of her maladaptive life style and she would need psychotherapy if she was ever to eliminate the effects of her personality disorder.

In the 1990s, Sara could have benefitted from the treatment modalities now available and her suicide could certainly have been prevented. However, it is by no means certain that she would have sought treatment or that her friends would have been able to persuade her to try it, especially since her psychopathology was not sufficiently severe as to require psychiatric intervention. Therefore, Sara Teasdale might still have died a suicide.

REFERENCE

Drake, W. 1979. *Sara Teasdale.* New York: Harper & Row.

15

Subintentioned Life-Threatening Behavior in the Elderly: The Story of Myra

Lenore S. Powell, EdD

As we have discussed throughout this book, the rate of suicide among the elderly—especially those 65 years of age and older—is high compared to the rest of the population. In the United States the suicide rate for the general population was 12.7 per 100,000 in 1987 and 21.7 per 100,000 for the elderly. In the 65 to 67 age group there is a 4 to 1 ratio of men to women; by the age of 85 the ratio is 12 to 1. The elderly, however, have lower rates of suicide attempts (Plutchik, Botsis and Weiner 1992).

Research indicates that more young people attempt suicide than complete it. For elderly people, roughly the same number attempt and complete suicide. Also, older people do not usually communicate their suicidal intentions openly (Gurland and Cross 1983). They attempt suicide less often as a means of gaining attention or as a cry for help and when they do commit suicide, they usually use violent and lethal means. Their suicide notes tend to express sorrow and they ask for forgiveness from specific persons who they believe they have troubled (Darbonne 1969).

Elderly people sometimes attempt suicide by not complying with medical treatment. Reasons for this behavior range from physical illness, pain, disability, isolation and loneliness to reaction to the threat of becoming dependent on another or fear of their own or their spouse's institutionalization. There appears to be varying statistical information on depressive disorder as a suicidal risk factor in the elderly, with estimates ranging from 48 percent to 80 percent. However, depression is a common factor and a precipitating cause of both successful and attempted suicides for the elderly (Blazer et al. 1986). Isolation, bereavement and widowhood in the first year (especially when a widow has a poor coping life style) can increase the risk of suicide.

Suicide may be a conscious and direct act as when a person hangs himself, overdoses on sleeping pills or shoots himself to commit suicide. When a person has an unconscious wish to die, it sometimes manifests itself indirectly; for example, being careless with one's life or provoking behavior that causes someone else to have homicidal feelings toward you (Levenson 1984). Heart attacks may also fall into this category.

A personality constellation that is related to survival and the ability to adapt to a crisis includes the traits of irritability, being demanding, aggressiveness and narcissism. As was discussed in Chapter 13, older people who are "crabby" seem to live longer because they are turning their bad feelings outward rather than against themselves; in other words, others are responsible for their problems. In contrast, those who lack the ability for introspection and an ability to maintain a self-system seem to experience greater hopelessness. They are less able to adapt to the massive changes that may occur when their resources are severely limited. Role loss, family problems, bereavement and its consequences and depression are some of the problems that, when coupled with personal illness, can lead to suicidal gestures, attempts and behavior that demand psychotherapeutic intervention (Seigler 1980).

THE CASE OF MYRA

Myra, a tall, stately, attractive woman of 71, was a member of my group of family members of Alzheimer's disease victims. She has been married 31 years to Alvin, a tall, handsome 77-year-old man, who had been a business whiz during the 48 years of his working life. Myra had originally been Alvin's secretary. They met, fell in love and married soon afterwards. Myra continued her secretarial work until the birth of their son, Harold. Then she retired to be Hal's mother, bottle-washer, tutor, chauffeur and all the other things that mothers do for their children. Fifteen years later when Hal was in high school, Myra resumed a secretarial job, although this time she did not work for her husband.

Their relationship was one of mutual intelligence and respect. They loved each other and Alvin indulged Myra's every whim. They were dependent on each other, a very close couple and family who enjoyed good health and financial success. When Alvin developed Alzheimer's disease, it came as a shock and a blow to both of them. As Alvin's ability to function deteriorated, Myra became more and more bewildered and devastated. All of her intelligence and emotional complacency were turned topsy-turvy. Her own abilities to function began to fail as Alvin's condition created the self-absorption, suspicion, flatness and shallowness of affect and lack of caring concern that is characteristic of some Alzheimer's victims.

Myra would get up early to clean the house and prepare sandwiches for Alvin, which she would leave in the refrigerator before she left for work. After work she would run home to prepare his dinner. When she opened the door, she was often confronted by chaos—clothes strewn about, food half-eaten and left rotting on the table, books turned over and Alvin screaming at her. One day he was nowhere to be found and Myra was beside herself. She called her son, their friends and former business associates to try and locate Alvin. Later that evening, with the help of the police, their son Hal found Alvin. He had gotten lost on his way to Hal's office.

During the weeks and months of slow but obvious changes in Alvin, Myra came to our support group and talked about her husband's deteriorating behavior. The group and I were very concerned with Myra's failure to take his situation seriously enough to ask for help. She waited until Alvin's condition worsened. We were concerned that Myra's grandiosity, shown as stubbornness, caused her to refuse to hire a home attendant to oversee Alvin during the day. Myra was operating under the fantasy that Alvin was still capable of eating his own lunch and traveling by himself and doing things around the house. To admit Alvin's deficiencies was, for Myra, an admission of her own fears that her dependency needs were no longer being met. In reality, they had stopped being met months before. Myra was suffering. The group encouraged Myra to share her fears about the meaning of Alvin's illness to her. Myra cried, worked harder at her job, lost weight, and developed insomnia and extreme nervousness that required her to take Valium and sleeping pills.

Myra fantasized that Alvin's behavior would change. She tried harder and harder to be good to him, caring and loving, but she was put off by his coldness and irascibility. She couldn't fully comprehend the organic impairment that is caused by Alzheimer's disease or the unwavering course of these changes.

One day when Myra came home from work, Alvin accused her of stealing his money and doing away with his real wife. Provoked by Alvin's behavior and failing to understand the often inexplicable catastrophic rages that many Alzheimer's patients experience, Myra got into a verbal battle with Alvin. They were both so upset and enraged that Alvin pushed

Myra down some steps and through the door. Myra was frantic. She ran to her neighbor and called her son Hal. Hal took charge of the situation and separated his parents physically. Myra's blood pressure soared and the next day she had a heart attack.

Was Myra's heart attack a subintentioned suicide attempt? Surely she did not consciously will such a fate on herself. Or did she, in the more subtle recesses of her unconscious, want a way of "escaping" from the painful realization that she was no longer her husband's favorite. The loneliness and feelings of emptiness that Myra experienced as a result of Alvin's illness apparently reawakened long-ago feelings of abandonment by her depressed mother and her absentee father. Myra had gone through her adolescence and early adult life searching for someone to whom she could devote her life and who in turn would devote himself totally to her and she found that person in Alvin. When Alvin's persona faded through the ravages of Alzheimer's disease, Myra was once again confronted with a void that she needed to fill. In individual therapy sessions we addressed the meaning of the vastness of that void. Myra's life was intertwined with Alvin's in a twinship merger. As a child, she had difficulty separating herself from a depressed mother and going to school was an overwhelming experience for her. In the same way she couldn't separate from Alvin. She also had difficulty in sharing me—the therapist—with the other group members.

Myra was lacking a strong cohesive self. She experienced Alvin as similar to and part of herself. She needed his constant admiration to support her fragile sense of self-worth. When Alvin's mirroring and attention stopped, Myra once again was confronted by her own deficits and neediness.

Myra denied her needs, although when she did allow me and the other group members to provide the self-object twinship and nurturance she required, she became less anxious about Alvin. Some of the group members became substitute siblings and children to Myra. They went out together and were responsive to each other's needs outside of therapy.

Myra kept putting off the decision to hire a home attendant to share in the care for Alvin, even when I and the other group members all encouraged her to do so. Her decision to act came at the point of her heart attack, which luckily was mild. Why did she wait so long?

Myra's grandiose self-sufficiency arose from insufficient caregiving by a depressed, unattuned mother. Myra's failure to trust anyone except Alvin and that he turned out to disappoint her prevented Myra from feeling that the therapist or the group could be relied upon to understand her or to provide the attunement she wanted and desperately needed.

Myra was confronted with her shame at not having attained some of her goals, for example, shame about not having achieved emotional independence. She became depressed as a result of her failure to take charge and master the situation of Alvin's illness. The depression immobilized Myra by shocking her ego into passivity. She could not live up to her narcissistic aspirations.

A self that is on the verge of fragmenting is overwhelmed with panic. Panic is the utmost enemy. Cousins (1983) reported that death was common after the emotional shock of learning that a loved one had a catastrophic illness. Sometimes suicides in later life reflect an attempt to wipe out the unbearable pain of mortifications and shame and an overwhelming sense of failure (Morrison 1989).

While Myra did not consciously attempt suicide, her inability to rest and her dogged perseverance in doing everything herself was, I believe, an attempt to let nature shock her body and mind into a state which she could not attain through self-control and self-willing. Thus, she provoked a heart attack. It was, I believe, an unconscious suicide attempt.

As a result of the heart attack, Myra was forced to share the caregiving with a nursing home into which Hal placed his father. After 2 months, Myra returned to the therapy group.

Understanding her heart attack as her ego's way of saying "Stop, I can't bear it any more," Myra was now willing to learn that she could express her own needs and feel supported and encouraged in being able to fulfill them. Her self-sacrificial behavior had caused her to suppress her anger (which was unacceptable to her) and her resentment over Alvin's difficulties as well as her own. Gradually Myra was able to make some changes including not having to visit Alvin on a daily basis and taking better care of herself.

CONCLUSION

The essence of life is change. But change itself produces various types of stress that can become overwhelming. When one's individual capacities and resources are drained, survival is threatened. A person must be able to look to family, friends, neighbors and supports in the environment for emotional, financial and spiritual strength.

Equally important is to instill in our young people, as well as the elderly, attitudes of acceptance of one's limitations, including the emotional constrictions that we all have and the limitations on our energies and capacities as we approach advanced age. Perhaps one step beyond the empathy and attunement that a nurturing psychoanalyst tries to give to her patients, society could be gentler and kinder and more attuned to the spiritual needs of its citizens. Spiritual bankruptcy is just as devastating as financial or emotional bankruptcy. We must take time to smell the flowers and to smile and acknowledge each other. In so doing we acknowledge our strengths, our humanity and our frailties. In simple ways, performing an act of loving-kindness every day is a mirror of the nurturance of the universe and the joy that can abound within our own spheres.

REFERENCES

Blazer, D.G. 1980. The Epidemiology of Late Life. In E.W. Busse and D.G. Blazer, eds., *Handbook of Geriatric Psychiatry*. New York: Van Nostrand Reinhold.

Cousins, N. 1983. *The Healing Heart*. New York: Avon Books.

Darbonne, A.R. 1969. Suicide and age. *Journal of Consulting and Clinical Psychology* 33:46-50.

Gurland, B.J. and P.S. Cross. 1983. Suicide Among the Elderly. In M.K. Aronson, ed., *The Acting-Out Elderly*. New York: Haworth Press.

Levenson, F.B. 1984. *Causes and Prevention of Cancer*. Calgary, Alberta: Vortex Enterprises.

Morrison, A.P. 1989. *Shame*. Hillsdale, NJ: The Analytic Press.

Peck, M.S. 1978. *The Road Less Traveled*. New York: Touchstone.

Plutchik, R., A.J. Betsis and M.B. Weiner. 1992. Clinical Measurement of Suicidality and Coping in Late Life. In G.J. Kennedy, ed., *Suicide and Depression in Late Life*. New York: Brunner/Mazel.

Powell, L. and K. Courtice. 1992. *Alzheimer's Disease: A Guide for Families*. Reading, MA: Addison-Wesley.

Siegler, I. 1980. The Psychology of Adult Development and Aging. In E.W. Busse and D.G. Blazer, eds., *Handbook of Geriatric Psychiatry*. New York: Van Nostrand Reinhold.

White, M.T. and M.B. Weiner. 1986. *The Theory and Practice of Self Psychology*. New York: Brunner/Mazel.

16

Assisted Suicide
and the Elderly

David Lester, PhD

The debate about whether individuals have the right to choose the method and timing of their own death remains unsolved after centuries of disagreement. Part of the problem is that there is a clash of absolute principles: "Thou shalt not kill" versus the presumed right that people have to make decisions about their own life and death. Utilitarians argue about the relative degrees of good and harm for the patient and his significant others in deciding which actions are the most beneficial (Beauchamp and Childress 1979). The issue has now reached the social-political sphere.

In the United States and in other nations, it is now legitimate for individuals to refuse life-prolonging treatment in cases of severe injury or disease. Individuals can sign do-not-resuscitate orders, draw up living wills and give power-of-attorney to others (West 1993). There are also guidelines available to those who must make decisions about the management of terminally ill people (such as those who are in an apparently permanent coma) relative to withholding or withdrawing life-sustaining measures (Miles and Gomez 1988).

Along with these changes, it has also been acknowledged that people have the legal right to kill themselves. Killing oneself is no longer illegal in most American states and has been decriminalized in most developed nations including Canada (Lester 1992) and New Zealand (Lester 1993).

Anthropologists have, however, made us aware of less well-known modes of voluntary death. In India a widow despite official government disapproval was, and sometimes still is, expected to die voluntarily on her husband's funeral pyre in a practice known as *suttee*. In Papua New Guinea, colonial administrators saw this practice as ritual homicide, but Durkheim (1897) called it altruistic suicide. Counts (1991) has described this practice in Kaliai, New Britain and New Guinea, where elderly widows of important leaders were strangled at their own request, if relatives agreed. The widow knelt on a mat and a relative, often her oldest son, either used a garotte to strangle her or broke her neck at the base of the skull with a special wooden sword. Counts' informants saw these decisions as rational choices made by women who were unwilling to tolerate their new status and who followed a ritual that avoided culpability in death. Indeed, the sword used became a treasured heirloom that was passed down to descendants with the accompanying story of her death. Counts viewed this act as assisted suicide.

However, rather than seeing such an act as having been willingly chosen by an autonomous person, it is possible to interpret this behavior as the result of extreme conformity to sexist oppression (Lester 1990a, 1990b). While widow-suicide has been a cultural practice, there has been no custom of widower-suicide. Furthermore, there is no evidence that widows voluntarily chose this option as opposed to merely conforming to societal expectations. Indeed, it would be difficult to propose criteria to distinguish between these alternatives. We know the power of social pressure in primitive societies, as shown, for example, by the notion of killing people by hexing them (Lester 1972).

Lester (1994) has recently studied a sample of cases of suicides by famous people or people who are interesting enough to warrant a biography. Two of these cases—Arthur Koestler and his wife and Stefan Zweig and his wife—were suicide pacts and both appeared to have been actions decided upon by husbands who did not want to live and who persuaded their healthy wives to die with them. Both women started out as secretaries to their future husbands and both were subservient, succumbing to their husbands' every demand throughout their married life.

With these introductory comments, let us examine the issues of assisted suicide with particular reference to assisted suicide in the elderly.

ASSISTED SUICIDE IN CROSS-NATIONAL PERSPECTIVE

Although in America, allowing people to die is a legally protected act, there is no legal provision for actively causing another's death. In Germany, however, the law presents an interesting paradox in this regard

(Battin 1993). While killing on request (including voluntary euthanasia) is prohibited, assisting suicide is not. There is a private organization (The German Society for Humane Dying) that provides information on how to commit suicide. To receive these instructions, a person must be a member for at least one year and must be terminally ill; he must not have received treatment for a psychiatric disorder within the previous 2 years. The instructions on how to commit suicide that the organization gives out must be kept a secret and the person who receives them must arrange to have the instructions returned to the society after his death. In difficult circumstances, the society can arrange for someone to obtain the necessary medications and can provide a companion during the dying process.

In the Netherlands, however, assisted suicide is protected legally as the result of a series of court decisions. Furthermore, there is a set of established procedures for approving an assisted suicide that require that the individual meet several criteria (such as that the person's request must be voluntary and his suffering intolerable). In addition, two independent physicians must approve the intended actions (Battin 1993). A recent survey showed that 1.8 percent of deaths in the Netherlands involved euthanasia at the request of the patient (with some physician involvement), including 0.3 percent unambiguous physician-assisted suicides (van der Maas et al. 1991). Public support for a liberal euthanasia policy in the Netherlands is about 81 percent (Borst-Eilers 1991).

RECENT TRENDS IN AMERICA

Recent court decisions have upheld a person's right to refuse life-saving treatment if the person's competency has been established, even when significant others object. Thus, Jehovah's Witnesses, who reject blood transfusions on religious grounds (they equate the procedure with cannibalism), have been granted the right of refusal for themselves (though not for their children) by a series of court decisions.

Recent court decisions have also permitted the withdrawal of life-sustaining treatment under certain conditions from a patient in a persistent coma. In the case of Nancy Cruzan in 1991, the United States Supreme Court permitted states to refuse withdrawal of life-sustaining treatment from incompetent patients unless there was clear and convincing evidence that to do so would be in accord with the patient's wishes (West 1993). Ms. Cruzan's parents provided this evidence by presenting testimony from her friends that she was opposed to being kept alive by tube feeding. Ms. Cruzan's feeding tube was removed and she died.

In a survey of elderly people in rural North Carolina, Gamble and his associates (1991) found that 86 percent of those he surveyed would want only basic medical care if they had a terminal illness. Ninety-three percent of them were happy to permit their family to make decisions about terminal care if they themselves were unable to participate in the decision, but only 45 percent had actually discussed this matter with their families. Furthermore, none had signed a living will and only 11 percent had discussed these issues with their physician.

Euthanasia means a "good death," but the term is used in many ways. It is often equated with intervention that results in a merciful death (West 1993). This intervention is also called *active euthanasia,* in contrast to simply withholding treatment which is called *passive euthanasia.* Family members have often deliberately murdered terminally ill or long-suffering relatives. For example, in 1985, Roswell Gilbert shot and killed his wife who was suffering from Alzheimer's disease. He was convicted of murder by the court, but granted clemency by the governor of Florida (West 1993). Physicians have also killed patients for humane reasons, as in the case of a gynecologist who responded to a 20-year-old woman who was suffering from ovarian cancer and who said to him, "let's get this over with" by administering a lethal dose of morphine (Anon. 1988).

Derek Humphry (1991), founder of The Hemlock Society, published a how-to book on committing suicide which quickly rose to the top of the best-seller list. Voices were raised both in support of and in opposition to the book. More recently, Jack Kevorkian, a physician, built a machine that enables people to kill themselves; he has been present and assisted them when they conducted their fatal suicidal action. The state of Michigan, which had no laws against such actions, tried to convict Kevorkian for murder, but they were unsuccessful. The state then reformulated its laws to make such actions subject to prosecution.

Kevorkian (1988) believes that physicians should go so far as to establish medical clinics where terminally ill patients could opt for death under controlled circumstances. This idea is not new. Indeed, Alfred Nobel, founder of the Nobel Prize, suggested this plan many years ago (Sohlman 1962). Public opinion surveys by both Harris and the Roper Organization have found that a majority of the general public believes in physician-assisted suicide (West 1993).

SOME PSYCHOLOGICAL AND SOCIAL ISSUES

There are complex social issues involved in active euthanasia and assisted suicide that go beyond the basic moral dilemma of whether it is "right" or "wrong." First, several commentators have pointed out that in the well-publicized Kevorkian assisted suicides, the first few people he helped to die were women. Although more recently men have also been assisted by Kevorkian (Gibbs 1993), feminists have noted that here we have a further example of possible female oppression. There is no proof that sexist oppression played any role in Kevorkian's cases, but the image of a man assisting women to kill themselves is not felicitous.

In the United States, about 30,000 people kill themselves each year without help from others. Why do some people want others to help them commit suicide by preparing the medication or arranging the apparatus for them? The Hemlock Society, which published Humphry's manual on how to commit suicide, will not assist people to kill themselves, but they will provide information. This raises the psychodynamic question of why some people want others to participate in their suicide. Even Freud, a physician who could easily have injected himself with morphine when he was terminally ill, wanted his physician to do it for him.

Psychologists have published much research on the personality dimension of belief in an external versus an internal locus of control. Some people believe that what happens to them is a result of powerful external forces or fate, while other people believe that they themselves are responsible for what happens to them. For example, if you failed an examination, was it your fault for not studying more or the teacher's fault for giving such a difficult examination? Or was it simply an unlucky day for you?

Psychologists consider an internal locus of control to be psychologically healthier than an external locus of control. People who want another person to kill them may want to avoid responsibility for their own death, consistent perhaps with an external locus of control, or perhaps they want to minimize the self-perceived sinfulness of the act of suicide. Is this a healthy choice?

It would be of great interest to collect information on the psychological state of those requesting assisted suicide so that we can assess the psychodynamics of the request better and perhaps decide whether such requests are rational and merit assistance.

OTHER ISSUES

Three other issues concerning assisted suicide are especially pertinent to the elderly. Those who object to assisted suicide often call upon the principle of the *slippery slope*. If society permits voluntary active euthanasia (such as assisted suicide), then society may slip to permitting less-than-voluntary active euthanasia and, eventually, involuntary active euthanasia. The latter situation, last practiced in Nazi Germany, leads to the decision by "experts" or "authorities" to terminate the life of those who are elderly, chronically ill, handicapped or retarded.

The slippery slope argument is commonly used to argue against policies such as gun control and abortion. However, experience in the majority of societies is that a compromise is reached, usually acceptable to the majority, and extreme positions are rare. This suggests that permitting assisted suicide will almost certainly not lead to involuntary active euthanasia.

A more likely danger is that the societal approval of assisted suicide may lead people to expect the elderly and terminally ill to choose this option. In days of limited health care resources, the care of the elderly— especially those who are chronically ill—consumes time, effort and money that could be used elsewhere. If society expects the elderly to choose suicide in order to free up resources for the rest of society, the elderly may well internalize this demand. This is especially likely if an elderly person feels that he is a burden (both interpersonally and financially) to others. The likelihood of this societal attitude is illustrated by the comments of Daniel Callahan, director of The Hastings Center for the Study of Medical Ethics, in support of comments by the governor of Colorado, Richard Lamm, who recommended that the government stop providing medical care to the elderly who have lived beyond their "natural span," presumably somewhere in their seventies (Richman 1992a).

Finally, many suicidal people are ambivalent about dying. They have problems with living more often than they have the wish to die (Richman 1992b). If the conditions of their lives could be improved, then they might not choose suicide. Perhaps society ought to give more consideration to improving the conditions of the lives of the elderly than to focus on assisted suicide.

For example, Betty Rollin's mother chose suicide and asked her daughter to help her in this because she could no longer bear the pain and nausea accompanying chemotherapy for her cancer (Rollin 1985). Betty Rollin could not find useful information on how to commit suicide from any physician in America and therefore called a physician in the Netherlands for guidance. Her mother managed to get a local doctor to prescribe Nembutal for her insomnia and she overdosed with this and Dalmane while Betty Rollin and her husband sat with her. There are ways to ameliorate the pain and nausea of patients undergoing chemotherapy, such as the prescribed use of marijuana. Unfortunately, the permitted use of analgesic marijuana is still limited.

The elderly, even those who are chronically ill, will often change their minds about dying if their living conditions are improved. Senator Jacob Javits, dying from a progressive neurologic disease, remained cheerful to the end because his pain was carefully managed, as it can be in many if not most cases. Cicely Saunders, Director of St. Christopher's Hospice in

London, affirmed this 20 years ago and there have been steady advances in pain management ever since.

The elderly often become suicidal in response to interpersonal stress, but social relationships can be improved. (Osgood and Covey in Chapter 9 have shown how simple changes in the conditions of living and interpersonal interactions for nursing home patients can change a person's attitude toward living versus dying.)

Psychotherapy can also be very effective for the suicidal elderly. Richman (1992b) has worked extensively with the suicidal elderly and is convinced that they can be helped to enjoy life with psychotherapy. He is concerned that the emphasis on suicide and assisted suicide, especially in connection with old age and chronic illnesses, will deter nursing home staff, social workers and psychotherapists from working with the suicidal elderly to improve the conditions of their life and their enjoyment of living.

SUMMARY

The growing acceptance of the right to refuse treatment and the mounting interest in assisted suicide in recent years raises the possibility that, rather than these actions becoming available choices for the elderly who are suffering, they may become demands placed upon the elderly by society. Voluntary euthanasia may become involuntary euthanasia. It is important to present patients with multiple options and they should also receive a full explanation of the alternatives. As well as providing how-to manuals on suicide and channels for obtaining help in committing suicide, the elderly should also be presented with the option of attempting to improve the physiological, psychological and interpersonal conditions of their lives as a means of relief. Only then can an informed choice be made.

REFERENCES

Annas, G.J. 1993. Physician-assisted suicide. *New England Journal of Medicine* 328:1573-1576.

Anonymous. 1988. It's over Debbie. *Journal of the American Medical Association* 259:272.

Battin, M.P. 1993. Suicidology and the Right to Die. In A.A. Leenaars, ed., *Suicidology*. Northvale, NJ: Jason Aronson.

Beauchamp, T. and J. Childress. 1979. *Principles of Biomedical Ethics*. New York: Oxford University Press.

Borst-Eilers, E. 1991. Controversies in the Care of Dying Patients. Paper presented at University of Florida conference on ethics, Orlando, Florida.

Counts, D. 1991. Suicide in Different Ages from a Cross-cultural Perspective. In A.A. Leenaars, ed., *Life-Span Perspectives of Suicide*. New York: Plenum.

Durkheim, E. 1897. *Le Suicide*. Paris: Felix Alcan.

Gamble, E.R., P.J. McDonald and P.R. Lichstein. 1991. Knowledge, attitudes, and behavior of elderly persons regarding living wills. *Archives of Internal Medicine* 151:277-290.

Gay, P. 1988. *Freud*. New York: W.W. Norton.

Gibbs, N. 1993. Rx for death. *Time* 141(22):34-39.

Humphry, D. 1991. *Final Exit*. Eugene, OR: The Hemlock Society.

Kevorkian, J. 1988. The last fearsome taboo. *Medicine and Law* 7:1-44.

Lester, D. 1972. Voodoo death. *American Anthropologist* 74:386-390.

Lester, D. 1990a. Suicide as a political act. *Psychological Reports* 66:1185-1186.

Lester, D. 1990b. The study of suicide from a feminist perspective. *Crisis* 11:38-43.

Lester, D. 1991. Sigmund Freud. *Proceedings of the Pavese Society* 3:52-57.

Lester, D. 1992. Decriminalization of suicide in Canada and suicide rates. *Psychological Reports* 71:738.

Lester, D. 1993. Decriminalization of suicide in New Zealand and suicide rates. *Psychological Reports* 72:1050.

Lester, D. 1994. A study of fifteen theories of suicide. *Suicide and Life-Threatening Behavior* (in press).

Miles, S. and C. Gomez. 1988. *Protocols for Elective Use of Life-sustaining Treatment*. New York: Springer-Verlag.

Richman, J. 1992a. Creative Aging. In D. Lester, ed., *Suicide '92*. Denver: American Association of Suicidology.

Richman, J. 1992b. The Neglected Epidemic. In D. Lester, ed., *Suicide '92*. Denver: American Association of Suicidology.

Rollin, B. 1985. *Last Wish*. New York: Simon & Schuster.

Sohlman, R. 1962. Alfred Nobel and the Nobel Foundation. In H. Schuck, ed., *Nobel: The Man and His Prizes*. Amsterdam: Elsevier.

van der Maas, P., J. van Delden, L. Pijnenburg and C. Looman. 1991. Euthanasia and other medical decisions concerning the end of life. *Lancet* 338:669-674.

Victoroff, V.M. 1983. *The Suicidal Patient*. Oradell, NJ: Medical Economics Books.

West, L.J. 1993. Reflections on the Right to Die. In A.A. Leenaars, ed., *Suicidology*. Northvale, NJ: Jason Aronson.